For Kerry Sutton-Spence and Harry Sieratzki

The Linguistics of British Sign Language

An Introduction

This is the first detailed explanation of the way British Sign Language works and is the product of many years' experience of research and teaching of sign linguistics. It assumes no previous knowledge of linguistics or sign language, and it is not structured around traditional headings such as phonology, morphology, and syntax. Instead it is set out in such a way as to help learners and their teachers understand the linguistic principles behind the language.

There are sections on BSL and also on the use of BSL, including variation, social acceptability in signing, and poetry and humour in BSL. Technical terms and linguistic jargon are kept to a minimum, and the text contains many examples from English, BSL, and other spoken and sign languages. The book is amply illustrated and contains exercises to encourage further thought on many of the topics covered, as well as a reading list for further study.

RACHEL SUTTON-SPENCE is Lecturer in Deaf Studies at the University of Bristol. BENCIE WOLL is Professor and Chair of Sign Language and Deaf Studies at City University, London.

A 90-minute video has been produced containing specially designed exercise material to accompany the book. The video is available from CACDP, Durham University Science Park, Block 4, Mountjoy Research Centre, Stockton Road, Durham DH1 3UZ.

The Linguistics of British Sign Language

An Introduction

RACHEL SUTTON-SPENCE AND BENCIE WOLL

CAMBRIDGE UNIVERSITY PRESS

CAMBRIDGE
UNIVERSITY PRESS

University Printing House, Cambridge CB2 8BS, United Kingdom

Cambridge University Press is part of the University of Cambridge.

It furthers the University's mission by disseminating knowledge in the pursuit of education, learning and research at the highest international levels of excellence.

www.cambridge.org
Information on this title: www.cambridge.org/9780521631426

© Rachel Sutton-Spence and Bencie Woll 1998

First published 1999
16th printing 2017

Printed in the United Kingdom by Print on Demand, World Wide

A catalogue record for this publication is available from the British Library

Library of Congress Cataloguing in Publication data
Sutton-Spence, Rachel.
The linguistics of British Sign Language: an introduction /
Rachel Sutton-Spence and Bencie Woll.
p.   cm.
Includes bibliographical references and index.
ISBN 0 521 63142 4 (hardback). – ISBN 0 521 63718 X (paperback)
1. British Sign Language – Handbooks, manuals, etc.   2. Sign
language – Study and teaching.   3. Deaf – Means of communication –
Great Britain.   I. Woll, B. (Bencie)   II. Title.
HV2474.S97   1998
419–dc21   98–20588   CIP

ISBN 978-0-521-63142-6 Hardback
ISBN 978-0-521-63718-3 Paperback

Contents

Acknowledgements

We would like to thank the following people: Mike George for the photographs of handshapes in the Conventions section; Bridget Peace for the drawing of the manual alphabet; Tasnim Ahmed, Tina Christou, Martin Hughes, Paul Scott, Shainal Vasant, Adam Walker, and Fiona Wood, students at the Centre for Deaf Studies, who modelled the sign illustrations; Frank Blades, Joseph Collins, and David Jackson for their assistance with the preparation and computerisation of the illustrations; David Brien for his kind permission to use the illustration conventions from the *BSL/English Dictionary*; Little, Brown for their kind permission to reproduce the extract from *Body of Evidence*, by Patricia Cornwell on pp. 126–7; Bryn Brooks and the BBC *See Hear* programme for providing the videos of Dorothy Miles's poems; Don Reed, for his permission to quote Dorothy Miles's poems; Daniel Jones for his assistance with the preparation of the manuscript; our colleagues at the Centre for Deaf Studies at the University of Bristol and Clinical Communication Studies at City University, in particular Frances Elton, for her comments on an earlier draft, and Hal Draper and Paddy Ladd, for their assistance with chapter 14. Finally, we would like to thank all the students we have taught sign linguistics to over the years for their input, suggestions, and comments.

Our apologies to anyone whom we have inadvertently omitted from this list.

Conventions used

Throughout this book we will frequently refer to BSL signs. Because of variation in BSL, a sign we describe may be different from one you know. There is no currently accepted, widely used writing system for BSL and we need to adopt a system for representing signs on paper. There are several sophisticated, accurate systems for representing signs from any language on paper ('notation' systems). However, these systems are complex and take time to learn. In this book we will not use these notation systems.

GLOSSING

We will use glossing as the main method of describing BSL signs. When we gloss a sign, we write its meaning using an English word or words, but it should be remembered that we are referring to the BSL sign and not to the English word used to write it down.

There are several conventions that are observed in the glossing used in this book:

(1) When we write the meaning of a sign using an English word, we write it in capital letters. For example, to write the sign that means 'cat', we write CAT.

(2) Many signs cannot be glossed by a single English word, because there is no exact English translation. In such cases, we write several English words to give the meaning of the sign, but each word is joined by a hyphen to show that we are referring to a single sign. For example, if we want to sign 'don't like' there is a single sign for this that may be written as DON'T-LIKE. The BSL verb that means 'I ask you' is a single sign in BSL that is glossed as I-ASK-YOU.

(3) If a verb sign is repeated, this is glossed to give its meaning, so that a sign that would be translated in English as 'knock on the door for ages', might be glossed KNOCK-FOR-AGES. However, we might also want to show

that the sign KNOCK was repeatedly made, and this can be shown by the symbol +++, to give KNOCK +++.

(4) There are other times when an English gloss is not so easy to provide, but the basic meaning of the sign still needs to be written. For example, when a signer points to a particular location, we write 'Index' to show that the signer has pointed to a specified location. If we need to know what grammatical information is included by the pointing, we may add 1, 2, or 3, where 1 would mean 'I' in English, 2 would mean 'you', and 3 would mean 'he', 'she', or 'it'. Index$_2$ LOVE Index$_3$ would be another way of writing YOU LOVE HER or, in English 'you love her'.

(5) If we are writing a fingerspelled word, we write it in small letters, with a '-' in between each letter. To write that someone has fingerspelled the English word 'cat', we would write -c-a-t-. Where letters from one-handed manual alphabets are referred to (e.g. in those from America, Ireland, and France), we write them in small letters, with a '.' between each letter. The two-handed British manual letter corresponding to the written letter 'f' is written -f-, and any manual letter from a one-handed alphabet is written .f.

(6) A great deal of information in BSL is shown by the face or by head movement. The meaning of this information is not easily translated into English but is often needed in a gloss, especially to give grammatical information. Information given by the face and head is shown by adding a line along the top of the words of the gloss, and writing conventional abbreviations to describe the information. The line extends over the glosses that are accompanied by a particular facial expression or head movement. Conventional abbreviations written along this upper line include:

q – this means that the facial expression and head movements are those normally seen during a question in BSL (see chapter 4)

neg – this means that the facial expression and head movements are those normally seen during negation in BSL (see chapter 4)

t – this means that the facial expression and head movements are those normally seen during the marking of the grammatical topic (see chapters 3 and 4)

hn – this refers to a head nod

br – this refers to a brow-raise

bf – this refers to furrowed brows, often with a frowning expression.

There are times when a sign is difficult to gloss in English because the sign is made up very differently from an English word or phrase. Where the handshape of a verb contains information about what class a noun belongs to (a "classifier"), the gloss includes this information. Thus, if the handshape tells us that an animal is involved in the action, the gloss will be written as animal-CL. If the handshape tells us that a vehicle is involved, the gloss will be written as veh-CL. If it is a person, the gloss is person-CL.

Proforms stand in the place of something previously identified, and include information about an object's shape. For example, if we want to say 'I looked at a picture', we represent the picture with a flat hand, indicating its two-dimensionality, while signing LOOK with the other. The gloss for the picture is written as pro-2D.

Pronouns in BSL are articulated by pointing to a location associated with the noun. The form of the point is the same in all pronouns, but the location of the point varies depending on the location assigned to the noun. Pointing has many other functions in BSL so we use the term 'index' to refer to pronoun pointing. This is glossed as Index with a subscript to indicate the location in space. If an Index has the meanings 'I', 'you', etc., it is glossed as $Index_1$ or $Index_2$. Otherwise Indexes have subscripts '$_L$' and '$_R$' to indicate left or right sides of signing space; or '$_A$', '$_B$', etc.

DESCRIPTION OF HANDSHAPES

Glossing is very useful for discussion of sign linguistics, but it has one major drawback: it only tells us the meaning of the sign, not about its form. On many occasions in this book, we will need to describe the form of the sign, as well as its meaning.

To describe a sign completely, we need to say what handshape was used, what location the sign was made at, exactly how the hands moved, what the orientation of the hands was, and what facial expression and other movements of the head and body were made. This can be quite a lengthy description, but there is a very quick way of noting the handshape of a sign. Often in this book we will use a description of the handshape in conjunction with a gloss, but we will not always specify the other parts of the sign, if this information is not required in the discussion.

There are many ways of representing sign handshapes on paper. They may be drawn, or allocated a symbol. In this book we will use symbols. Readers new to this system may need some time to get used to the conventions, but it is a very simple system, once the basic rules are understood, and it allows very quick and easy description of handshapes.

Single letter labels are assigned to different handshapes to describe them. Many of the label names come from the American manual alphabet (which is different from the British manual alphabet, and uses only one hand). When a sign's handshape is the same as a letter in the American manual alphabet, we give it that letter name. For example, a closed fist is similar to the American manual letter 'A', so instead of writing 'fist', we can say 'A' hand. The flat hand with all the fingers together is similar to the American letter 'B', so we label this a 'B' hand. Sometimes, a numeral is used instead, so that an open hand with all the fingers spread out is called a '5' hand because it is the same as the American numeral 5. Some of the handshape names use additional symbols to describe a handshape fully. Most commonly, we might need to say a handshape is 'bent' or 'clawed'.

The following symbols will be used in this book: A, Å, Â, B, B̈, C, E, F, G, H, I, K, L, O, Ô, bO, R, V, V̈, Y, 4, 5, 5̃, 8. You may want to refer to the illustrations here as you read the book until you become more familiar with the system.

A   Fist

Å   Fist with thumb extended

Â   Fist with 'hat'

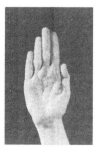

B   Flat hand, fingers extended and together

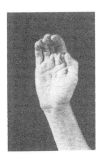

B̈   Curved hand, thumb at side

C   'C' shaped hand

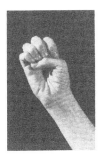

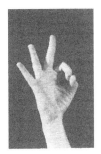

E   Fist with thumb alongside
fingertips

F   Thumb and index finger form
circle, other fingers straight

G   Index finger extended from fist

H   Index and middle fingers extended
together

I   Little finger extended from fist

K

L   Index and thumb extended
at right angles

O   Circle with thumb and fingertips
touching

bO   'X' with index finger and thumb
touching to form 'baby O'

R   Fist with index and middle fingers
extended and crossed

V   Fist with index and middle fingers extended and spread

V̈   'V' hand with index and middle fingers bent

4   All fingers except thumb extended and spread

5   All fingers extended and spread

5̈   All fingers extended, spread and loosely curved

8   Index, ring and little fingers extended and spread, thumb and middle finger form circle

DOMINANT AND NON-DOMINANT HANDS

Many signs in BSL are made only using one hand. However, there are also signs made using two hands. When we describe a sign, we will also want to describe the actions of the two hands. Reference to the two hands is complicated by the fact that left-handed and right-handed signers will use opposite hands for the same sign. For this reason, we will not refer to 'left' and 'right' hands. Instead, we will refer to the 'dominant(d)' and 'non-dominant(nd)' hands. For the right-handed signer, the dominant hand is the right hand. This is the signer's stronger, more easily controlled hand and if a sign is one handed, the dominant hand will usually be used to articulate the sign. The non-dominant hand is the weaker, less easily manipulated hand. In many uses of two-handed signs, the dominant hand will move, while the non-dominant hand remains stationary.

ACCEPTABILITY

On some occasions we will describe a sign construction that is linguistically unacceptable or ungrammatical in BSL. When such a construction is glossed, it will have a '★' in front, to show this.

There are also times in this book when it is necessary to refer to socially unacceptable language. When a sign is described that is socially unacceptable, it will have a 'ˣ' in front to show that many signers consider it socially unacceptable.

OTHER CONVENTIONS

When we refer to a sign gloss, we will use capital letters. When we refer to an English word or phrase, we will use italics. When we refer to an idea that may be expressed in any language, we will use ' ' around the words.

Where it is necessary to refer to the sounds of a spoken language, we will use / / around the letters to show that they represent the phonemes of a language. Where we use [ ], we refer to the physical sounds (see chapter 6).

ILLUSTRATIONS

The photographs in the book have been taken from video recordings. We have tried to select video frames which contain the most important features of the example. However, since still images cannot show movement, symbols for movement have been added where necessary. These symbols are the same as those used in the *BSL/English Dictionary*.

Arrows and lines show direction and path of movement. The arrowhead indicates the main direction of movement.

Direction symbols

Open arrowheads indicate movement towards or away from the signer; closed arrowheads indicate movement to the left or right; or up or down. Double arrowheads indicate repeated movement in the direction of the arrowhead; pairs of doubled arrowheads indicate repeated movement in two directions: up and down, side to side, or towards and away from the signer.

> *movement towards or away from the signer*

▲ *movement to the left or right or up or down*

>> *repeated movement towards or away from the signer*

▲▲ *repeated movement to the left or right or up or down*

<< >> *repeated movement towards and away from the signer*

▲▲ ▼▼ *repeated movement from side to side or up and down*

Path symbols

A line is used to indicate path of movement of the hand. When the symbol appears in a curved arrow around the wrist, it indicates a twisting movement. It may also be used to show wrist or finger bending. An interrupted line indicates slow movement; a doubled line, fast movement; a line with a bar at the end indicates firm movement or abrupt ending of the movement.

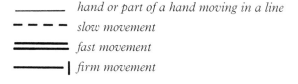

——————— *hand or part of a hand moving in a line*

− − − − *slow movement*

═════ *fast movement*

——————| *firm movement*

Circular movement

Circles indicating movement have direction symbols in line with the path of movement. Each circle shows the movement of one hand, unless both hands move along the same path. The arrowheads indicate whether the movement is single or repeated, and the direction of movement. Arrowhead position indicates whether the hands move in parallel or alternating movement. Circles are also used to indicate signs where the hands maintain contact throughout the movement (see interacting movement symbols below).

Internal movement symbols

Several symbols are used to indicate movements of the finger(s). These include 'tapping' movements of the fingers, 'crumbling' movements, and 'wiggling' movements.

M   *tapping movement in which the hand touches another part of the body several times quickly*

⚲   *crumbling movement in which the pad of the thumb rubs the pads of the fingers*

〰   *wiggling movement of the fingers*

⟩—   *opening or closing of part of the hand*

⟨—   *closed hand opening or open hand closing*

1 2 3   *movements occurring in sequence*

Interacting movements

A circle with a cross in it placed over one hand indicates that the hand does not move; a large circle over both hands indicates that the hands maintain contact throughout the movement of the sign. Direction and path symbols attached to a circle indicate that the hands are held together and move together.

⊗ *stationary hand – no movement*

○ *hands maintain contact throughout the movement*

Examples of symbols in combination

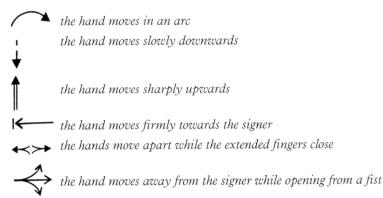

the hand moves in an arc

the hand moves slowly downwards

the hand moves sharply upwards

the hand moves firmly towards the signer

the hands move apart while the extended fingers close

the hand moves away from the signer while opening from a fist

1   2 2   1

the hands make two parallel upwards movements

the hand moves in a clockwise horizontal circle

the hands move at the same time in circles parallel to the signer's body; the left hand moves anticlockwise, the right hand moves clockwise

the hands move rightwards together, maintaining contact throughout

EXERCISES

These sections are designed for students of BSL who wish to apply some of the concepts introduced in the book to BSL data. Exercises are found at the end of each chapter. Suggested further reading for each chapter follows each set of exercises.

Where an exercise involves collecting, identifying or analysing samples, students may wish to use the CACDP Sign Linguistics video, which has been specially made to accompany this book, and which provides video material specifically designed to be suitable for the exercises. Alternatively, source material such as the *BSL/English Dictionary*[1], the BSL CD-ROM[2] series, video recordings of such programmes as *See Hear*, or materials provided by tutors will also be useful. Students will benefit most from the exercises if they discuss their findings with their BSL tutor.

[1] *BSL/English Dictionary*, D. Brien (ed.). Faber & Faber (1993).
[2] BSL CD-ROM. Microbooks (1997).

Chapter one

Linguistics and sign linguistics

Linguistics tries to find out the rules that explain what language users know, so that we can understand how language works.

People who know a language use it without thinking. They can use a language very well, and get it right nearly all of the time. But, if we ask them to tell us the rules of their language, they often find that they cannot because they have never had to think about it before. Most users of a language do not think in terms of 'rules' for their language and often do not stop to think about it. As sign linguists, we want to stop and think about language, most especially British Sign Language, so that we can find the rules that explain how the language works.

If we are to understand how BSL works, sign linguistics needs to ask questions like:

- Is BSL just a pantomime?
- Is sign language the same around the world?
- How do we ask a question in BSL?
- How do we say 'no' in BSL?
- What is the order of signs in BSL?
- Does BSL have adjectives and adverbs like English does?
- How do we show something happened a long time ago in BSL?
- Are there some handshapes that are not part of BSL?
- Can we sign with a straight face and give the full meaning?
- Do all signers sign in the same way in BSL, or are there differences?

A linguist looks at the language and tries to find out the answers to questions such as these.

One of the tasks for linguistics has always been to find out everything possible about a language and write it down, so that someone else could learn it. Linguists have written dictionaries of languages so that learners could learn the vocabulary of the language. In many cases they have made a written form for the language, if it did not have one (it may seem strange to users of English to think that a language may not have a written form, but many of the world's languages are only spoken and do not have a written form). The linguists have then tried to work out and write down as many of the grammatical rules of the language as possible. The main aim of this sort of work was to describe the language. Many linguists were also missionaries who wanted to learn different languages so that they could teach their religion to the people who used those languages. Other linguists worked for the governments of countries that had colonised the speakers of these new languages and needed to know the languages in order to rule the people.

Missionaries and other church workers in Britain may have been some of the first sign linguists. They hoped that their descriptions of sign languages would make it possible for hearing people to learn to communicate with deaf people so that deaf people could share in church life.

Linguistics was revolutionised in the 1960s by Noam Chomsky, an American linguist. He pointed out that to just describe languages was not very challenging or very helpful for understanding language as a whole. His view was that it was a bit like collecting stamps – all very pretty to look at, but it did not answer any deep questions about the way language worked. Chomsky wanted to ask bigger, more important questions like: 'Why do we use language?', 'How do we learn language?', 'How do all human languages work?'

Linguistics now has two main aims: it still tries to describe languages, but it is now also interested in asking why the languages are like this.

Some sign linguistics is very theoretical and uses theoretical ideas from mainstream linguistics. This is useful and important work, to help increase our understanding of human languages generally. However, that is not what this book is about. From the point of this book, we will be trying to describe the way that BSL works. Sometimes we will ask why it works like this, but really our first job is to be able to explain what happens in BSL.

A knowledge of the linguistics of BSL is important for many people. Learners of BSL need to know how it works, so that they can learn it better, and understand how to use the language more like a fluent signer. They can also use sign linguistics to compare the English language (which they know) with BSL (which they are learning). People who are working as sign language teachers need to understand how the language works if they are going to teach it well. When a student signs something wrong, the tutor needs to be able to explain why it is wrong, and how to sign it right. A sign tutor who is a fluent BSL signer still needs to be aware of the rules of BSL, in order to explain the language in a structured way to learners. Tutors could just teach people all the signs in the BSL dictionary, but that would not be the whole of BSL. All languages are very much more than just vocabulary and tutors need to know how to explain this to students.

Linguistics is not easy. Even the best users of a language cannot always tell us the rules of their language. We can use an analogy here to think about the problems for fluent language users talking about their language. Many people can ride a bicycle, but very few people can explain how it is done. If we ask them, they may stop and think about it, and come up with some basic rules (e.g. you have to put your feet on the pedals and you have to keep going forwards, otherwise you fall off), but what is important is that they never normally think about it.

If a person knows BSL, they may be able to think for a while and be able to answer a question about it. For example, a linguist may ask 'When do you use fingerspelling in BSL?' or 'Why do deaf people nod their heads a lot when they sign?' They will probably have a few immediate answers, but as they think more about it, they will probably find that they have to add things or change their mind. Maybe they will have to watch themselves signing, or look at other people. Just because a person uses nods or fingerspelling, it does not mean that they can explain it easily to someone else.

Any person describing their language also must be careful, because if they have never thought about something before they could give the wrong answer. A person might tell a linguist that they never use one particular sign, when really they do, but think that they do not. For example, one British deaf signer said that she did not use the American sign OK, and only used the British sign OK (fig. 1.1). Ten minutes later, in conversation with the same people, she used the American sign. She was not lying when she said she never used the American sign. She really believed that she never used it.

Again, it may seem odd that someone who is fluent in a language is not aware of what they are doing. If we go back to the bicycle analogy we can see that it is not so strange. If we ask someone how to ride a bike, they might tell us that we need to steer by moving the handlebars. They really think that we do turn the handlebars when we ride a bike. In fact, we normally lean to steer and if we tried to turn the handlebars, we would probably fall off.

Fluent users of a language are very useful to linguists, but we cannot always expect them to get things right, especially when it comes to asking them for rules about their language. So, linguists need to study language for themselves. Linguists have to try to be detached and view a language as if they were nothing to do with it.

We can say that the job of a linguist is to find out how a language works, so we need to ask what it is that users of a language 'know'. We can say that they will know the sounds or gestures that are allowed in the language, they will know the words or signs that are in the language (and what they mean) and they will know how to string the words or signs together to make larger units of meaning.

Fig. 1.1a OK (BSL)

Fig. 1.1b OK (ASL)

WHAT DO WE KNOW WHEN WE 'KNOW' A LANGUAGE?

(1)   Someone who knows a language has knowledge of its forms (sounds, gestures, etc.). This includes knowledge of what forms are in the language and what forms are not. People who know English immediately know if a word could be a word of English. People who know BSL immediately know if a sign could be a sign of BSL. In both cases, we know what is acceptable in the language and what is not.

If we use a word from another language that has forms that are *not* in our language, we have three main options. We can use a substitute from our lan-

Fig. 1.2 EIGHT (Portuguese Sign Language)

guage, we can add that form to our language or we can mark it in some way as being 'foreign'.

Some handshapes appear very odd to British signers, such as the hand-shape for the Portuguese number EIGHT (fig. 1.2) . At first, British signers may even wonder how people can get their fingers into such positions, but for Portuguese signers, it is no problem, because it is a part of their language.

In BSL there is no native sign handshape identical to the American manual letter 'e' (although it can be made if the shape of the referent requires that handshape). There is a sign EUROPE that uses this handshape (for example, in French Sign Language). Users of BSL who borrow this sign need to deal with a form outside their language. One solution is to change the handshape to fit BSL by relaxing the handshape into a looser O-shaped hand (see fig. 1.3). Signers usually do this without thinking about it. They may even be surprised that they do it. Another solution is to use the handshape but note in their minds, perhaps subconsciously, that it is foreign in some way.

BSL does not use certain parts of the body for making signs. There is a set signing space in BSL, and signs are normally not made outside this space. For example, there are no established signs that use the buttocks, or the back of the head, or the inside of the upper arm as a location. Some strongly visually motivated signs (see chapter 10) can be made outside the normal signing space (e.g. SMACK-ON-BACK-OF-HEAD or BEE-STING-INNER-UPPER-ARM) but these are exceptional. The BSL sign ASDA is derived from the supermarket chain's logo of patting the rear trouser pocket. BSL does not have established signs on the buttocks, so many signers relocate the sign to the side of the hip.

BSL has handshapes in its signs that other languages do not. Greek signers do not use a handshape with the fist closed and only the little finger and ring

Fig. 1.3a EUROPE (French Sign Language)

Fig. 1.3b EUROPE (BSL)

finger extended. In BSL this is used for the numeral SEVEN in some dialects, and found in signs such as NEXT-WEEK (fig.1.4). American Sign Language (ASL) does not have the handshape with the fist closed and only the middle finger extended. BSL uses this in HOLIDAY and MOCK (fig. 1.5). Any ASL signer would know automatically that this handshape is not a part of ASL. If we asked them to make a list of every handshape in ASL, they would probably not be able to, but if they saw the BSL sign MOCK, they could easily say that ASL did not use that handshape.

These differences between languages can be seen in spoken languages as well. Standard British English does not use the sound made in the back of the

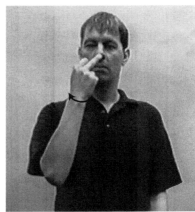

Fig. 1.4 NEXT-WEEK

Fig. 1.5 MOCK

Fig. 1.6 IT (Irish Sign Language)

throat, that is found in Scottish words like *loch* and German words like *Bach*. English speakers often change the sound to a /k/, so that *loch* and *Bach* are pronounced like *lock* and *bark*. Alternatively, they may keep the 'foreign' sound for any words that they know use it in the original language but they certainly would not make a new English word using it.

A user of the language knows what could be a part of their language, and what could never be found in it. For example, the word *mbwa* (the Swahili word meaning 'dog') could never be part of English, but *wamb* could be, if someone invented it. The first word has a sound combination that cannot occur in English. The second word contains a combination that is seen in English.

A BSL user also knows what could be in the language, and what could never be found in it. For example, we would have to reject a sign made on the back of the knee as a possible sign of BSL. The Irish Sign Language sign IT uses a handshape foreign to BSL, so that sign is not part of BSL (fig. 1.6). However, there is no reason why BSL could not have a sign that uses the little finger extended from the fist, circling in contact with the cheek. It just happens that no such sign exists – at least, not at present – although it would be allowed by the rules of BSL.

It is worth noting that speakers of different languages often cannot even hear different sounds from other languages and very often cannot make these sounds accurately. Signers usually can use the locations or make the hand-shapes from other sign languages, perhaps because sign elements can be easily seen, while the articulators for spoken language are largely invisible. It is even possible to mould a signer's hand into the right configuration if they have problems forming it (although this is not good manners if the signer is an adult). The fact that sign languages still reject certain forms as being foreign, even if they are not difficult to make, shows that the sign languages are working in a similar way to spoken languages.

(2)   **Someone who knows a language also knows the sign/words in
the language and how to relate these forms to meanings.** This means that
they know the lexicon (the mental vocabulary) of the language, and they
know what signs or words mean. This is probably what most people mean
when they say they 'know' a language.

The relationship between forms and meanings is 'conventional'. This
means that everyone who uses a language has agreed that a particular sound
or gesture has a certain meaning. Here we need to understand the term 'referent'. A referent is something referred to by a sign or a word. If we see a
mouse, we use the word *mouse* to describe it. The real animal we are talking
about is the referent, and the word *mouse* or the sign MOUSE is the symbol
that refers to it. We can say that the symbol MOUSE has a conventional relationship with the referent 'mouse'. *Mouse, souris*, and *rato* have been agreed
by speakers of different spoken languages to refer to a small furry creature
that lives in a hole and eats cheese. So there is a different convention in each
language. If speakers did not agree, someone could use another word such as
dog to refer to a 'mouse' and it would be very confusing.

In sign languages this is also true, even for signs that seem very visually
motivated. Users of a sign language must all agree on a symbol for a referent.
The BSL and ASL signs for the referent 'pig' are both clearly visually motivated, but very different in form: the BSL sign focuses on the shape of a pig's
snout, and the ASL sign focuses on a pig eating from a trough. The BSL sign
UNIVERSITY is visually motivated and focuses on the shape of a mortar-
board, while the equally visually motivated Spanish Sign Language sign
focuses on the idea of students carrying books under their arm (fig. 1.7). Two
similar signs in ASL and BSL represent a beard but in ASL this means 'old'
and in BSL it means 'man'. These examples show that signs must be agreed
conventionally by the language users, even when they are visually motivated.

There are many different signs for MOUSE, even within BSL, but users
are agreed that their sign means the same small furry animal that lives in a
hole and eats cheese. This means that the signers know the lexicon, and know
what the lexicon means. If we know a language, we are able to name a mouse
when we see it. We do not know a language fully if we know that one sign is
formed as 'bent index finger at the side of the nose' but we do not know that
it means MOUSE, and refers to the small furry animal. We will discuss this
topic in more detail in chapter 9.

(3)   **Someone who knows a language, knows how to combine
words/signs to form phrases and how to combine phrases to form sentences.** It means having knowledge of the syntax of the language. It gives the
user of the language the opportunity to be creative.

Dictionaries contain many words, and a good dictionary may be expected
to contain most of the 'words' in a language. However, there are no diction-

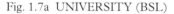
Fig. 1.7a UNIVERSITY (BSL)   Fig. 1.7b UNIVERSITY (Spanish Sign Language)

aries to tell us the sentences allowed in a language. This would be impossible because there are an infinite number of sentences that can be made in any language. This is not a problem for a person who 'knows' a language because if we know the rules of the language, we can understand and produce new sentences. We may not know how we do it, but we can do it.

This is why it is not enough to teach someone BSL by teaching them every sign in the dictionary. Even after learning the entire lexicon, a person still would not know how to put the signs together to make a sentence.

In BSL, users also know how to add grammatical information to signs. Signers can also take parts of signs and put them together to make new signs. This is unlike English, where words are mostly fixed and a speaker does not often create a new word. We will discuss this in more detail in chapter 11.

IS BSL A FULL, REAL HUMAN LANGUAGE?

All too often, people (including some linguists) have dismissed sign languages as not being 'real' languages. The popular view of sign languages is that they are merely some sort of limited pantomime or gesture system, and very much inferior to spoken languages. Here we will consider the possibility that BSL may not be a real language. We will reject this idea, and show that it is – in every way – a full human language.

One of the most important results of sign linguistics studies over the last 30 years has been to demonstrate to everyone (who cares to look) that BSL is a language just as good as English, or any other language.

This is important because some powerful people have thought that BSL is not a language at all, so it has not been used in many settings, including schools, churches, or on television, and deaf people have suffered by having their language ignored or insulted. The Abbé de l'Epée, the great French educator of deaf children in the late eighteenth century, believed that deaf people should use signs, but even he believed that the 'natural gestures' of deaf people needed changing to follow the grammar of French. Many deaf people have been told by English speakers that deaf signing is not as good as English, and they have come to believe this. Because of this prevailing attitude, it is worth making two points very clear:

- **BSL has got a grammar, just as good as English.** Its rules are very different, and in some ways they are more flexible, but it still has got a grammar. BSL sign order is different from English word order, but it still has its own rules of sign order.

- **BSL has got a lexicon, just as good as English.** The lexicon is not as big, but the size of the lexicon is not as important as being able to say anything necessary. It sometimes happens that there is not a single BSL sign to express something for which English uses a single word or phrase, but there are also some BSL signs for which there is no easy translation into English. Many languages lack exact translations for words in other languages. A well-known example is that English does not have a single word for the German word *Schadenfreude* (the pleasure derived from another person's discomfort), and yet English can still express this meaning if necessary. If BSL really needs a specific item for a concept, it can create new signs just as English can make new words. BSL can also borrow new signs from other languages, just as English can borrow new words.

A linguist named Charles Hockett suggested in the 1960s that there were several 'essential characteristics' of all human languages which are not found in other communication systems. This approach to defining language is very different from traditional dictionary definitions. It can also help us to see what characteristics are common to both spoken and signed languages. We will consider some of these characteristics here.

Language has broadcast transmission and directional reception

Human language is 'broadcast'. That is, it is not beamed to an individual receiver, but can be received by anyone within hearing (for spoken languages) or sight (for sign languages). Anyone within range can receive what is being communicated and identify the person communicating.

Rapid fading

Both speech and sign have rapidly fading signals. The channels remain open for use and re-use. Language users need complex memory abilities to process and store the short-lived signals of language.

Interchangeability

All people are both senders and receivers of language. Animal communication systems are often 'uni-directional' – for example, only worker bees dance to communicate information. Other types of human communication systems that are not language are also often 'uni-directional' – for example, road signs. Language also offers feedback so that speakers and signers can monitor their own linguistic output, can talk or sign to themselves, and can alter their communication as they desire.

Arbitrariness and conventionality

Words and signs have the meanings they do because users of the language agree that those are their meanings. There is no reason why the word *cat* means what it does – it does not look like a cat or sound like a cat. Even those words which do sound like what they mean are conventional. In BSL, although many signs are not completely arbitrary, their meanings are always conventional. For example, we have seen that the BSL sign MAN clearly is related to 'beard', but a nearly identical form in ASL means 'old'. Many other signs are completely arbitrary, such as WHY.

Creativity and productivity

Users of a language can create and understand an infinite number of new sentences. The rules of a language allow us to combine the vocabulary we know to create new meanings. Humans can talk about anything, even things that are impossible. Even as strange a sentence as English: *The geranium pulled a six-foot high strawberry gateau from his pocket and watched while it stood on one leg and combed its hair* or BSL: FLOWER g-e-r-a-n-i-u-m- POCKET PULL-FROM-POCKET CAKE STRAWBERRY CAKE Index SIX-f-t- HIGH FLOWER WATCH CAKE Index STAND-ON-ONE-LEG COMB-HAIR can be understood, even though no one has ever seen these sentences before, and has never been in a situation where this is true.

Users of a language can also produce new words or signs which have never appeared before in the language. They can be made either by combining existing words or parts of words in new ways, or by making up new words using the rules of the language (see chapters 3 and 11).

Discreteness and duality of patterning

Discreteness refers to the fact that human languages are made up of elements distinguished from each other. In English the sounds /b/ and /p/ are perceived as different from each other. There are no intermediate sounds halfway between /b/ and /p/. In BSL, 'B' and '5' are distinguished in the same way. A handshape produced with slightly spread fingers is understood as either a 'B' or a '5', not as some other intermediate handshape (see chapter 9 for further discussion of BSL phonology).

Duality refers to the observation that languages combine basic units that have no meaning into meaningful signs or words. In English, the sounds that make up the word *dog* have no meanings on their own, but if we combine them in the right order, they make the word *dog*. The same characteristic is true for BSL as well. Each sign is made up of a handshape, a sequence of movements and holds, and a location. Each alone is meaningless, but when they are put together, a sign is formed. For example, FLOWER has a handshape (also seen in other signs like PERFECT and ASK), a location at the nose, and a movement from one side of the nose to the other.

The feature of duality means that a small set of meaningless features can be used to build up a large set of meaningful signs. There are only a small number of handshapes in BSL, but they can be used at different locations with different movements, so that many different signs can be made.

Displacement

Users of a language can construct messages about the past, present and future, and about imaginary worlds as well as the real world. Animal communication does not have the same flexibility. As a philosopher once said: 'No matter how eloquently your dog may bark, he cannot tell you that his father was poor but honest.'

In the past educators often believed that deaf children could only refer to things that were present in the environment, or talk about things happening at that time. These educators thought there was no way to talk about the past and future in BSL. We now know, however, that BSL is no more tied to the here and now than English.

Cultural transmission

Human language is passed on to children within a culture. The specific language children acquire depends on the linguistic group into which they are born. No one is 'programmed' to acquire a specific language. All languages are equally learnable, provided that there is adequate exposure. Deaf babies often use gestures, even if their parents do not sign to them, because they have a natural urge to communicate, but neither these, nor the 'home signs' that families create, are language. BSL has to be learned from other users of BSL.

Talking about language itself and lying

Language can be used to talk about language – just as we are doing here. In contrast, dogs do not bark about barking. Language can also be used other than to provide accurate information: it can be used to lie and mislead.

Languages are based on sound

The vast majority of human languages make use of the 'vocal-auditory' channel – they are produced by the mouth and perceived by the ear. All writing systems also derive from or are representations of spoken language. Sign languages are different; they make use of the 'corporal-visual' channel – produced by the body and perceived by the eyes. Why sign languages are almost never found in hearing communities is not known. However, what we have seen so far in this chapter is sufficient to show that BSL is a human language, even though it does not use sound. This means that theories based on language as essentially spoken are wrong.

WHAT IS AND WHAT IS NOT BSL?

Studying sign linguistics, we will be looking at BSL. But often there is great confusion over what we mean by BSL. BSL is the natural language of signs that has developed in Britain over centuries. It is the language used by the British Deaf community. In the last part of this chapter we will briefly review visual forms of language that are not BSL. We will discuss Cued Speech, Paget-Gorman Sign System, Signed English, Sign Supported English, and fingerspelling.

Cued Speech

Hand cues are made near the mouth, to identify the different speech sounds which look the same on the lips (e.g. /p/, /b/, and /m/) or those which cannot be seen on the lips at all (e.g. /k/ and /g/).

This system does not use signs at all. It focuses on speech. Eight handshapes show groups of English consonants, and when these handshapes combine with different lip patterns, it is possible to identify each sound.

The Forchhammer hand-mouth system in Denmark is a similar system. Ultimately, a person is not expected to rely on Cued Speech, but rather to use it as a tool to learn spoken English.

Cued Speech is not BSL because it does not use BSL signs, and it always follows spoken English mouth patterns. The cues have no meaning on their own (fig. 1.8).

Fig. 1.8 Cued Speech configurations for 'wall'

Paget-Gorman Sign System (PGSS)

It is important to remember that this is what it says it is: a sign system, not a sign language. It provides a one-to-one, sign-to-word match. It was designed in the 1930s (and refined in the 1950s) to be used in the classroom with deaf children. Nowadays it is mostly used with children with learning difficulties or specific language impairments, but who have normal hearing.

The signs do not come from any sign language, but have been created to represent English words and English grammar. There are signs for pronouns, prepositions (e.g. 'at', 'on', 'under', 'through', etc.), and also separate signs for grammatical endings to English words like '-s', '-ing' and '-ed'.

It has thirty-seven basic signs for categories such as 'colour', 'time', 'animals', 'buildings', 'food', and 'surfaces'. One hand makes the sign for the basic category, and the other hand makes the sign for the particular meaning referred to.

For example, the non-dominant hand makes the category sign for 'colour', and the dominant hand makes the sign that means 'red'.

In the signs meaning 'school' and 'classroom', the specific sign is the same, but the basic category sign differs. In the sign used to mean 'school', the basic sign is the 'building' category, and in the sign used to mean 'classroom', the basic sign is the 'room' category (Fig. 1.9).

This system may seem a little unusual to English speakers, but there are many languages in the world that include categories in their words. They are called 'classifier languages' (see chapter 3). However, English is not one of them. This means that the aim of teaching English to children may be confused by making an important principle out of something that English does not use.

It also means that all signs are equally complicated. In 'natural' languages, most simple words that we use often are easy to sign or say. It is usually more effort to sign or say more complicated concepts. In Paget-Gorman, signs

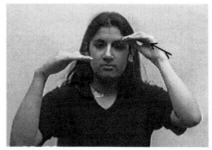

Fig. 1.9a SCHOOL (Paget-Gorman)

Fig. 1.9b CLASSROOM (Paget-Gorman)

for simple ideas may be just as complicated as those for more complicated concepts.

The Paget-Gorman Sign System does have advantages, though. Importantly, it has been a way for deaf children to have better access to English than they would through lip reading. It is also quite easy for English speakers to learn. However, it is not the language of the British Deaf community.

Paget-Gorman is not BSL because it uses a different lexicon and grammar from BSL, and it is not used by the British Deaf community.

Signed English

This uses basic BSL signs in English word order, and also has sign markers to show English grammar (e.g. articles and past tense) (fig. 1.10). It also uses fingerspelling (see below). It is almost always used with speech.

Fig. 1.10a THE (British Signed English)

Fig. 1.10b -ED (British Signed English)

There are problems with the use of Signed English. It is very slow, and a message takes longer in Signed English than in either BSL or English. This means that spoken English accompanying Signed English becomes unnaturally slow, and many English speakers let speech take over and drop some signs. Many BSL signers using Signed English insert features of BSL grammar so that the grammar is not 'pure English' any more.

Signed English is not often used in everyday communication. It is mostly a teaching tool, so that signers can learn more about the structure of English. Many deaf children recognise the usefulness of Signed English when sitting in an English lesson, but use BSL in the playground.

There is also the problem that there is no one-to-one match between the English and BSL lexicons: one word in English does not correspond to one sign in BSL. For example, the word *open* in English can be translated by many different signs, as in: 'open a window', 'open a door', 'open a can of fizzy drink', 'open a tin of cat-food', 'open a drawer', 'open curtains', etc. Therefore it is not clear whether different signs should be used for these different meanings. However the benefits of Signed English are that it does use BSL signs, it is easy for English speakers to learn, and it reflects the structure of English.

Sign Supported English

In Sign Supported English (SSE), the key words of a sentence are signed, while the person speaks. This means the main vocabulary is produced from BSL, but much of the grammar is English on the mouth.

It is quite easy for users of English to learn, which means it is easy for English-speaking, hearing parents to use. This is important. Hearing parents of a deaf child may not have the time or ability to learn full BSL, but SSE allows some communication and some access to signing. However, the child has no access to any grammar words except English through lip-reading.

It is important to remember that SSE does not refer to a single way of communicating. Someone who is fluent in both English and BSL will use SSE differently from someone who is fluent in BSL but knows only a little English, or someone who is fluent in English but knows only a little BSL.

Fingerspelling

This represents the written form of English, not speech. It is possible to recreate any written English word by fingerspelling, with twenty-six hand-arrangements corresponding to the twenty-six letters of the English alphabet. By using these, fingerspellers can produce the spelling of an English word on their hands (fig. 1.11). Fingerspelling is not BSL though, because it does not use BSL vocabulary. However, BSL does use fingerspelling quite a lot, especially in some dialects.

People may say that the manual alphabet is not a 'natural' part of BSL. There is a 'political' aspect to this. The manual alphabet was invented by hearing people and fingerspelling is always derived from English, so it can be seen as a threat to BSL because of the power of English.

However, it is not a good argument to say that fingerspelling has no part in BSL just because it is derived from another language. Many languages take words from other languages and make them their own (English certainly does). Also, the manual alphabet is used so much in BSL that it cannot really be ignored. It is the responsibility of linguists to describe what they see, not what they think should be there.

Younger people fingerspell less than older people, but older deaf people fingerspell quite a bit. It is important for linguists to understand how fingerspelling fits into BSL.

The manual alphabet is used for fingerspelling whole words that do not have equivalents in BSL, and for the names of people and places. In fact, this accounts for about a third of all uses of fingerspelling. Even people who do not fingerspell very much will often fingerspell names. Fingerspelling may often accompany a sign with a similar meaning, as well. For example, someone may spell a personal name and then give a personal name sign (e.g. -n-e-l-s-o-n- EYE-PATCH), or fingerspell the name of a place and then give its sign (e.g. -t-h-a-i-l-a-n-d-, NEAR CHINA, THAILAND). This may also happen with other signs where a word is fingerspelled and followed by a sign with the same basic meaning, but with more information.

Many fingerspellings are of words that do have a sign synonym in BSL, so there must be other reasons for fingerspelling. Some reasons are as follows:

(a) to introduce an English word which has no sign equivalent (yet), often occurring with new technology, current affairs, or in academic discussion (e.g. -f-a-x-, -s-e-r-b-, or terms like -m-o-r-p-h-e-m-e- from linguistics);

(b) to accompany a new concept expressed in sign, (e.g. 'computer mouse');

(c) to explain a regional sign that may not be well-known to a signer from another region (e.g. the Scottish sign TUESDAY);

(d) to produce English idioms while signing BSL (e.g. 'there is going to be a happy event' or 'he got away with murder');

(e) to produce euphemisms (e.g. s-e-x-, -g-a-y-, -t-t- (toilet));

(f) for convenience and time-saving (e.g. if everyone knows the English word); and

(g) to use as part of the core lexicon of BSL (e.g. MOTHER, SON, JANUARY produced as -m-m-, -s-n-, and -j-a-n-).

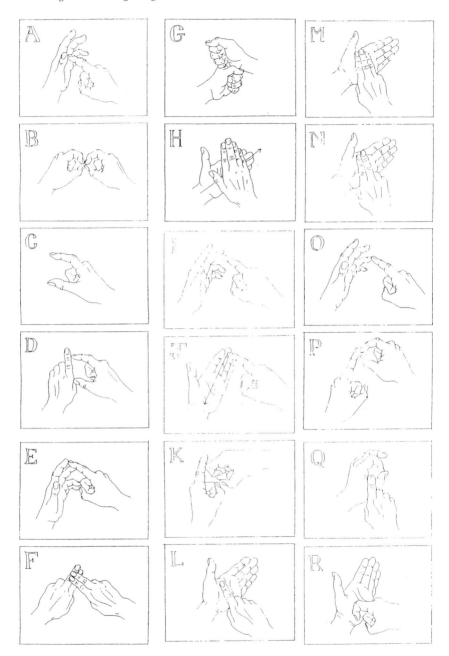

Fig. 1.11 The British manual alphabet

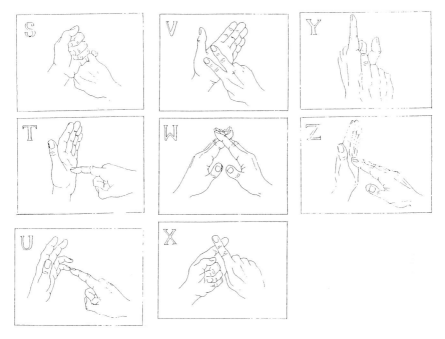

Fig. 1.11 *(cont.)*

Signers whose first language is English may also use fingerspelling even though an equivalent sign exists throughout the sign community. For example a learner may ask how to sign -b-i-o-l-o-g-y- or -u-n-i-v-e-r-s-e-. Interpreters may also use fingerspelling while interpreting into BSL, especially if they are tired.

Abbreviations of fingerspellings are often made into signs, and the use of only the first letter of words is very common. We will discuss fingerspelling further in chapter 12.

Relationship between visual language and BSL

None of the five forms of visual language described above is BSL. However, languages are not in closed boxes, and some of these forms may 'leak' into BSL.

PGSS is not a part of BSL, but some children use PGSS vocabulary with BSL grammar, and some adults use some PGSS signs when they are signing BSL.

Fingerspelling and cued speech are often borrowed by sign languages.

Many sign languages are influenced in some ways by fingerspelling. Danish Sign Language has several signs borrowed from the Forchhammer system of hand-mouth cueing.

The whole area of Signed English is complex. It takes most of its vocabulary from BSL. If it is 'pure' Signed English, with all English grammar, then it is not much like BSL. Certainly its vocabulary is much more limited because it does not have many of the ways of creating signs that BSL does. However, many deaf people use signing that is more or less influenced by English for various reasons, and they often feel that it is BSL. In the end we must rely on a social definition: does the person believe that the language they use is BSL?

None of these ways of communicating is better or worse, from a linguist's point of view. They may have different social value but they are not 'better' or 'worse' as languages. In the past, many people felt that BSL was 'bad' and Signed English was 'good'. Now that we accept BSL, Signed English and SSE are sometimes felt to be 'bad'. That is not very good for the self-esteem of someone who uses SSE or Signed English. Linguistic discussions should try to avoid resulting in value judgements.

As a last point, we must remember that BSL is independent of English, but it has still been influenced by English. Any minority language that is surrounded by a majority language will be influenced by the majority language, and BSL is no different (as we will see in chapter 12).

SUMMARY

In this chapter we have discussed what linguistics is, and why sign linguistics is important. We have discussed what it is that we know if we 'know' a language. We know what is allowed in the language, what words or signs are in the language and what they mean, and how to put these words and signs together in the right order. We have seen that BSL is a full human language, just like any other. It can do all the things that any human language can do. We have also considered visual forms of language that are not BSL. Cued Speech, Paget-Gorman Sign System, Signed English, Sign Supported English, and fingerspelling have all been invented for use with deaf people, but they are not the natural language that BSL is.

EXERCISES FOR CHAPTER 1

1. Consider some possible and impossible signs in BSL.
   (a) Think of a nonsense sign that uses a handshape never used in BSL.
   (b) Think of a nonsense sign that uses a location never used in BSL.
   (c) Think of a sign that obeys all the rules of BSL (i.e. uses a legal handshape and location) but simply does not exist.

2. The importance of knowing the language rules as well as vocabulary is considered here.
   (a) Translate the sentences using a BSL dictionary.
       (i) *The priest doesn't like fish.*
       (ii) *Twenty cows crossed the road yesterday.*
       (iii) *Send the new school a letter.*
       (iv) *Who is that person hugging the dog?*
       (v) *The proof of the pudding is in the eating.*
   (b) What problems did you find in doing this?
   (c) Translate the sentences into 'well-formed BSL'. What differences do you see between the well-formed BSL sentences and the ones based solely on your dictionary work?
   (d) What does this tell us about the importance of knowing how to combine signs?

3. What are the communication limitations of traffic lights, road signs, and the washing instructions on clothes that we do not see in human communication?

4. Make up a sentence in BSL that you are fairly sure nobody has ever signed before. (You should not make up any new signs – just use signs that you know are already used in BSL, but have never been used together before.)

5. Observe the fingerspelling of fluent BSL signers. Note down the different uses and put them into the categories we have discussed in this chapter.

FURTHER READING FOR CHAPTER 1

Aitchison, J. 1983, *The articulate mammal,* London: Hutchinson.
Crystal, D. 1988, *Rediscover grammar,* Harlow: Longman.
Fromkin, V., and Rodman, R. 1993, *An introduction to language,* London: Holt, Rinehart and Winston.

Chapter two

BSL in its social context

The main part of this book concerns the structure of BSL. We will be describing the way that the language works and how it can express different types of linguistic information. However, it is important to remember that all languages are used within a social context. To understand how a language is used, it is important to understand the interaction between the language and the communities that use it.

By now it should be clear that British Sign Language is the language of the British Deaf community. Its lexicon is different from other sign languages. Sign languages are not universal, and most sign languages are mutually unintelligible. The sign languages of all Deaf communities are independent of (even if they are influenced by) the spoken language of the surrounding hearing communities. For this reason there is very little similarity between American Sign Language, Irish Sign Language, and British Sign Language. The three Deaf communities are independent of each other, and so are the three sign languages.

However, some sign languages are historically related to each other. They are more similar to each other than to languages that are not related. In a similar way, some spoken languages are related. If we know German, we can read some Dutch, to which German is closely related. If we know Spanish, we can read Portuguese fairly easily, again, because the two languages are related. However, knowing Dutch and German will do us little good if we try to read Finnish, to which neither is related. Knowing Spanish and Portuguese will leave us totally unprepared to deal with Basque, which is spoken on the borders of France and Spain. We can see the same pattern in sign languages. For example, French Sign Language (Langue de Signes Française – LSF) and American Sign Language have a common language ancestor. As a result, signers of LSF can recognise many ASL signs and vice versa. Australian Sign Language (Auslan) is closely related to BSL, because of the historical links between the Deaf communities and deaf education in the two countries, and BSL signers can understand Auslan fairly easily. Users of Scandinavian sign languages are reported to be able to understand each other fairly well, again because the sign languages have a common history.

Although BSL is a language in its own right, and different from other national sign languages, British signers do not all sign in exactly the same way all the time. Just as there are variations in English according to region, social group membership and the social situation, so there are regional, social and situational differences in BSL. It is important to be aware of these differences in BSL, if we want to have a really good understanding of the language.

SOCIAL VARIATION IN BSL

We will begin by considering social variation in BSL. In spoken languages, linguists generally expect to find differences according to different social groups within the language community. We can expect differences in language according to the social class of the speaker, their age, sex, ethnic identity, religious identity, and whether they have experienced bilingual situations. We will look at all these for BSL.

Social class

Sign linguists need to ask if there is a class distinction in sign languages. In order to be able to answer this, we need to decide what is meant by 'class'. In British English, social class labels are based upon a person's income, educational background and family background. However, there is no reason why 'social class' should have the same defining points for British deaf people. Research has shown that deaf people are more likely to have unskilled and semi-skilled jobs than hearing people, so income is not necessarily a good guideline. Few members of the Deaf community were able to go to university until very recently, so there is not the same educational parallel with hearing people. In American deaf society, however, there is a recognised 'social class' grouping of deaf people who have attended Gallaudet University, the national university for deaf students. In Britain, we might think that the educated elite of the Deaf community would be those who attended the Mary Hare Grammar School for the Deaf. There has been no formal research into the BSL of Mary Hare alumni, but since this school has not used sign language officially, having been a pupil at Mary Hare might not necessarily have a strong influence on BSL usage.

The most noticeable 'social class' distinction in BSL derives from family background. Only 10 per cent of deaf children in Britain are born to deaf parents, while 90 per cent have hearing parents. Exposure to sign language at an early age is different for the children of deaf parents and the children of hearing parents. Those born to deaf parents are more likely to have had early exposure to a fluent model of adult BSL. Those born to hearing parents often (although by no means always) only begin to learn BSL when they start school, or even after they have left school. Consequently, those deaf people coming from deaf families are seen as members of a linguistic elite. Research comparing adult signers from deaf and hearing families has shown that their signing differs significantly. Deaf signers from deaf families use features of BSL such as syntactic space, mouth patterns, and proforms (all of which will be discussed in more detail in later chapters) very differently from signers from hearing families.

Social class in relation to the hearing community may also have some effect upon BSL, although this has not been researched. In English there is a class dialect or variant which is very similar across different regions. This is often called Standard English. We will discuss the idea of a standard form later, but it is worth mentioning that there is no evidence yet of a social class form in BSL unrelated to region.

Age dialect

The form of a language also varies according to the age of the person. There are many features that differentiate older and younger signers. It is important to ask why language varies in different age groups. In spoken English, differences between generations are fairly small. They are often limited to the lexicon: slang, and words that have currency when people are young and then are retained as they get older. For example, some older people in England still talk about the 'gramophone' and 'wireless', while younger people do not. On the whole though, there is a reasonable ease of communication between the two generations.

In sign languages the differences are often far greater than in established languages such as English. This arises especially because of the breaks in passing the language from generation to generation. Some young deaf people claim that they cannot understand the signing of older deaf people. As a broad generalisation, older deaf people (for example, those over seventy) often use much more fingerspelling and many fewer clear English mouth patterns than younger deaf people. Many younger deaf people (for example those under twenty) use a form of BSL that is more heavily influenced by English grammar, and use relatively little fingerspelling. Signers from different age-groups also use different signs for the same referents.

Many of the differences we see in the signing of deaf signers of different ages are due to three major factors. First, as we have seen, there are few deaf children with deaf parents. This means that children rarely learn sign language from their parents. This in itself results in large changes in sign language between generations.

Second, educational changes have had a large impact on the signing of deaf people. Before the 1940s, English was taught through lip-reading and fingerspelling, with the result that the fingerspelling of older deaf people is fluent and a prominent feature of their signing. Since the 1940s, improvements in hearing-aid technology have meant that deaf people have been expected to use more of their residual hearing to listen to and learn English. Until fairly recently, most deaf schools used English in the classroom and signing was proscribed with varying degrees of severity. However, most schools were residential, so that deaf children signed together (often in secret) and therefore learnt BSL in the playground, in dormitories and at weekends. Since the 1970s there have been increasingly tolerant attitudes towards some use of signing in the classroom, and most recently in some schools, even of BSL. At the same time, however, deaf schools have been closing down as more deaf children are sent to local 'mainstream' schools. Although this new policy of educating deaf children in the mainstream has many advantages, one major loss is that of exposure of children in schools to a relatively large signing community. It remains to be seen what effect this will have upon BSL.

A third reason for age differences in BSL arises from the way in which many signs in BSL reflect some aspect of the appearance of items, or the way they are used, as we will see in chapters 10 and 11. As technology has changed, so younger signers have changed signs to reflect the new appearance or means of operating or handling new appliances, while older signers often maintain the sign in its earlier form. The BSL sign TELEPHONE has changed over time as telephones have gone from a two-part apparatus with the mouthpiece held in one hand and the earpiece in the other, to a dumb-bell-shaped apparatus, and now to one with an aerial, that is held in the palm of the hand (fig. 2.1). Similar changes may be seen in signs such as TRAIN, CAMERA, and WATCH (the timepiece) where technology, and consequently the form, have changed greatly over the last seventy or eighty years. This same pattern is seen in other sign languages as well as BSL.

Old signs also die out. For example, signs such as PAWN-BROKER and ALMS are no longer in widespread use, although they are given in a very basic list of signs from 100 years ago. Young people today might not need signs for these referents, but would need signs such as FAX, LOTTERY, or LASER to refer to new inventions (fig. 2.2).

Men and women's dialects

In most languages women and men use language differently. There has been a great deal of research on this topic, especially in the last thirty years. The extent and type of difference vary in different languages. Again, the important question is why differences occur.

Fig. 2.1 Changes in TELEPHONE

Theories explaining differences in the English of men and women usually focus on the different social status of men and women (women traditionally having a lower social status), or on the different social roles of men and women (women traditionally having a more caring role in society and men being more prone to confrontation and assertion) or on the different aims of conversation (women using language to construct friendships more than men do). Although there is something useful in many of these theories, the differences described between men and women in English are relatively small. Only very rarely do they result in a complete breakdown in communication between the sexes.

In some sign languages the difference between men and women's signing is very great, to the extent of mutual unintelligibility. This is not the case in BSL, where the differences in the language of men and women are as slight as they are in English, if not even less important. It has been theorised that since most teachers working with deaf children in primary schools are women, they may be the major source of signing for both boys and girls, so that at an early age boys do not have adult male role models for signing.

Fig. 2.2 FAX

However, there has been no research to confirm this. In Ireland, there are greater differences between men and women's signing than in Britain because boys and girls were educated separately. This is also true in Belgium, and in other Roman Catholic countries where boys and girls are traditionally educated separately.

Two researchers, Barbara LeMaster and John Dwyer, found substantial lexical differences between the signing of Dublin deaf men and women. The two schools of St Mary's (girls) and St Joseph's (boys) used totally different sign vocabulary. When deaf young people left school, they had to learn a new vocabulary to communicate with the opposite sex, with the girls tending to adopt the boy's signing. Strict segregation of the children no longer exists, but knowledge of the two forms of Irish Sign Language still persists, particularly among older signers.

Variation linked to ethnic group

In America, there are some dialects of ASL that are easily identifiable as 'Black' ASL and others that are clearly 'White' ASL. In America, until the 1960s, Black and White children were segregated for education. Deaf clubs also had, and continue to have, a tradition of being separate, although they are no longer segregated by law. This history of segregation has led to language variations based on racial group. Black signers often know both the White and Black varieties of sign, while the White signers often only know the White signs.

The variation in BSL between Black and White signers appears to be less marked. There were relatively few Black people in Britain until the 1950s, and Black deaf children all went to 'mixed' deaf schools, where they were often in the minority, so they learned the general 'White' dialect of BSL. This is not to say that the signing of British Black and White signers is identical. Until recently there has not been a strong Black deaf identity in Britain. Black deaf people saw themselves as part of either the Black community or the Deaf community, but not both. However, some Black deaf adults have adopted a style of signing that marks their identity as Black. As this joint identity grows, a more distinctive 'Black' dialect of BSL may emerge.

The British Asian Deaf community is relatively small. However, since genetic deafness appears more common in the British Asian community, we may see an emerging 'Asian' variety of BSL in time.

Religious groups

There are some differences in BSL arising from membership of religious groups. Again, there are clear reasons for this, especially in relation to education or membership of social groups. Different religious groups do have special signs relating to practices or beliefs of their religion. For example, Jewish deaf people have signs for 'rabbi', and for religious festivals like 'Chanukkah'; and Hindu deaf people have signs for their gods and religious festivals.

Muslim signing in BSL has never been formally researched. We would need to consider why British Muslims might sign differently from non-Muslim signers. Certainly Britain's deaf Muslims have their own signs for specifically religious terms as do other religious groups.

One clear difference in BSL is in Roman Catholic and Protestant signing. The signing of deaf British Catholics is strongly influenced by Irish Sign Language because Irish monks and nuns have provided education for Catholic deaf children that is suitable for Catholic beliefs, and Irish-trained priests serve the Catholic Deaf communities in Britain. The Catholic signing uses many initialised signs that are based on the Irish manual alphabet (see chapter 12 for more about initialised signs).

British Jewish signing has an interesting history. At one time there was a school for Jewish deaf children in London. This was an oral school, but some signing was permitted after the arrival of deaf German refugee children in the late 1930s, to ease communication. Where children remained within the Jewish community, they continued to use this signing after they left school, and did not mix much with other deaf people. After the deaf school closed (in the early 1960s) the Jewish School for the Deaf dialect began to decline and very few people use it now. However, Israeli Sign Language is now influencing the signing of British Jewish deaf people. Many Jewish deaf people visit Israel and they are increasingly adopting Israeli signs.

Different spoken language identities

This is not a major feature in BSL, as there is only one dominant national spoken language in Britain. But it is worth remembering that some British deaf people's home language may be neither English nor BSL, but another language (such as Greek or Urdu). In many other sign languages, however, this is important. For example there are dialects of ASL that are different depending on whether the deaf person's family uses English or Spanish. In Canada, deaf people from English-speaking families use a dialect of ASL; deaf people from French-speaking families use a different language: LSQ (Langue de Signes Québécois). In Nigeria, the sign languages vary depending on membership of different tribes, as they do to some extent in South Africa.

We have seen, then, that social group identity may have an effect on the signing of BSL users. Another important factor is the signer's regional identity within Britain. It is this type of dialect we will now consider.

REGIONAL DIALECTS

Regional variants are what most people think of as 'dialects', even though in linguistics social dialects are just as important as regional dialects.

Researchers from Bristol University a few years ago presented a list of English words for translation to signers in different parts of the country. Regional lexical differences were identified, particularly in some semantic fields, for example colour terms, days of the week, and numerals (fig. 2.3).

This is very interesting in itself. It is important for anyone wanting a good command of BSL to know regional variants of signs. However, in linguistics, it is not enough just to collect and describe different regional signs. We also have to consider why regional signs exist. It is possible to say that BSL regional dialects arose because deaf people were quite isolated, and only knew the BSL of the people around them. There is no way to send letters in BSL to distant places (because there is no written form), and BSL cannot be used on the telephone. So when spontaneous changes arose in one dialect of BSL, no one outside the dialect area knew about it. Now that we have national broadcasting of BSL on television, people can see more varieties of BSL, and differences between regional dialects may be decreasing.

This may explain why dialects have not merged until recently, but it does not explain how they arose in the first place. It suggests that there was once a single BSL which split up as deaf people spread throughout the land. That is likely to be only partly true.

Dialect differences in BSL have probably arisen from schools where signs

Fig. 2.3 Regional variants of ELEVEN

have been used informally by children for many years. When young people leave school, they may not use school signs in contact with deaf people from other areas, but continue using those signs with other local people. Signers will have two variants of BSL: one that they use when they meet people from outside their local region, and one that they use locally. Fluent signers are as skilled at switching between regional varieties as speakers of English are.

Dictionaries may also be responsible for the lessening of sign language dialect differences. If a regional sign does not get into a dictionary (or only with the title 'regional sign') it will lose out to signs that are in the dictionary. All these factors are likely to lead to regional dialects becoming more uniform in the future.

SITUATIONAL VARIETIES OF BSL

The language used by any member of a language community will vary according to the social situation. 'Social situation' includes the topic of conversation, the reason for the conversation and the person or people who

Fig. 2.4a WHAT (child-directed BSL)   Fig. 2.4b WHAT

make up the conversational partners. As with all languages, BSL changes according to whether a signer is addressing one person, a small group, or a large gathering. It also changes when a signer meets someone who does not have good command of BSL (either a foreign deaf person or an English-speaker). It changes when a signer is signing to a small child, rather than an adult. It also differs depending on whether a situation is informal and relaxed and the group present know each other well, or whether a situation is formal and the conversational partners are strangers. Knowing about the situational varieties of BSL is important for anyone who wants to have a thorough under-standing of the language.

In more casual BSL the signing space used tends to be larger and more expansive than in formal signing. Informal BSL uses less fingerspelling and a greater variety of non-manual features, including more marked facial expressions (see chapter 5 for further discussion of non-manual features). There is less influence from English and the sign lexicon may include signs appropriate only to informal conversation, including idiomatic signs and creative metaphors, or to conversation with young children, for example, use of a special sign WHAT (fig. 2.4).

Signs may be less clearly articulated, so that, for example, a two-handed sign may be made with only one hand, or may be articulated in the space in front of the body, rather than at a specific location on the body. There may be greater use of signs more like 'gestures', for example, a simple shrug, instead of the sign DON'T-KNOW.

When deaf people meet foreign deaf people, they change their signing to include more gestures. More non-manual features are used, and there is considerably more paraphrasing and negotiation of meaning. Deaf people who are experienced in communicating with foreign deaf people may not use

BSL, but instead use a form of communication known as 'International Sign'. This is a mixture of mime, international gestures that are mutually known (perhaps borrowed from another language or perhaps not) and signs made up for that encounter only and with meaning only in that context.

Often, however, the person using International Sign uses a high percentage of their own sign language. One study by Bencie Woll found up to 70 per cent of signs produced by a BSL user as part of International Sign were BSL signs. For this reason, we might want to say that International Sign is not a separate form of communication but a situational variant of BSL. This approach is further supported by the fact that the grammar used in BSL and International Sign is often very similar.

CHANGES IN BSL

If we are to understand BSL in its social context, we also need to understand its development through time. Knowing about the way BSL has been used and thought about in the past can tell us a lot about the way BSL is used and thought about today. This section will identify some of the changes that have occurred in BSL, and propose some reasons for these changes.

All living languages change, and BSL is no exception. We have already seen that older signers sign differently from younger signers, and this is an example of language changing.

There are four processes by which signs change over time. Sometimes, a new sign arises for a new concept. This often happens for developments in science, technology or medicine (FAX, LASER, INJECTION, AIDS) (see pages 24–5 earlier in this chapter and also chapter 11). Sometimes a new sign replaces an old one with exactly the same meaning. Sometimes a new concept arises, but a sign already in use takes on that new meaning. For example, the sign SOCIAL-WORKER is the sign previously glossed as MISSIONER. Although social workers do not wear the distinctive clothing of church workers seen in the sign, they replaced missioners' work, and the old sign was maintained but with altered meaning. Finally, there can be a change in a concept, and this change is reflected by a new sign replacing the older form. In the past, the concept of 'interpreter' was signed as 'missioner sign for me'. With the change to recognising the function of an interpreter as signing for *both* participants, a new sign INTERPRETER was developed (fig. 2.5).

Problems with studying the history of BSL

Before we can consider change in BSL we need to look at some of the very real difficulties in historical research on BSL. The study of the history of BSL is hampered by the lack of written records. There never has been a way of writing BSL. It is much easier to do historical research on languages with a

Fig. 2.5a SOCIAL   Fig. 2.5b INTERPRETER
WORKER/MISSIONER

literary tradition. The history of English, for example, can be traced through surviving texts that date back for many hundreds of years. These texts reveal the history and development of English words, grammar and even pronunciation. Historical sign linguistics cannot use a corpus of BSL literature in the same way, simply because one does not exist.

Although data about BSL's history is limited, it is not non-existent. Information about the past of BSL can be found from several sources. It is possible to read about BSL from written descriptions in English, and there are some printed records containing drawings and photographs of signs. There is also some film of British deaf signers dating from the 1920s. With the widespread use of video now, we will have a better record of BSL to pass on to future generations of historians.

Another important source of information is the linguistic knowledge of deaf people themselves. Sometimes linguists have the opportunity to study the signing of very old deaf people. For example a 100-year-old deaf woman has been interviewed on television. Information can also come from those members of the Deaf community with deaf grandparents, and even great-grandparents. They may have considerable knowledge of the ways that people used to sign. Deaf people in their eighties, who had deaf grandparents, would know of the signing used by someone who had been born as long ago as the 1840s or 1850s. Sign linguists and members of the Deaf community are now realising the importance of recording linguistic information from older deaf people.

Information written in English

Written descriptions or comments about signing in the past are not uncommon, but they were usually written by people with little detailed knowledge of deaf people's sign language. Many of these references simply mention that signing was used. There are, however, a few descriptions of the signs themselves. The earliest known of these comes from 1575. The parish register of St Martin's, Leicester, mentions that in February 1575 a deaf man, Thomas Tillsye, was married to a woman named Ursula Russel (who was probably hearing), making his vows in sign.

The sayd Thomas, for the expression of his minde, instead of words of his owne accord used these signs: first he embraced her with his armes, and took her by the hande, putt a ring upon her finger and layde his hande upon her harte, and held his handes towardes heaven; and to show his continuance to dwell with her to his lyves ende he did it by closing of his eyes with his handes and digginge out of the earthe with his foote, and pulling as though he would ring a bell with divers other signs approved.

One major drawback to these descriptions is that it is not always possible to tell exactly how the signs were made. In the passage above, the parish clerk mentions that Thomas made a sign 'digginge out of the earthe with his foote'. This might have meant that he gestured digging with a spade, or simply that he dug his heel into the ground, or even his toe. There is no way of knowing.

Drawings of signs

Illustrations solve the problem of vague English descriptions, but illustrations have always been expensive to produce in texts, and they are rare before the nineteenth century.

Illustrations show the form of signs much more clearly than written descriptions ever could. They also show some facial expressions accompanying signs. However, they are only lexical lists. There are very few references to any morphological features or to the syntax of the language.

There are a few French dictionaries of the signs used in the late eighteenth and early nineteenth centuries in the Paris deaf school, providing an excellent record of the sign vocabulary used in France. There is no known similar record in Britain because of the different histories of the two countries' education systems. Thomas Braidwood, who ran the first non-private school for deaf children in Britain, claimed to use an entirely oral method of teaching, because he believed this gave him greater prestige. In 1809, his grandson Joseph Watson revealed that the teaching methods used in the school had always used a combination of lip-reading, signs, fingerspelling, writing, and pictures. There is no record of what these signs were, though.

From the middle of the nineteenth century onwards, several sets of illustrations of signs used by British deaf people were produced. Many deaf men were trained to work as printers, and deaf people ran their own magazines and newspapers for the Deaf community. Occasionally these papers carried illustrations of signs, often drawn by deaf artists.

Other sources of pictures are texts published by missioners to the deaf, which often contain a few pictures of signs. These signs were often connected to religion, although some common signs were also shown. It is these illustrations that allow some discussion of changes in signs over the last century (fig. 2.6).

History of sign language in schools

The history of BSL is closely bound up with the development of deaf education and the growth of schools for the deaf. Deafness is not common and before schools existed, deaf people rarely, if ever, met other deaf people. Aside from some basic home signs which they would have used for communication with their immediate family and friends, they did not possess a full sign language. The same is true today in many parts of the world. For example, in India today, many rural deaf people are isolated and have to resort to the creation of their own signs.

In eighteenth-century Britain, it was these isolated deaf people in particular who benefited from being brought together in schools. Their sign language was profoundly influenced by the social community created by the schools. In these schools deaf children were able to learn a shared language for the first time.

However, it is clear that deaf people were signing before the schools and institutions for the deaf opened. Signing existed 200 years ago, wherever there were groups of deaf people. Although deaf people in rural communities have often been isolated, deaf people have gathered in larger towns and cities, and sign languages have been used there for centuries. Deaf people who moved into the new towns and cities created by the industrial revolution would have found other deaf people with whom they could socialise. Pierre Desloges in the 1780s referred to the many deaf people in Paris who would meet and discuss all manner of things in sign language, without having had the benefit of any education. In England, Pepys described a deaf servant who signed to his master, George Downing, to tell him of the Great Fire of London in 1666.

The lexicon of sign language used in British schools from the mid-eighteenth century onwards developed from a mixture of signs used by the deaf children themselves, and those signs introduced by the teachers.

CHANGES IN ATTITUDE TO THE LANGUAGE

Widespread changes in BSL occur because of the way that the language is officially accepted and used in public places. BSL changed when schools started using it nearly 200 years ago, and again when it was banned in schools. It has also changed as a result of its introduction to TV.

1.—The R. hand is rubbed circularly on palm of L. 2.—The three fingers are drawn upwards. 3.—The R. thumb is pressed hard down on L. palm. 4.—The R. hand is scooped across L. palm from fingers to wrist. 5a.—The R. hand is extended and closed. 5b.—The R. hand, palm upward, is turned sharply downwards and to the R. 6.—Rich, grand, gentleman. Fingers as drawn are moved slowly downwards. 7.—Better: R. thumb passed over L. thumb TWICE. Best: the same ONCE emphatically. (NOTE.—3a "best" some use the L. first finger, as drawn, instead of the thumb). Worst: R. little finger passed over L. emphatically once. 8.—Move R. hand upwards in short stages. 9.—Pass R. hand as drawn slowly down lower part of face. 10.—As drawn, making forward and upward small circles with upward thumbs. 11.—R. hand moved smartly upward from mouth. 12.—Hands as drawn, shivered. 13.—As drawn, wrist first elevated, then down, as in drawing.

П. ASH.

Fig. 2.6 Nineteenth-century drawings of signs

The lack of continuity between generations of signers may also have contributed to change in BSL. Many deaf children have, in recent generations, learnt their sign language from other children (often the children of deaf parents) rather than from adult language models.

Another possibility is that adults cause the change deliberately. They may use, and teach, the language the way they think it should be used rather than the way they actually use it. Some BSL teachers teach BSL that they never use, because they believe it should be like that.

One of the causes of change in sign languages has been language planning. Ever since public education of deaf people has existed, hearing people have attempted to alter the language used by deaf people. Even the great sign language enthusiasts of the eighteenth and nineteenth centuries, such as the Abbé de l'Epée in France, and Thomas and Edward Gallaudet in America, tried to alter the 'natural signs' of the deaf children they taught, to match the structure of the spoken language of the country. Interestingly, the earliest writer to criticise this was Joseph Watson, nephew of Thomas Braidwood, and headmaster of the first school for the deaf in London. He wrote in 1809:

Never let any thing so chimerical be thought of as an attempt to turn master to the deaf and dumb, in the art of signing . . . What should we expect from an European who should undertake to teach his own . . . language, to a South-Sea Islander, who was henceforward to live among Europeans . . . Should we suspect that the teacher would set about new modelling, methodizing and enlarging this . . . language as the readiest method to make the islander acquainted with the European tongue . . . (p. 77)

Unfortunately for the language planners, the changes have not been as great as they would have liked. Hearing people often try to invent new signs or sign systems for deaf people (e.g. new fingerspelling alphabets or complete new systems such as Paget-Gorman) but these have never been totally accepted.

STANDARDISATION

One of the causes of language change is standardisation. The standard form of a language is the one used by the educated elite of the language community and so it has high prestige. It cuts across regional differences and is an institutionalised norm which can be used in the mass media, to teach foreigners, etc. It is usually the form of the language that is written, has had its grammar described and is found in the dictionary. Once it has developed it changes very slowly.

It is by no means clear that there is a standard form of BSL. Standard English is the language used by the hearing social elite, and is not regionally identifiable. The BSL of the social elite, however, is regionally marked. Standard English is the dialect that is taught to second language learners of

English; learners of BSL learn local dialects of BSL. Standard English is written, taught in schools and is validated by being preserved in dictionaries (any words from non-standard forms of English that do make it into dictionaries are clearly marked as being non-standard). However, there is no written form of BSL, and BSL has only recently been officially reintroduced to schools, where it is not always taught by native signers. The *BSL/English Dictionary* has only recently been published and contains a limited number of signs. Standard English is used on television and radio and by government organisations. BSL on television is not standard and deaf television presenters use different regional signs. Despite these major differences, there is no doubt that British deaf people recognise BSL as one language. We have seen that there are certain signs that are accepted as being those one uses across regions. Sometimes standardisation of a particular sign can be traced to the influence of single individuals or small groups. For example, in the past there were a number of different regional signs for 'people'; many of these have been lost and have been replaced by the sign PEOPLE (a compound of MAN + WOMAN) thought to have been spread by social workers. The sign GOVERNMENT used on television (and consequently spreading throughout BSL) was imported by people who had attended international conferences. It is possible that some form of Standard BSL is slowly emerging, but with the social context of BSL being so different from that of English, there is no certainty as to what form it will take.

SUMMARY

This chapter has described some of the variety seen within BSL in relation to different social contexts. We have seen that the lexicon and grammar of a sign language differs in different social groups within a Deaf community. We have also seen that there are regional dialects in BSL, just as there are in English. Situation will also affect the choice of BSL variety. Looking at BSL in a historical context, we have seen that like all living languages, BSL has changed to reflect changing society.

EXERCISES FOR CHAPTER 2

1. Here you need to think about the way that the social situation will affect a signer's language.
    (a) Consider different contexts for conversation (e.g. legal matters, education, deaf politics, lunch, cars, health, linguistics, fishing, world politics). How would the context affect your signing?
    (b) Consider how you would change the signing you use with different conversational partners (e.g. a child, your mother, your best friend,

your partner, a hearing person who can sign quite well, a hearing person who signs very little, a foreign deaf person, a television audience, an older person, a meeting of five colleagues, a room of fifty people, etc.).

(c) Consider different reasons why you might be talking or signing (to tell a story, to arrest someone, to deliver a lecture, to tell someone off, to make friends, to interview someone, to build up and solidify a friendship, to seduce someone, to ask a favour, etc.). How would this affect your signing?

2. Compare video clips of the same signer in two different social situations. Watch the two clips and identify linguistic features that you find different in the two contexts. Include the following:
   (a) the different use of mouth patterns (is one more 'English' and one more 'BSL'?)
   (b) the different facial expressions
   (c) the varying amounts of 'gesture' in the signing
   (d) the different amounts of fingerspelling
   (e) the size of signing
   (f) the speed of signing
   (g) the use of space

3. Compare video clips of three signers of different ages. Try to find one signer over seventy, one in their forties, and one a teenager. What differences are there in their signing that might be attributed to their ages?

4. What signs can you think of that must have come into BSL during your lifetime because the concept did not exist before then?

5. Think about the idea of a 'standard' dialect of BSL.
   (a) Is there a standard form of BSL?
   (b) Is there a single dialect that is used by the educated elite of the Deaf community?
   (c) Is there a single dialect that has high prestige?
   (d) Is there a single dialect that cuts across regional differences?
   (e) Is there a single dialect that is an institutionalised norm which can be used in the mass media?
   (f) Is there a single dialect that is used to teach 'foreigners' (i.e. hearing people)?
   (g) Is there a single dialect that is written?
   (h) Is there a single dialect that is found in the dictionary?
   (i) Might there be one in the future?
   (j) Should there be one?
   (k) Is there a dialect that is not a standard yet but you think should be? Why?

FURTHER READING FOR CHAPTER 2

Aitchison, J. 1981, *Language change: progress or decay?*, London: Fontana.

Aramburo, A. 1989, 'Sociolinguistic aspects of the Black Deaf community', in C. Lucas (ed.), *The sociolinguistics of the deaf community*, San Diego, CA: Academic Press, 103–21.

Hay, J., and Lee, R. 1994, *A pictorial history of the British manual alphabet*, Edinburgh: The British Deaf History Society.

Edwards, V., and Ladd, P. 1983, 'British Sign Language and West Indian Creole', in J. G. Kyle and B. Woll (eds.), *Language in sign*, London: Croom Helm, 147–58.

Jackson, P. 1990, *Britain's deaf heritage*, Haddington: Pentland Press.

Jepson, J. 1991, 'Urban and rural sign language in India', *Language in Society* 20, 37–57.

Joos, M. 1968, 'The isolation of styles', in J. Fishman (ed.), *Readings in the sociology of language*, The Hague: Monton, 185–91.

Kyle, J. G., and Woll, B. 1985, *Sign Language: the study of deaf people and their language*, Cambridge University Press.

Lucas, C., and Valli, C. (eds.) 1992, *Language contact in the American Deaf community*, London: Academic Press.

Nowell, E. 1989, 'Conversational features and gender in ASL', in C. Lucas (ed.), *The Sociolinguistics of the deaf community*, San Diego, CA: Academic Press, 273–88.

Sutton-Spence, R., and Woll, B. 1990, 'Variation and recent change in British Sign Language', *Language Variation and Change* 2, 313–30.

Woll, B. 1987, 'Historical and comparative aspects of BSL', in J. G. Kyle (ed.), *Sign and school*, Clevedon: Multilingual Matters, 12–34.

Zimmer, J. 1989, 'Toward a description of register variation in American Sign Language', in C. Lucas (ed.), *The Sociolinguistics of the Deaf community*, San Diego, CA: Academic Press, 253–72.

Chapter three

Constructing sign sentences

Syntax is the term for the way that words or signs are put together to create meaningful sentences and phrases. Although there are conventions in written English to mark the beginnings and ends of sentences, there is no formal agreement on what a sentence is. It is very difficult to define a sentence, but most people have a rough feeling that they know a sentence when they see or hear one.

Although words have their own meanings, the order of words or signs in a language is just as important in relation to meaning. If words and signs are not combined according to the syntactic rules of the language, the meaning is either lost, changed, or becomes unclear.

Before we can address the syntax of BSL sentences in much depth, we need to consider the idea of 'proforms', and how and why BSL uses them. Understanding and using proforms in BSL is essential for the understanding of the syntax of BSL.

A proform is anything that refers to, and stands in the place of, something previously identified. The identification may have been made using a sign for the referent, or the referent may be present for all to see. For example, the sign CAR has a related proform (a 'B' hand (see Conventions for an explanation of this and other symbols)) that is used to provide more information about the location of the car and the action it is involved in. This type of structure is also found with MAN and CAT ('G', 'V' or 'V̈', depending on the context), CAKE ('5' hand), PLATE ('B' hand), and many other signs.

Pronouns are a familiar type of proform to those who know English. A pronoun stands in place of a previously mentioned noun. 'Pronoun' literally means 'in place of a noun'. A 'proform' is any form that stands in the place of, or does the job of, some other form. It is often a noun, so the terms 'proform' and 'pronoun' may seem to be the same, but we keep the term 'pronoun' to mean *I, you, he, she, it, we, them*, etc., and we use 'proform' for a more specific BSL structure.

Pronouns contain information relating to who is being talked about, and how many of them there are. This information is called 'person' and 'number'.

Person refers to who is being talked about: in first person, the speakers or signers refer to themselves, or themselves and some others. In second person, the speakers or signers refer to the conversational partner(s). In third person, the speakers or signers refer to anyone or anything else, apart from speaker or signer, and conversational partners.

Number tells us how many individuals are involved. The English number system only has singular and plural, so we only know if there is only one person involved or more than one. The BSL number system is more complex.

Pronouns can only have meaning when the referent can be identified. In the sentence *That's his book* we need to know who 'he' is. In *She won't like it*, we need to know who 'she' is. 'I' and 'you' are easier to identify, because the referents are often present. If a speaker says 'I' we know who is being referred to, and we know who 'you' refers to, because 'I' is talking to 'you'. In writing, or on the telephone, however, we may not know who 'I' refers to, because the speaker or signer is not present. 'We' in English is a bit harder to identify. It includes the speaker, but who else? If a person says, *We will go shopping on Saturday* does that mean 'the speaker and a friend', or 'the speaker and their family' or 'the speaker and the whole of London', or 'the speaker and the rest of England' or 'the speaker and the conversational partner'? The context of the sentence almost always identifies 'we'.

Pronouns in BSL are articulated by pointing to a location associated with the noun. The form of the point is the same in all pronouns, but the location of the point varies depending on the location assigned to the noun. Pointing has many other functions in BSL so we use the term 'index' to refer to pronoun pointing.

Pronouns in BSL are similar to those in English, but there are five main differences.

(1) **BSL does not distinguish between 'he' and 'she', but English does.** Many languages do not mark this difference, for example Finnish and Hungarian. This does not mean that these languages are somehow less perfect than English. It just means that they are different. Even English does not always make this gender distinction in its pronouns, because 'they' can be used to refer to more than one woman, or more than one man, or a group of men and women.

(2) **BSL has many more pronouns than English.** English has pronouns for one, and pronouns for more than one. For 'singular' (pronouns referring to one), we have *I, he, she, it,* and *you.* For 'plural' (pronouns referring to more than one we have *we,* and *they. They* covers *he, she* and *it,* while *you* is the same whether it is singular or plural.

BSL has pronouns for (individual) one, two, three, four and five (although there is some disagreement about five) and for (plural) many. This means that instead of being limited to *we*, as English is, BSL has WE-TWO, WE-THREE, and possibly WE-FOUR and WE-FIVE as well as WE-ALL and EACH-OF-US. The same applies to 'you' and 'they'.

(3) **BSL does not always use possessive pronouns the way English does.** In BSL, pointing is also used for possession, such as 'my', 'your', 'ours', etc., where this is regarded as 'inalienable', or 'permanent', for example 'his name', 'your husband', 'their children', 'my kidneys'. The usual possessive pronouns with closed fist (MY, OUR, YOUR) are only used for possession regarded as transitory, temporary, or capable of being changed.

(4) **BSL pronouns include additional information about the noun.** In the signed form: TEACHER Index$_3$ (where we sign TEACHER, and then point – meaning 'the teacher, he . . .') the pronoun refers both to the teacher, and also to where he is. English pronouns do not tell us where a person is.

(5) **The English pronoun *it* refers to almost anything that is not a person.** English uses *it* to refer to a house, a dream, an aeroplane, a 6-foot strawberry gateau, the whole of the USA, the whole world, or a tiny virus. So English *it* is used for anything of any size or shape, just so long as it is not human (with a few exceptions).

BSL can use a simple point with the index finger to refer to any 'it', but it also uses so many different handshapes for different shaped and sized referents, that we give this group of pronouns the special name 'proforms'.

There are many proforms in BSL but we are going to focus on three basic groups of proforms used frequently in BSL (and a fourth handshape which is slightly different):

(1) A single finger ('G'): this stands for referents which are considered to be long and thin: PERSON, PENCIL, TOOTHBRUSH, TUBE-TRAIN, etc.

   The 'G' hand is used when an object is represented as having one dimension (length or height).

(2) A flat hand ('B'): this stands for referents represented as having two dimensions: BED, PLATE, TABLE, CAR, PICTURE, etc.

   The same handshape can be used as a proform for many signs, e.g. a flat 'B' hand can stand for nouns such as WALL, VEHICLE, TABLE, CARD, FAX, BICYCLE, PLATE. The 'B' hand occurs in different orientations: palm-down (e.g. in FAX); palm-up (e.g. in PLATE); and palm-sideways (e.g. in WALL).

   The Swedish linguist, Lars Wallin, has said that this handshape is used when objects are represented as having a top and a bottom, and with two dimensions as most important (or 'salient'). It is interesting that Irish Sign Language and ASL proforms for cars and other similar vehicles have the palm facing sideways (representing length and depth), while the BSL proform has the palm facing down (representing length and width). The languages are focusing on different dimensions, but all still 'see' cars as two-dimensional.

(3) A curved 'clawed' hand ('5'): this stands for referents represented as having three dimensions, whether square or round: a building, a rock, a cake, a bush, etc. Two slightly different handshapes are used, one with the palm facing down (e.g. for HOUSE) and one with the palm facing sideways (e.g. for MUG), but both are represented as three-dimensional, with length, width, and depth.

(4) Two fingers extended and spread ('V' or 'V̂'). These are slightly different from the previous examples, because they do not focus on dimensions. They focus on the legs (or sometimes the eyes) of a person or animal. They are included here because although they do not replace the signs LEGS or EYES, they are used to represent the movement or location of a person or animal previously identified. For example, this proform would be used in 'the child ran down the stairs' and 'the cat shot out through the cat-flap'.

In BSL the full sign is normally produced first, followed by the proform. The full sign is usually needed to identify the referent. Otherwise, while it will be possible to identify some features of the referent as, e.g., flat or long, it will not be clear what it is.

Pronouns, unlike the proforms described here, do not have 'dimensions'. In some ways, pronouns are 'zero-dimensional'. They point out a grammatical area where a person or thing is placed, but there is no reference to shape.

Proforms allow signers to move signs freely in signing space. The importance of proforms can be seen most clearly when we think about full signs which either use two hands or are anchored to the body. Because proforms use only one hand, and are not body-anchored, they can be placed in different locations, repeated and moved. This freedom of movement is often not possible for the full signs. There are some one-handed signs, made in the space in front of the body, for which proforms are not used, because the signs themselves are free to move. This freedom is important because BSL uses space to provide so much grammatical information. The placement and movement of signs in space indicate their relationship to each other.

When we consider proforms, it is also worth discussing classifiers, because proforms are among those signs that contain classifiers. Classifiers are found in many languages, not only in sign languages. In the broadest sense, they label referents as belonging to a particular meaning group, such as referents that share the same shape, or are living, or are male. French uses *le* and *la* to classify nouns' referents as masculine or feminine. English does not have

Fig. 3.1 (SOMEONE) PASS

many classifiers, but there are some examples like *sheet of paper, piece of fruit, head of cattle, stick of wood,* or *blade of grass.* All these words put the nouns' referents into certain classes. Using *-ess* as a suffix to mark females (e.g. *stewardess, hostess, actress,* etc.) is also an example of classifier use. Other languages use classifiers much more, such as Chinese and many South American languages. In one South American Indian language, *ma-mamak* means 'banana' and *ma-kanu* means 'canoe'. At first glance these two referents do not appear to belong to a common category, but people with an interest in sign linguistics often quickly spot that canoes and bananas have a similar shape, so the language uses the classifier *ma* for both nouns. All the classifiers mentioned above are 'noun classifiers'; they label nouns as belonging to specific categories. Languages also have 'predicate classifiers'. In order to understand these, we need to define what a predicate is.

PREDICATES

A predicate is anything that makes a statement about a noun or a noun phrase. Predicates can be nouns, verbs, verb phrases or adjectives. In the BSL sentence (SOMEONE PASS) 'A person passed by', the subject is SOMEONE and the predicate PASS (fig. 3.1); in MAN ILL 'The man is ill', the subject is MAN and the predicate is ILL.

In BSL sentences relating to location or movement, the predicate contains information about the location or movements of the subject. In the first example above, the predicate PASS not only carries information about the movement, but the handshape shows that the subject is an individual human. However, in the sentence MAN ILL, there is no information in the handshape of ILL to indicate that the subject is an individual human. Unlike the 'G'

Fig. 3.2a Ungrammatical sentence
*DENMARK-IS-SURROUNDED-
BY-WATER

Fig. 3.2b Grammatical sentence DENMARK 3D-PRO-SURROUNDED-BY-
WATER

handshape in SOMEONE, not all noun handshapes can occur in predicates.
Elisabeth Engberg-Pedersen points this out in her research on Danish Sign
Language. In the sentence 'Denmark is surrounded by water' the handshape
of the subject DENMARK cannot occur in the predicate IS-SUR-
ROUNDED-BY-WATER. Hence the example in figure 3.2a is ungrammatical. The handshape of DENMARK can be replaced with a '5' hand in the
predicate to create a grammatical sentence (fig. 3.2b).

   In other examples, the handshape in the predicate does not appear in the
subject noun phrase. For example, in 'The car drives up the hill' (CAR Veh-
CL-DRIVE-UP-HILL) the classifier handshape for the car (the 'B' handshape) only occurs in the predicate (fig. 3.3).

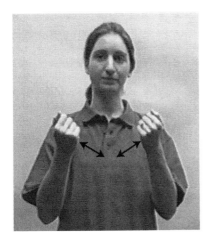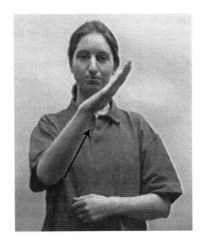

Fig. 3.3 'The car drives up the hill'

The language identifies different referents as belonging to the same class (e.g. bus, lorry, boat, etc.) so they use the same predicate classifier even if the noun signs are different. The term 'classifier' is used because the handshape 'classifies' the referent as belonging to a particular group. We can see from this where proforms fit into the idea of classifiers. The handshapes of the proforms are defined by the class of the nouns (e.g. objects seen as one-dimensional, two-dimensional, or three-dimensional, etc.).

Predicate classifiers form parts of verbs. DENMARK in the earlier example is not part of a classifier group, because it does not belong to any class and is not part of a verb.

CLASSIFIERS

Linguists have described classifiers in two ways. One way has been to use the term 'classifier' to mean any handshape which is used in signs referring to similar objects ('noun classifiers') and the other is to restrict the term 'classifier' solely to predicates. Mary Brennan's definition, in the *BSL/English Dictionary*, is very broad. Any handshape that can be used to denote a group of referents that share any similar features is called a classifier. The shared features can be the shape and size (e.g. something small and round), or the way they are handled (e.g. something held between finger and thumb), or some shared abstract meaning (e.g. all motorised vehicles). This broad definition weakens the use of the specialist term classifier. Any sign with some visually motivated link between form and meaning in this definition is labelled as a classifier. Most sign linguists in the USA and elsewhere restrict the use of the term classifier to elements that meet the following criteria:

Fig. 3.4 'The cat sits.'

(a) they refer to a group that shares some common features;

(b) they are proforms (that is, they substitute for more specific signs);

(c) they occur in verbs of motion or location.

A clear definition of the more specific concept of classifier has been given by Clayton Valli and Ceil Lucas: 'A classifier is a handshape that is combined with location, orientation, movement and non-manual features to form a predicate. It is a symbol for a class of objects.' In 'The car went past', the subject is CAR and the predicate is Veh-CL-PASS. The classifier handshape is a flat hand, with palm facing down. The same handshape would be used with any motorised four-wheeled vehicle.

In 'The cat sits', the subject is CAT and the predicate is Animal-CL-SIT (fig. 3.4). The same classifier handshape would be used for any animals with similar features. We can see from Valli and Lucas's definition that classifier predicates have two parts – a movement morpheme and a classifier handshape morpheme. Movement morphemes may be of the following types:

(1) Existence – the hand movement does not mean that the noun itself is moving. For example, in order to describe the shape of a bus, or a stack of coins, the movement of the hand outlines the shape (fig. 3.5a).

(2) Motion – the movement of the hand represents the motion of a moving referent, e.g. BICYCLE-PASS (fig. 3.5b).

(3) Location – the movement of the hand places a referent in a particular location, e.g. ANIMAL-LOCATED-AT, HOUSE-LOCATED-AT (fig. 3.5c).

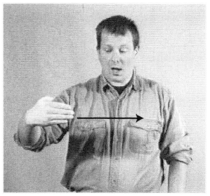

Fig. 3.5a Existence: STACK-OF-COINS

Fig. 3.5b Motion: BICYCLE-PASS

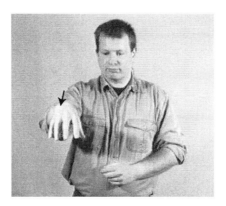

Fig. 3.5c Location: HOUSE-LOCATED

Classifier predicate handshape morphemes may include Whole Entity, Handling, and Extension. In a Whole Entity-CL the handshape represents a whole referent. This may be in terms of features (such as 'animate' or 'human'); or in terms of its dimensions or shape (also called Size and Shape Specifiers). In a Handling-CL, the handshape shows the configuration of the hand as it moves, uses or tracks an object or part of an object. Extension-CLs trace the shape of an object and include handshapes used to represent surface areas.

The same referent can be represented by different handshapes depending on the predicate. For example, a sheet of paper can be represented by a Whole Entity-CL, (in this case, a 'B' hand) in the sentence 'The sheet of paper was lying on the table', and by a Handling-CL (in this case, an 'Ô' hand) in the sentence 'Someone was carrying a sheet of paper'(fig. 3.6).

Fig. 3.6 Predicate handshapes representing SHEET-OF-PAPER ('Ô' and 'B')

The sentence I-LOOK-AT-YOU does not contain a predicate classifier because the handshape does not represent a class and LOOK here is not a spatial verb (it does not describe the existence, location, or movement of the subject). The handshape is visually inspired in some way at a metaphorical level, but it is not within the grammatical system of predicate classifiers (see fig. 8.9).

Is the handshape in WALK a classifier? It occurs in a verb of movement, and it has a meaningful handshape. It has 'two things sticking out', but it is not clear that there is a natural class of referents with 'two-things-sticking out'. In LOOK and WALK it would seem that we have classifiers, but the former represents gaze direction, and the latter, legs. The nouns FORK and SNAKE represent further examples of different referents with 'two-things-sticking-out'. In contrast, classifiers need to form a genuine and natural group with shared meaning, e.g. 'vehicles'.

Understanding proforms and classifiers in BSL is essential for understanding the rules of sign order in BSL. We will return to classifiers again when we discuss verbs in chapter 8.

SIGN ORDER

One area of BSL that many people are confused by is the question of sign order. There is no full description of correct sign order in BSL. This can make it very difficult for people learning BSL, and also for people teaching it.

However, it is important to understand that BSL does have its own rules for the order of signs, and that these rules are different from English. This is important for people who want to use simultaneous signing and speaking. It is impossible to speak English and sign BSL at the same time. It is sometimes possible for very short phrases, but not for more than that. If there are more than two or three signs, either the signs have to follow English order, or the words have to follow BSL order.

People whose first language is English often think in English and translate into BSL as they go along. This can result in signing following English order. It is important to note that using BSL signs in English order may help communication if someone does not know much BSL. It might be better to communicate with some signs rather than not at all, or only in spoken English. But it would not be BSL.

Before introducing the rules of BSL order, it is important to be familiar with the terms used to refer to the parts of sentences. Sentences can be divided into two basic parts: the subject and the predicate. The subject is the theme or topic and is most often a noun, noun phrase, or pronoun. The predicate is the rest of the sentence and serves to say something about who or what is receiving the action (the goal, or, grammatically, the object).

Linguists traditionally distinguish 'direct' from 'indirect' objects. The direct object is directly affected by the action of the verb, while the indirect object receives the object of the action, benefits from the action, or experiences it. For example, in the sentence *Maud gave Millicent a tomato*, *Maud* is the subject, and *gave Millicent a tomato* is the predicate. Within the predicate *gave* is the verb; *a tomato* is directly affected by the action, and is therefore the direct object; while *Millicent* receives the object, and is therefore the indirect object. Another way in which a sentence can be described is as consisting of a topic and a comment, which we will discuss in more detail below. Some rules of BSL order arise from the features we have already discussed in this chapter.

Full signs and proforms

To use a proform, it is usually necessary to sign the full sign and then the proform. In BSL, to sign 'The car goes under the bridge', 'car' and 'bridge' come in twice, as a sign and as a classifier, as may be seen in figure 3.7. See also figures 3.3 and 3.4.

Adjectives

Another important rule in BSL relates to the order of adjectives and nouns. An adjective describes a noun. The signs BOOK, MAN, and DOG are nouns. The signs HOT, COLD, TALL, SHORT, OLD, YOUNG, FRENCH, GERMAN, NEW, HANDSOME, RED, and GREEN are all examples of adjectives.

In some languages, the noun goes first and the adjective second (e.g.

Fig. 3.7 'The car goes under the bridge'

Hebrew: 'sefer atik' translated as 'book old'), and in other languages the adjective goes first and the noun second (e.g. Russian 'staraya kniga' translated as 'old book'). BSL usually puts the adjective second, and English *usually* puts it first. We will discuss adjectives in more depth in a later chapter, but it is useful at this point to recognise that the choice of order in BSL depends to an extent on the sentence and context. For example, a person offering a choice of hot food or cold food would sign HOT FOOD, and in this context FOOD HOT would be odd. For now, it is worth making a general rule that adjectives usually come after nouns in BSL. This is another example of why signing and speaking at the same time is difficult.

It is important to note that BSL can also build adjectives into nouns, by changing the form of the noun. For example, while it is possible to sign BOX SMALL, it is more common to articulate the sign with the size or shape incorporated, so we have the sign SMALL-BOX, or LARGE-BOX, or ROUND-BOX (see fig. 3.8a). As well as incorporating adjectives into nouns, they can be incorporated into the noun's proform, for example BOOK THICK-BOOK (fig. 3.8b).

Fig. 3.8a SMALL-BOX

Fig. 3.8b BOOK THICK-BOOK

Setting the time

When signing, a time framework is set up to establish when events happened. This is necessary in BSL because information about time (such as reference to the past) is not in every verb as it is in English, as we will see in more detail in chapter 7. Therefore a time frame (e.g. YESTERDAY) is marked at the beginning of a signer's first sentence. All following sentences are assumed to have followed in time order until the time frame is changed: YESTERDAY GIRL EAT CAKE vs. English *The girl ate the cake yesterday.* *GIRL EAT CAKE YESTERDAY is ungrammatical. A more general time marker like BEEN can also be used to set the time frame, with more specific information later in the sentence. For example in YESTERDAY BEEN LECTURE ME, the framework is established first, but BEEN LECTURE ME YESTERDAY is also acceptable, because the general time frame 'past' is set up at the beginning.

Asking questions

In questions, the question sign is usually placed at the end in BSL:

KEYS WHERE vs. *Where are the keys?*
TOM WHO vs. *Who's Tom?*
LINGUISTICS WHAT vs. *What is linguistics?*
TICKETS HOW-MANY vs. *How many tickets?*
TRAIN LEAVE WHAT-TIME vs. *What time does the train leave?*

It is also worth noting that since BSL question signs are different from English, questions like 'what time' are single units.

The question sign may also be placed both at the beginning and the end of the sentence, for example:

WHERE KEYS WHERE

Pronoun copy

In pronoun copy, the index used for the pronoun is repeated at the end of the sentence. It is very common in BSL, for example:

GIRL Index$_3$ RICH Index$_3$ ('The girl is rich') (fig. 3.9)

Index$_1$ DEAF Index$_1$ ('I am deaf')

In English we might say *The girl's rich, she is*, or *I am deaf, I am*, but this is unusual in Standard English, and much less common than pronoun copy in BSL.

Pronoun copy is often accompanied by a head nod, especially if the sentence is emphatic. It is also possible to leave out the manual sign altogether and just nod in the direction of the pronoun.

Nouns and verbs

Sometimes in BSL nouns come before verbs, and sometimes verbs come before nouns. The reasons for the difference are clear. We have already said that the full sign must come before the proform. This means that if a proform is used in a verb, then the noun must come first, e.g. CAR Veh-CL-BACK-UP. Where proforms are not involved, other factors are important. In MAKE CAKE or LIGHT FIRE or PAINT PAINTING, the verb comes first

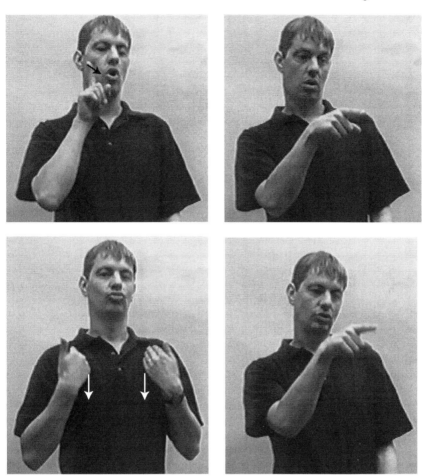

Fig. 3.9 'The girl is rich'

and then the noun. In FOOD PACK, GLASS BREAK, or WALL PAINT, the noun comes first and then the verb. This is because verbs are of two types – 'effective' and 'affective'.

(a) Effective verbs make something exist – e.g. 'bake', 'make', 'light', 'paint' (a picture).

(b) Affective verbs act on something that already exists – 'eat', 'hit', 'break', 'pack', 'paint' (a wall).

In other words: the fire does not exist until we light it; the painting does not exist until we paint it, etc. But the lunch is there to pack; the glass is there to

Fig. 3.10a I-ASK-YOU   Fig. 3.10b YOU-ASK-ME

break; the wall is there to paint, etc. BSL represents this logic by ordering the nouns and verbs accordingly.

MAIN ELEMENTS IN SENTENCES

So far we have considered the order of some signs within a sentence. We will now consider the general structure of the whole sentence. Linguists have categorised the world's languages according to the order of the main elements in sentences: the subject, the verb, and the object. Information about which word is the subject or the object may be given in three basic ways: through inflectional morphology, the form of the word, and word order.

Inflectional morphology

An example of information through inflectional morphology in English is the addition of /-s/ to the ending of a verb to mark if a 3rd person singular (he, she, it, the man, etc.) is performing the action, e.g. *He asks mother* vs. *I ask mother*. BSL includes even more information in the verb, e.g. the direction of movement is different in I-ASK-YOU vs. YOU-ASK-ME (fig. 3.10), as we will see in chapter 8 (see also figures 8.4 and 8.5).

The form of the word

In English, pronouns change depending on whether they are the subject or object of the verb. *I* and *he* are used for subjects, e.g. *I like mice* or *He likes mice*. *Me* and *him* are used for objects, e.g. *Mice like me* or *Mice like him*.

In BSL there is no difference (in the manual component) between the pronouns for the subject and object. Many spoken languages also do not distinguish subject and object pronouns.

Word order

Word order can show which element is the subject and which the object. In English, for example, the subject comes before the object.

Given that there are three basic elements (S, V, and O), there are six ways they can be ordered. Different languages order them differently. Where languages are highly inflected (see inflectional morphology above), word order is often less important grammatically because the relationship between subject and object is shown by the inflectional morphology. Some languages have free word order because they are so highly inflected, e.g. Latin, Quechua, and Navaho. Others have a preferred order for sentence elements.

SVO – e.g. English, French, and Thai 'the girl won the race'
VSO – e.g. Welsh, Biblical Hebrew 'won the girl the race'
OVS – e.g. Hixkaryana 'the race won the girl'
OSV – e.g. Hurrian 'the race the girl won'
VOS – e.g. Tzutujil 'won the race the girl'
SOV – e.g. Turkish, Japanese 'The girl the race won'

Seventy-five per cent of the world's languages use SVO or SOV. Standard English follows an SVO order, e.g. *Jane smiled at Mary. Jane* comes first because she is the subject. If *Mary* had done the smiling, she would have come first. However, this rule is less strong in casual spoken English than in formal, written Standard English. It is probably better to talk about preferred order, rather than what is allowed. In poetry and songs we can take even more liberties. David Crystal gives the following examples:

Hear thou our prayer – VSO
Strange fits of passion have I known (Wordsworth) – OSV

Just as spoken languages vary in their preferred order, so do sign languages. To a certain extent the order of the signs may be influenced by the spoken language of the surrounding community and the written language the signers know. However, the preferred order for Italian Sign Language is like that of spoken German and that of German Sign Language is like that of spoken Italian.

In English, word order is very important for identifying the subject and object. In our earlier sentence *Jane smiled at Mary* only word order tells us who smiled at whom. In BSL, sign order is not always so important. This is partly because of extra information carried in the verb, for example in 'I telephone you' (this will be discussed later). There are also other cues (especially non-manual ones such as role shift and eye gaze changes – which will also be discussed later) which make the meaning clear.

It has been claimed that there is no fixed order in BSL, but only general preferences. In the past, it was said that this flexibility indicated that BSL was not a real language. However, fixed order is only one way of creating meaning. Also like other languages (for example Spanish) BSL often omits the subject completely, especially where the subject is 'I'.

Influence of the spoken language on signers

English can influence the order of signs in BSL. This influence can come in many ways:

(1) It may occur for some signers because sign language is their second language and the order of the spoken language dominates their signing. Signers whose first language is English often use English word order to a greater or lesser extent, even if they do not intend to.

(2) Other signers who are fluent in both English and BSL may choose to use a more English sign order when communicating with signers with good English skills but limited BSL.

(3) In formal situations signers often feel that signed English is required. There is no exact definition of signed English or BSL, but there may be times when signers use rather more English sign order in their BSL.

(4) Signing is particularly influenced by English word order when the signer is signing while translating from a text. TV presenters who are signing from an autocue may follow a more English order than if they are signing out of the studio.

Real world knowledge

Real world knowledge plays a role in deciding on word order in BSL at the sentence level. The order of signs can be flexible if there is no question of who is doing the action or receiving the action. For example,

GIRL CAKE EAT or CAKE GIRL EAT

MAN NEWSPAPER READ or NEWSPAPER MAN READ

are all acceptable because cakes do not eat girls and newspapers do not read men.

The American linguist Scott Liddell has pointed out that being able to work out the likely meaning of a sentence does not necessarily mean that it is grammatically correct. For example in English if we heard *The newspaper the*

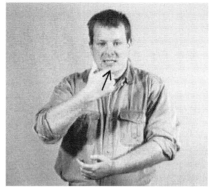

Fig. 3.11 PIZZA EAT-PIZZA

man read, we would be able to guess that the man read the paper and not vice versa, but we would still not feel the sentence conformed to the rules of Standard English.

Note that in these examples, however, that the verb comes after the object. This is necessary because the form of the BSL verb can vary, depending on the object. For example, the handshape in EAT is different in EAT-PIZZA, EAT-APPLE, and EAT-HAMBURGER (fig. 3.11). In order to establish the correct form of the verb, the object often comes before it.

Nouns receiving the action can be built into the verb

Sometimes there is no need to think about the order of the signs because there is only one sign. For example, there is no need to worry about whether the correct order is WASH FACE or FACE WASH because WASH-FACE is signed as a single unit (fig. 3.12). The same is true of SMOKE-CIGARETTE or OPEN-DOOR, etc.

Topic-comment

In BSL, the topic is usually established first, and then commented about. The topic is the subject of the sentence. It is also the focus, the old information, the theme of the discourse, or the person or thing about which the conversation is taking place.

The comment is what is said about the topic. It is also the predicate, and the new information about the topic.

The topic sets up a spatial, temporal, or individual framework within which the predication takes place.

Temporal framework - e.g. 'During the war...' After the topic has been set

Fig. 3.12 WASH-FACE

up, everything that follows is set in the time of the war. 'When I was at school...' sets up a time framework so that everything which follows is in that particular time. 'When I go on holiday next summer...' sets up a time framework for talking about the future.

Spatial framework – e.g. 'I saw a lovely house...' After this topic has been set up, everything that follows belongs to that spatial framework of talking about the house.

Nominal framework – e.g. 'Let me tell you about my sister...' This sets up the nominal framework of talking about the signer's sister.

In topic-comment structures, the topic is set up and re-established each time it is changed. BSL is not the only language that sets up topics and then comments upon them; topic-comment languages are common around the world.

So, in BSL, the topic is important. It is marked in several ways.

(1) It comes first.

(2) It is followed by a pause – e.g. SCHOOL (pause) LETTER SEND. An English translation would be *It was the school that sent the letter.*

(3) The eyes are widened during the topic, followed by a pause, e.g.

    _____wide eyes   _____question

SISTER BEFORE LIVE AMERICA (pause) NOW COME-BACK

'Is your sister who was living in America, back now?'

(4) It can be accompanied by a head nod, e.g.

    __hn

DOG CAT CHASE

'It's the dog that chases the cat.'

Fig. 3.13 READ-NEWSPAPER

(5) The topic may be signed and held with one hand while producing the comment with the other hand, e.g.

NEWSPAPER (nd) NEWSPAPER
        (d)   READ

'It's the newspaper that I'm reading.' (fig. 3.13)

Because different parts of a sentence can serve as topics and comments, the order of signs can vary, depending on what has been made the topic. Any of these is orders is possible if the topic is marked.

GIRL EAT CAKE   SVO   'As for the girl, she ate the cake'
CAKE GIRL EAT   OSV   'As for the cake, the girl ate it'
EAT CAKE GIRL   VOS   'As for eating the cake, the girl did it'

Topics are sometimes established by making the sentence into a 'rhetorical' question. For example, the signer may sign:

_____q _____hn
GIRL WHAT EAT CAKE
'What about the girl? She's eating cake.'

_____q ___hn
EAT CAKE WHO GIRL
'As for eating the cake, who's doing it? The girl.'

_____q ___hn
GIRL EAT WHAT CAKE
'What's the girl eating? Cake.'

It is important to realise that these look like questions but are not really questions, and an answer is not expected. They merely serve to emphasise the topic.

SUMMARY

In this chapter we have considered pronouns and proforms in BSL. BSL has a rich system of signs to represent referents, and this system is rather different from English.

Proforms vary depending on the shape and size of referents. Proforms are particularly important for BSL because BSL is a spatial language which moves signs in space.

We have considered many of the influences on sign order in BSL. BSL has definite rules about sign order, which are different from word order rules in English, so that speaking English and signing BSL at the same time is not possible.

Full referents usually must come before proforms. Adjectives often come after the noun (or are incorporated into the form of the noun). Question signs are sentence-final, or can occur both at the beginning and at the end of a sentence. Pronoun copy permits the repetition of a pronoun at the end of a sentence. Nouns may precede or follow verbs, depending on whether the verb is affective or effective.

The order of signs is influenced to some extent by English, but also by common sense and the way that nouns can be built into the verb. Finally, BSL sign order is controlled by the topic of the sentence, with whatever the topic is coming first.

EXERCISES FOR CHAPTER 3

1. Consider further the importance of proforms in BSL.
    a) Try placing the following signs in space in front of the body. Which are possible and for which do you need proforms?
    (i)   CUP
    (ii) VIDEO-CAMERA
    (iii) AEROPLANE
    (iv) TRAIN
    (v)   CAR
    (vi) WOMAN
    (vii) ROSE BUSH
    (viii) BED
    (b) Translate each of these examples into BSL and note where the full sign and the proform come:

(i)   *video cassettes on a shelf*
(ii) *books piled on a table*
(iii) *tables stacked on top of each other*
(iv) *a bomb under a car*
(v)   *a limpet stuck to the side of a ship*
(vi) *a sheep jumping over a hedge*

2. Adjectives
   (a) Create sentences including translations of the following into BSL and see how you use the adjectives in BSL:
       (i)   *a short list*
       (ii) *my blue car*
       (iii) *the pretty girl*
       (iv) *the thick book*
       (v)   *his hot food*
       (vi) *the German President*
   (b) What positions are acceptable? Is the idea of a 'position' always relevant? Which adjectives go before the sign, after the sign, at the same time as the sign, are represented by proforms, or are incorporated into the sign?

3. Translate the following sentences into BSL, using pronoun copy.
   (a) *What is linguistics?*
   (b) *The boy stole the TV.*
   (c) *She won a gold medal.*

4. Sign order
   (a) Translate the following sentences into BSL, thinking in particular about sign order. Is there only one acceptable sign order, or can each sentence be signed in different ways?
       (i)   *The man likes the woman.*
       (ii)   *The woman likes the man.*
       (iii) *I like your sister.*
       (iv)   *The man reads a newspaper.*
       (v)   *The boy stole a television.*
       (vi)   *The girl eats cake.*
       (vii) *The car hit the bus.*
       (viii) *I phone you.*
       (ix)   *You phone me.*
       (x)   *The cake ate the girl.*
   (b) Translate the sentences above into BSL using topic-comment structures.
   (c) Vary the topics of the sentences. For example make *the man, the newspaper,* or *the reading of the newspaper* the topic in the sentence *The man reads the newspaper.*

5. Using a BSL video clip, identify the pronouns and proforms that are used.
   (a) For each pronoun that you identify:
       (i) say if the referent is present in the signing environment or if it needs to be specified by a separate sign
       (ii) say how many people are referred to by the pronoun.
   (b) For each proform that you identify:
       (i) say what full sign it replaces
       (ii) say if the proform describes one, two, or three dimensions, or the legs or eyes of the referent, or if it is another sort of proform
       (iii) say why you think the proform was used, e.g. to locate the sign, to indicate whether there was more than one referent, or to show how the referent moves.

6. The following tasks address central 'grammatical' ideas that we use when discussing sign linguistics.
   (a) Mark the subject and predicate in the following English sentences:
       (i)   *The cat sat on the mat.*
       (ii) *Elisabeth Engberg-Pedersen and Carol Padden have written some interesting papers on sign linguistics.*
       (iii) *I love the way you smile at me.*
   (b) Mark the subject in the following English sentences. Also mark the direct and indirect objects (where applicable).
       (i)   *You won the argument.*
       (ii)   *The rabbit ate a lot of lettuce.*
       (iii) *Maud handed Millicent the offending photograph.*
       (iv)   *Mary is a doctor.*
       (v)   *The sun set slowly.*
       (vi)   *I like mice.*
       (vii) *Disraeli was the prime minister.*
       (viii) *I rode my bicycle up the hill.*

FURTHER READING FOR CHAPTER 3

Bergman, B., and Wallin, L. 1985, 'Sentence structure in Swedish Sign Language', in W. Stokoe and V. Volterra (eds.), *SLR 83*, Silver Spring, MD: Linstok Press, 217–25.

Crystal, D. 1988, *Rediscover grammar*, Harlow: Longman.

Deuchar, M. 1983, 'Is British Sign Language an SVO language?', in J. G. Kyle and B. Woll (eds.), *Language in sign*, London: Croom Helm, 69–76.

Engberg-Pedersen, E. 1993, *Space in Danish Sign Language*, Hamburg: Signum Press.

Friedman, L. 1975, 'The manifestation of subject, object and topic in American sign language', in C. Li (ed.) *Subject and topic*, Academic Press: New York, 125–8.

Liddell, S. 1980, *American Sign Language syntax*, The Hague: Mouton.

Chapter four

Questions and negation

QUESTIONS

All languages can ask questions. In chapter 1, where we discussed character-istics of communication systems, we found that animals and traffic lights cannot ask questions in the way humans can with language. BSL can ask questions, just as well as English can.

Language users know how to ask a question, but actually a 'question' is quite difficult to define. Questions can be defined by their function (the reason for asking a question), or by their form or structure (how a speaker or signer knows that a sentence is a question, and not a command or a declarative statement).

Anyone who knows English has no problem saying what is and what is not a question. The same is true for sentences in BSL; signers know what is a question and what is not. However, it is much more difficult to describe the rules for forming questions.

QUESTION FUNCTION

Questions have a basic function in language – they can be treated as requests for information. One definition of a question is that it expects (although does not necessarily get) a response, and preferably an answer.

A response is something that follows and relates to what another person has said, whether or not that other sentence was a question.

Mary: *Lovely day!*

Jane: *Yes, and I've heard it'll last.*

In this example, Jane is responding to what Mary has said, but Mary's sentence was not a question and Jane's response is not an answer.

An answer provides information that is requested in a question, e.g.

Mary: *Is the cat upstairs?*

Jane: *Yes.*

There are also occasions when information can be requested without asking a question, for example by a command to give information, e.g. *Name!*

QUESTION STRUCTURE

Linguists have found that questions differ from sentences that are not questions (called 'declarative' sentences) in all languages, because they have one or more of the three features below:

(a)   a word or sign that signals a question

(b)   a characteristic intonation pattern or facial expression

(c)   a characteristic word or sign order.

There are three main forms of question in BSL that we will discuss here: Yes–No, Wh-, and Alternative. We will look at the role of question signs, facial expression and sign order in each of these three question forms.

Yes–No questions

These occur when the person asking the question asks for an answer that is 'yes' or 'no' (also called 'confirmation' and 'negation'), e.g.

Mary: *Is there a king of France?*

Jane: *No*

Other examples include: *Did you go to the deaf club yesterday? Have you got any children? Is there life on the moon? Is it really true that you drive a BMW? Do you like ice-cream?*

All these questions only expect *yes* or *no* as answers, although it may be possible for the person answering to give a different answer.

It has sometimes been said that BSL does not have single manual signs meaning 'yes' and 'no'. The nodding of an 'A' hand or a 'Y' hand, or the side-to-side shaking of an 'A' hand are used by some people for NO and YES, but these have been introduced into BSL through signed English. Many signers use only non-manual signs for YES and NO. There are many other manual signs that have some sort of 'no' meaning, but these all have more specific negation than just 'no' (as we will see later in this chapter). Other languages do not have single words for 'yes' and 'no', for example Irish.

Questions are often answered in BSL by repeating part of the question (most often the verb). For example:

```
                                  q            _____hn
Mary: MOON LIFE EXIST-THERE Jane: EXIST-THERE
```
Mary: 'Is there life on the moon?' Jane: 'Yes.'
```
                        q        __hn
Mary: ICE-CREAM LIKE Jane: LIKE
```
Mary: 'Do you like ice cream?' Jane: 'Yes.'

```
                        q          ___hn
```
Mary: BUDGIE HAVE Jane: HAVE

Mary: 'Do you have a budgie?' Jane: 'Yes.'

Some questions look like Yes–No questions, but they are really requests for more information than a simple 'yes' or 'no'. For example, if Mary asks: 'Have you seen the cat?', it is rarely usefully answered if Jane says: 'Yes'. The question is understood as meaning 'Where is the cat?' even though it is not asked like that.

Tag questions are a form of Yes–No question. They are attached to the end of declarative sentences. In BSL tag questions are formed by signing a sentence that is not a question, and then adding a sign that can be glossed as RIGHT or TRUE, with the appropriate facial expression for a question. For example:

```
                  _____q
```
THREE CHILDREN HAVE RIGHT

'You've got three children, haven't you?'

```
                  _____q
```
LAST-YEAR WENT FRANCE TRUE

'You went to France last year, didn't you?'

In both examples, only RIGHT or TRUE is accompanied by question facial expression, but it makes the whole utterance a question. These tags ask for confirmation of information, rather than for additional information.

English also has tag questions with a similar structure, e.g. *There are three children, right?* However, there is a more common way to form tag questions in English: e.g. *You haven't seen the cat, have you?*

In a Yes–No question in BSL there is no special question sign to show that the question is a question. While English does have special structures for Yes–No questions, it is possible to ask questions in English without using them: e.g. *The cat's upstairs? Linda has children? This happened in the USA?* This type of question is quite common, especially in spoken English.

Instead of using special question signs, Yes–No questions in BSL are signalled by facial expression. A Yes–No question is usually accompanied by raised eyebrows, opened eyes, and a slight backward thrust of the head and shoulders.

However, the 'brows raised' rule, abbreviated *br*, does not always hold, because emotional facial expression is also important. For example, if a person is puzzled, or angry, the eyebrows may be down, even though the question is a Yes–No question.

Sign order does not change in BSL Yes–No questions. For example, the manual part of CHILDREN HAVE could be a question or declarative sentence.

Wh- questions

These request new information from a wide range of possibilities. They are called 'Wh- questions' because in English all Wh- questions contain a question word that begins with *wh-* (*what, why, where, when, who, which,* and *how* (in the past *how* also began with *wh-*)). Unlike Yes–No questions, in BSL these questions do have a special question sign. Examples of Wh- questions include *Where did you go for your holiday? When does this programme finish? Who is that man? Why are you late?* None of these questions can reasonably be answered by a simple *yes* or *no*.

French also has similar 'qu- questions' including the words *qui, quelle, quoi, quand, comment,* and *combien* (although *où* does not fit in). In BSL there is less similarity between these question signs, although many do have some sort of repeated movement (WHAT, WHAT-FOR, WHO, WHICH, and WHERE have a side-to-side movement and WHEN, HOW-MANY, HOW-MUCH, HOW-OLD have an internal movement). WHY and HOW fit less well into this pattern, although they are also question signs.

Facial expression is also important in Wh- questions. The general rule for Wh- questions is that the brows are furrowed (abbreviated as 'bf'), the eyes are slightly closed, and the head is thrust slightly forward or slightly tilted to one side.

Again, though, this is just a general rule. As we said earlier with Yes–No questions, puzzlement or anger can lead to lowered eyebrows. If the person asking the question is surprised or just showing polite interest, then even though the question has a Wh- sign, the eyebrows are raised.

The British linguist Margaret Deuchar has said that the facial expression is not so much a distinction between Wh- and Yes–No questions, as between ones which request a lot of information and those which do not.

The brows are furrowed to show a puzzled face for Wh-, but only if the questioner genuinely does not know the answer. A mother talking to a toddler may ask 'Where's Teddy?' in order to get the child to point at a picture. In this case her eyebrows are raised and not furrowed. This is in contrast to a genuine question where the mother does not know where the child put the teddy (fig. 4.1):

    _____bf
TEDDY WHERE
'Where's Teddy?' (questioner does not know the answer)
    _____br
TEDDY WHERE
'Where's Teddy?' (question with known answer)

Raised eyebrows are also used in BSL to signal turn-taking. This means that signers raise their brows when they are ready to hand the signing turn to the other person. For this reason, a Wh- question may end with raised brows.

Fig. 4.1a Wh- question with unknown answer WHERE?

Fig. 4.1b Wh- question with known answer WHERE?

Sign order is also relevant here. We said earlier in chapter 3 that in BSL, the question signs most often come at the end of the sentence. Sometimes the Wh- sign comes both at the beginning and at the end of the sentence, as for example, in WHERE CAT WHERE. This can be analysed as a sort of 'question copy', like 'pronoun copy'. It may also occur for emphasis.

The sign glossed as WHAT and another question sign made with palms turned upwards are often used as general question markers and as general markers for turn-taking. These are always placed at the end of the sentence.

Alternative questions (or Which-questions).

These questions only allow for an answer already provided in the question. For example, If Mary asks *Would you like tea, coffee or milk?* she allows Jane only the possibility of answering *tea, coffee,* or *milk.* She does not expect *orange squash* and also does not expect the answer *Yes.* In BSL these questions are mainly distinguished from Yes–No questions by the optional use of the question sign WHICH at the end: LIKE TEA COFFEE MILK WHICH.

Note: it is possible to use the sign WHICH in a Wh- question as well. For example, TODAY SANDWICHES, WHICH FILLING? is an ordinary Wh-question because no choice is given in the sentence. TODAY SAND-WICHES HAM, CHEESE, PEANUT-BUTTER WHICH? is a 'Which' or 'Alternative' question because the choices are given in the sentence.

Rhetorical questions

We have said that questions ask for information, but there are also times when this is not their function. Rhetorical questions are one type of question that

Fig. 4.2 True rhetorical question: 'Are we finished? Not yet'

does not expect an answer. They are not real questions because they are not a request for information. Their form is the same but their function is different. The task of a rhetorical question is to emphasise what the person is saying and draw attention to a point.

Rhetorical questions imply a closeness with the conversational partners because the use of a rhetorical question implies that the conversational partners know the answer and are thinking in the same way as the speaker or signer. Consider this example: 'And why have we asked this? Because we know they won't tell us!'

Rhetorical questions occur when speakers or signers ask a question with no expectation that it will be answered by the conversational partner, or when talking or signing to themselves. In the latter case the question may be answered by the signer or speaker themselves: e.g. 'Where did I put that? Oh, yes, in the kitchen.'

The American linguist Ronnie Wilbur has described three types of question which do not expect an answer. True rhetorical questions (e.g. 'Are we finished? Not yet') have appropriate facial expression (furrowed brows for Wh- questions, raised brows for Yes–No questions) (fig. 4.2).

Echo questions are a response to a previous utterance and mimic part of that utterance – Mary: 'Where are the keys? Jane: Where...? Maybe in the kitchen.' BSL has similar constructions (fig. 4.3).

The third type Wilbur describes have often been confused with true rhetorical questions, but are characterised by always having raised brows despite having the form of Wh- questions, for example (fig. 4.4):

          _____br
(SEE) KEYS WHERE KITCHEN

Fig. 4.3 Echo question: 'Where ... Maybe in the kitchen'

These serve to introduce a topic, and are therefore a type of topic-comment structure, having a parallel with English sentences of the type: *Where the keys were last was in the kitchen.*

When interpreting from BSL to English, it is sometimes tempting to translate START WHEN FOURTEEN YEARS–AGO as *So, when did it start? Fourteen years ago.* In fact it would be more appropriate to translate this as *When it started was fourteen years ago* or *It was fourteen years ago when it started.*

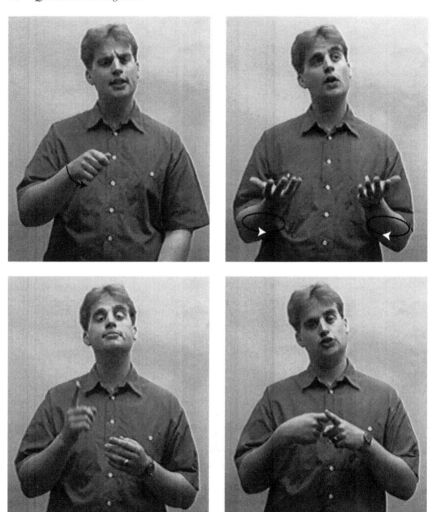

Fig. 4.4 Topic-introducing question: 'Where I saw the keys was in the kitchen'

NEGATION

Negation is a grammatical construction, just as a question is. It is very difficult to define negation exactly, but, as with questions, people who know a language know if a sentence has negation in it. English users know that the second of each of the following pairs contains negation: *I like mice* vs. *I don't like mice*; *Mice are nice* vs. *Mice are not nice*; *Henry missed the bus* vs. *Henry did not miss the bus; She always goes to London* vs. *She never goes to London; There were mice in the house* vs. *There were no mice in the house.*

It is easy to confuse the linguistic notion of negation with 'bad' meanings or things that have 'negative emotions' in them. Some words have a 'bad' or 'negative' meaning attached to them, e.g. *sad, disappointed, depressed,* or *lie.* But this is different from a sentence that has negation. Sentences contain negation because they say that something is not the case. They are nothing to do with how someone feels. We may not like the idea of spiders in the bath, but *There are spiders in the bath* is positive and *There are no spiders in the bath* has grammatical negation (even if we feel happier about that). *I was very sad* is a positive sentence; *I was not very sad* is a negation of that sentence.

There are three main elements of negation in BSL:

1) facial expression
2) head movement
3) negation signs, or signs with negation incorporated in them.

Facial expression

Facial expression alone does not negate a sentence (although it can accompany 'bad' feelings, or it can express doubt). For something to have grammatical negation, there also needs to be a shaking of the head, or a negation sign. This is also true in English, where negation is not carried by intonation (although sarcasm and disbelief can be).

There is more than one negation facial expression. There are different degrees of general negation facial expression. At its mildest level, negation (abbreviated 'neg') facial expression can be signed by having the lips pushed out a little bit and the eyes slightly narrowed. At a very extreme level, the eyes can be almost closed, the nose very wrinkled and the mouth very turned down, or the lip very curled (fig. 4.5).

Facial expression also involves mouth patterns. There are several negation mouth patterns in BSL that accompany negation signs. Without the mouth pattern, the sign is not complete. Examples include mouth patterns we call 'boo', 'vee', and 'thaw' (see fig. 4.6a, b and i below).

Head movements

There are two kinds of negation head movement in BSL.

(a) The 'negation head turn'. The head turns and is held there. It may then be returned to a forward facing position. This half head turn often occurs as part of a negation sign, rather than as a way of negating a sentence. It

Fig. 4.5a Weak negation   Fig. 4.5b Strong negation

occurs with some specific negation signs, such as those that are accompanied by 'boo' and 'vee' (see the section above on non-manual features).

(b)   A repeated side-to-side movement of the head. This may occur together with other non-manual markers such as nose-wrinkling or drawn-down lips. This head-shake on its own can negate either a sentence or a sign.

The repeated side-to-side head shake can occur all through a sentence, or just at the end of it, in order to negate all that has come before. For example: 'The woman didn't watch television' could be signed

_____neg
WOMAN TELEVISION WATCH

with a negative head shake all through it; alternatively the sentence can be signed with the negation element added at the end:

__neg
WOMAN TELEVISION WATCH NO

This also occurs in non-standard English, most famously in the film *Wayne's World*, e.g. 'Great body! Not!' In Old English, it was quite a common way of negating sentences.

Sentences can also be negated by adding the head shake after the final sign, with no extra manual component.

__neg
WOMAN TELEVISION WATCH

Negation signs

English has many negation words, e.g. *no, not, never, nobody, none, nought, zero*. It also has affixes, such as *un-* and *dis-* which work in the same way to change the sentence meaning. For example, *unhappy* is the negation of *happy*, and *displeased* is the negation of *pleased*. There are many negation signs in BSL. The following, found in the BSL dictionary, are some of the most common:

(1) flat hand, palm down and twisting up, with the 'vee' mouth pattern. It can be used alone or can be attached to a verb as a sort of suffix, e.g. SEE + neg, or HAVE + neg. It is often used for denial of possession, presence, or experience (fig. 4.6a).

(2) flat hand across the mouth, with the mouth pattern 'boo' or 'poo'. This uses the half head turn that we discussed earlier. It is often used for denial of existence (fig. 4.6b).

(3) flat hands, palm down, crossed, moving out in a cutting action. This, too, uses the negation half head turn. It is often used with commands or instructions, so may be translated in English as 'don't'. It is often used in association with signed forms of English (fig. 4.6c).

(4) 'O' or 'F' hands circling. They are sometimes glossed as NOTHING and NOBODY (fig. 4.6d).

(5) fists, with palms away from the body, moving left and right, with a mouth pattern 'shhh'. This is usually glossed as NOT-YET (fig. 4.6e).

(6) fist with the thumb extended moved out from under the chin. Often used to mean 'not'. This is common among northern and Scottish signers and also in signing influenced by English (fig. 4.6f).

(7) the 'B' handshape moved from side to side. This is particularly used to deny something or as a negative answer to a rhetorical question (fig. 4.6g).

(8) spread '5' hand that may be used as a suffix by some signers, for example WON'T, WHY-NOT, NOT-BAD and SHAN'T (fig. 4.6h).

(9) the regional Welsh sign (an open '8' hand). This manual sign is accompanied with the mouth pattern 'thaw', and can be glossed as NOTHING. This BSL sign is not very well known outside Wales, but is widely used in New Zealand Sign Language, which is related to BSL. There are many people in New Zealand whose families originally came from Wales, so this sign may have been taken there from Wales (fig. 4.6i).

(10) the BSL verb SAY-NO. Some people claim that this has been borrowed from ASL; some people say the Americans borrowed it from BSL; and some people say it is chance that the two signs are similar. It is sometimes glossed as simply meaning NO, but actually it is a verb (fig. 4.6j).

Fig. 4.6a HAVEN'T-SEEN ('vee')

Fig. 4.6b NOT-EXIST ('boo')

Fig. 4.6c DON'T (command)

Fig. 4.6d NOTHING/NOBODY

Fig. 4.6e NOT-YET

Fig. 4.6f NOT

Fig. 4.6g NO (to deny)

Fig. 4.6h WON'T

Fig. 4.6i NOTHING (Welsh) ('thaw')

Fig. 4.6j SAY-NO

Separate signs

There are also signs that have their own negation form. These are often verbs of experience or sensation, such as DON'T-KNOW, DISAGREE, DON'T-REMEMBER, SHOULDN'T, DON'T-LIKE (fig. 4.7).

In BSL it is common to have more than one negation marker in the sentence. In Standard English, only one negation marker can appear in a sentence. However, many forms of non-standard English use multiple negation, just as BSL does, e.g. a person might say *We ain't going nowhere* or *I don't know nothing*. In BSL, a sentence such as DON'T-KNOW NOTHING is just a strong form of negation.

Fig. 4.7a LIKE   Fig. 4.7b DON'T-LIKE

SUMMARY

In this chapter we have discussed the importance of two grammatical constructions in BSL. We have seen that there are different types of questions that have different roles in the language. We have also seen that it is possible to describe rules about the way that non-manual features and different signs are used to make different questions. These rules are not simple, because the facial expression that is used will vary depending on other factors.

It is possible to negate positive sentences and say that something is not true. BSL does this in a variety of ways: facial expression, head movement, special negation signs, and changes to signs.

EXERCISES FOR CHAPTER 4

1. Yes–no questions
   (a) Translate the examples of Yes–No questions given below into BSL.
   (b) See if your questions feel correct with raised or furrowed eyebrows.
       (i)   Is there a king of France?
       (ii)   Did you go to the Deaf club yesterday?
       (iii)   Have you got any children?
       (iv)   Is there life on the moon?
       (v)   Is it really true that you drive a BMW?
       (vi)   Do you like ice-cream?
   (c) Imagine that you were puzzled while asking your questions, or very angry. See if they feel correct with raised or furrowed eyebrows.
2. Wh- questions
   (a) Translate the examples of Wh- questions given below into BSL.

(b) See if your questions feel correct with raised or furrowed eyebrows.

   (i)   *Where did you go for your holiday?*
   (ii)   *When does this programme finish?*
   (iii) *Who is that man?*
   (iv)   *Why are you late?*
   (v)   *What's her name?*
   (vi)   *How many cakes did you eat?*

(c) Imagine that you were surprised while asking your questions, or trying to encourage an answer. See if they feel correct with raised or furrowed eyebrows.

3. Negation

   (a) Translate the following sentences into BSL and think how you would sign them and how you would sign them with negation.

      (i)   *The cat's asleep.*
      (ii)   *I like fish.*
      (iii) *She hit the child.*
      (iv)   *He's very sad.*
      (v)   *There is life on the moon.*
      (vi)   *The flowers are dead.*
      (vii) *I know him.*
      (viii) *She agrees with me.*
      (ix)   *There are spiders in the bath.*
      (x)   *You catch the bus.*

   (b) Try signing these sentences with a negation facial expression only. Is this sufficient to negate them?

   (c) Describe the special 'negation' non-manual features that go with each of your sentences above. You will need to describe the facial expression, including the mouth pattern and the head movement.

   (d) Describe the manual sign that was used for the negation.

4. Other types of questions

   (a) How would you translate the following four BSL sentences into English?

              _____bf
   (i)   START WHEN 14 YEARS AGO
              _____br
   (ii) STEAL TELEVISION WHO BOY
              _____bf
   (iii) TODAY DEBATE WHERE SOUTH WALES
              _____br
   (iv) MURIEL PAINT WHAT HER HOUSE

   (b) What is the difference between the ways that BSL and English express these ideas?

FURTHER READING FOR CHAPTER 4

Bouchard, D., and Dubuisson, C. 1995, 'Grammar, order and position of Wh- signs in Quebec Sign Language', *Sign Language Studies* 87, 99–139.

Coerts, J. 1990, 'Analysis of interrogatives and negatives in SLN', in S. Prillwitz and T. Vollhaber (eds.), *Current trends in European sign language research*, Hamburg: Signum Press, 265–78.

Vogt-Svendsen, M. 1990, 'Eye-gaze in Norwegian Sign Language interrogatives', in W. Edmondson and F. Karlsson (eds.), *SLR '87: Papers from the fourth international symposium on sign language research*, Hamburg: Signum Press, 153–62.

Woll, B. 1981, 'Question structure in British Sign Language', in B. Woll, J. G. Kyle and M. Deuchar (eds.), *Perspectives on British Sign Language and deafness*, London: Croom Helm, 136–9.

Chapter five

Mouth patterns and other non-manual features in BSL

'BSL is a language that uses the hands to communicate instead of the tongue.' This statement is only true up to a point, because other parts of the body are also very important in BSL. Signers actually look at each other's faces, not their hands, when communicating. This chapter will explore the role of non-manual features in BSL, focusing especially on the role of the mouth, but also on the rest of the face, and the head.

There are many mouth patterns that convey grammatical and phonological information in BSL (see also chapter 9).

Although BSL is independent of English, it has been influenced by English, and has borrowed from English. One of the things it has borrowed is the mouth patterns from English words. BSL has not just borrowed randomly, though, and there are times when English mouth patterns are borrowed, and times when they are not. More importantly, BSL changes the English mouth patterns, so that when they are used, they are not always used as they are in English.

Understanding the use of mouth patterns in BSL is important. Knowing how and when to use appropriate mouth patterns is a difficult skill for learners of BSL.

This discussion of mouth patterns also reinforces the point that it is not possible to sign BSL and speak English at the same time, because we will see that there are many occasions when an English mouth pattern is inappropriate while signing BSL.

The Dutch sign linguist Trude Schermer has contrasted 'spoken components' and 'oral components'. These are the terms that we will use here. Spoken components are derived from spoken languages, and oral components are not. We will consider these two types in turn.

SPOKEN COMPONENTS

These have various uses:

(a) to represent spoken language mouth pattern in combination with signs;
(b) to represent spoken language mouth patterns with first-letter signs; and
(c) to distinguish other manual homonyms.

Spoken components have been under-researched in BSL. Because researchers put emphasis on the independence of BSL, they have tended to ignore spoken components. Now that this independence is established, we can show how BSL is influenced by English.

There are some mouth patterns that are easily identifiable as corresponding to English words, and there are 'word-pictures' which are borrowed from English but are not English. There is no clear distinction between the two, but the two types definitely exist. For example there are some mouth patterns used in BSL that come from English but a non-signing English speaker would not recognise them as English.

When we talk about spoken components, we have to remember that often we interpret what we see because we know what the English word might be. In fact, we might be seeing things that are not there. For example, some speech sounds look the same on the lips, so 'bill' and 'pill', or 'tan' and 'Dan' would look the same. But if a deaf person fingerspelled the name -b-i-l-l-, we would say that the spoken component we saw was 'Bill', not 'pill'. This is rarely a problem in practice, but it is important to be aware of this. For example, linguists might believe that a signer is saying the whole English word, when he is really only saying a part of it, and the linguists are filling in the rest with their knowledge of English.

Spoken components in signs

Hearing and deafened people, and fluent signers who are being kind to learners, use many spoken components and many English grammatical markers, (like 'hous*es*', 'want*ed*', 's*a*ng', 't*oo*k'). This often looks like whispered English. Using spoken components may help non-fluent signers to recognise the accompanying sign. For example, the spoken component from 'room' and the sign ROOM may be much easier to understand together than when each occurs on its own.

In BSL less influenced by English, there is still considerable use of spoken components. They frequently serve to identify or establish a sign. They are used especially for proper names, e.g. of people, towns, countries. Most of the spoken components are found with nouns. Spoken components accompany far fewer verbs, perhaps because (as we will see later) verbs often use other special BSL mouth patterns. An exception is the group of verbs, such as KNOW, WANT, THINK, which do regularly occur with spoken components. Where spoken components are used for verbs, the components are often in their most basic, uninflected forms, for example, mouthing 'take', not 'took' or 'taking'. So they are not grammatically part of English, but part of BSL. In phrasal verbs, part of the verb is often mouthed. For example, 'off' in SWITCH-OFF or 'out' in THROW-OUT or 'home' in GO-HOME. Spoken components often do not represent the full English word, even with nouns, e.g.

Fig. 5.1 'Are you deaf?'

'hsp' with HUSBAND and 'fsh' with FINISH. Often the spoken component does not coincide exactly with the sign. When an index follows a noun, verb, or adjective, the mouth pattern of the noun will often extend over the index:

/def/_____⌐
DEAF-Index₂ ⌐
'Are you deaf?' (fig. 5.1)

Sometimes the hands and mouth give the same information, but in a different order, for example the hands may sign WORK NONE while the spoken component is 'no work'. It is also possible for the signer to sign different elements on the hands and mouth. For example, WORK FINISH? may be signed with WORK on the hands and mouth articulating 'fsh'. NO CHILDREN may be signed with CHILDREN on the hands and 'vee' on the mouth to show negation. So some mouth patterns have no accompanying manual component.

It is also not uncommon for signers just to use a spoken component without any manual signs at all. This occurs especially in casual signing. A signer may mouth 'What you mean?' without bothering to sign, especially if they happen to have their hands full. This, however, is probably not a part of BSL, but an example of a signer switching between BSL and English. Signers may also mouth English with no manual signing if they are reporting the speech of a non-signer, e.g. *Do you lip-read?* or *Are you all right?* These fully non-manual components are usually quite short.

Spoken components with first-letter signs

There are many single manual letter signs in BSL that are derived from the first letter of fingerspelled English words (as we will see in chapter 12). These usually have accompanying spoken components to make the meaning clear. Context is important, obviously, but the spoken component helps, too. For example, the signs given below are all formed by producing the first letter of the fingerspelled English word, so they look the same on the hands:

GEOGRAPHY, GOVERNMENT, GARAGE, GUARANTEE, GLOUCESTER, GLAMORGAN, GINGER, and GEORGE
VIRGIN, VODKA, and VEGETARIAN
MOTHER, METRE, MONTH, MEMBER, and MONDAY

Spoken components are also often used to accompany full fingerspellings. Individual letter names are not produced. The only time the names of the letters are produced is when spelling an abbreviation such as BBC or RNID.

Spoken components to distinguish other homonyms

Sometimes pairs or small groups of signs have identical manual components. One group are 'coincidental' manual homonyms (that is, signs that have the same form but different meanings), such as FINLAND and METAL, or BATTERY and UNCLE, where the spoken component is used to disambiguate them. Other, semantically related pairs, such as HUSBAND and WIFE, AUNT and UNCLE, FOUR and NINE, are always contrasted by the addition of spoken components. In some cases, such as APPROPRIATE and AGREE, the signs are similar in meaning, and spoken components may be used by signers who know English to distinguish them.

ORAL COMPONENTS

There are a great many other uses for the mouth in BSL. We will consider here: enacting mouth movements; parallel mouth/hand movements ('multi-channel' signs); manner and degree adverbs; and negation.

Enacting mouth movements

In these movements, found in signs such as LAUGH, VOMIT, APPLE, and BITE, the mouth performs an action that imitates the real action, although often in a stylised way (fig. 5.2).

Parallel mouth/hand movements

There are lexical items which have a compulsory BSL oral component. It is not an extra piece of information, but is part of the sign itself.

These have often been called 'multi-channel signs'. This was once a useful term, for drawing attention to non-manual features, but it suggests that only a small group of signs have non-manual features, whereas in fact almost all signs do.

A more useful and interesting observation about the signs previously called multi-channel signs, is that the movement of the mouth parallels the move-

Fig. 5.2 BITE

ment of the hands. For example, in the sign EXIST, the hand is held still in space while the fingers flutter gently. The mouth articulates 'sh' at the same time, which is a continuous and gentle stream of air.

In DISAPPEAR, the hands close abruptly, while at the same time, the mouth closes abruptly. In SUCCEED, the hands move apart abruptly, while at the same time the mouth opens abruptly. In REALLY, the active hand hits the passive hand and is held there, while at the same time the mouth closes and lips are held together (fig. 5.3).

Fig. 5.3 REALLY

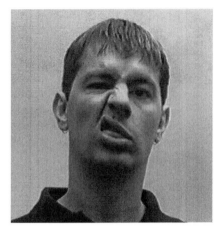

Fig. 5.4a 'th-curl' ('unpleasant')

Fig. 5.4b 'relaxed mm'('average')

Fig. 5.4c 'tense mm' ('exact')

Fig. 5.4d 'ee' ('intense')

Manner and degree adverbs

Oral components which serve as adverbs can be added to give extra information about the manner or effort of an action. (An adverb is any part of speech that tells us more about an action.) The same oral components are used to show the extent or size of an object or the degree (e.g. 'bigger', 'biggest') of an adjective. These are basically the same components, although the meaning of manner or size depends on what is being modified. For example, if an action is performed with no special effort, the oral component 'relaxed mm' is used. The same oral component is used when describing an object as being of average size.

Fig. 5.4e 'puffed cheeks' ('large/long')   Fig. 5.4f 'shh' ('large/long'(Northern))

Fig. 5.4g 'sucked-in cheeks' ('small')

The following are the important manner and degree markers in BSL (fig. 5.4):

'th-curl' (tongue protrusion with curled upper lip) – boring, unpleasant

'relaxed mm' (relaxed closed lips, slightly protruding) – easy, effortless, average

'tense mm' (tense closed lips) – determined, firm, exact

'ee' (teeth together, lips drawn back) – intense, with effort, very near in time or space 'brr' (lips vibrating) – movement, either through space or time. The mouth configuration is the same as in 'relaxed mm' (fig. 5.4b)

puffed cheeks – long duration, many, large, difficult

'shh' (rounded lips) – long duration, many, large, difficult (originally Northern, but now used more widely)

sucked-in cheeks – few, thin, small.

These oral components are not the same in all sign languages. There are manner and degree oral components in other sign languages, but they are different, e.g. in ASL 'th' means carelessness and in Finnish Sign Language, 'hyu' is similar to relaxed 'mm' in BSL.

Negation

Negation can be expressed manually, as we have seen in chapter 4, but there are also important 'negation' mouth patterns. A downward turned mouth, curled lip etc. are part of negation. They can also be used to express doubt if they are not accompanied by a head shake. There are also specific negation signs that must have oral components like 'vee' or 'boo'.

FACIAL EXPRESSION

It is not always easy (or desirable) to separate oral components in BSL from information given on the rest of the face. We will now consider information carried on the rest of the face that may be phonologically or grammatically important. Important parts of facial expression to note here are the actions of the cheeks, brows, eyelids, and eye gaze.

Facial expression may have several functions, including lexical distinctions (obligatory for some signs), to mark questions, to mark topics, to mark conditionals ('if'), and to show emotional state.

Lexical distinctions (the facial expression is part of the sign)

Like the signs with parallel mouth patterns, the facial expressions are obligatory for some signs (e.g. RELIEVED, SHOCK, BEG) where the facial expression reflects the emotion associated with the meaning.

To mark a question

We mentioned these when we discussed questions in chapter 4. Basically the eyebrows are furrowed for puzzlement and Wh- questions, and raised for Yes–No questions and those where the questioner has an idea of the answer.

To mark the topic

This was mentioned in chapters 3 and 4 when we talked about topics as part of topic-comment constructions. The brow-raise as a topic marker is an example of the use of facial expression as a grammatical feature.

To mark a conditional ('if')

A conditional clause can be marked by brow movement as well as head tilt and (optionally) the sign IF.

                            br
IF WANT SWEETS SIT
                      br
WANT SWEETS SIT

Both can mean 'If you want sweets, sit down' (fig. 5.5a).

Sometimes conditionals look like rhetorical questions discussed earlier in chapter 4: 'Do you want sweets? Then sit down' (fig. 5.5b).

The difference is that there is a longer pause after the rhetorical question,

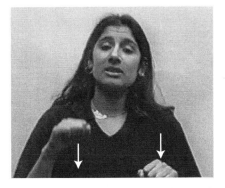

Fig. 5.5a 'If you want sweets, sit down'

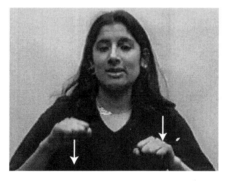

Fig. 5.5b 'Do you want sweets? Then sit down'

and the eyebrows are higher and the head further back in the rhetorical question than in the simple conditional. It is worth noting however, that BSL can use rhetorical questions where Standard English would use a conditional. Non-standard English may use a construction very similar to the BSL 'rhetorical question'.

To show emotional state

This is a complex area, because signers show emotions on their face, the same as speakers, and these facial expressions are definitely outside the language.

However, emotional facial expressions are also used linguistically. They must accompany the relevant sign for an emotion, e.g. sad for SAD, angry for ANGRY, surprised for SURPRISED. However, they can also be super-imposed on other signs. In the sentence: SAD ME WHY RABBIT DIE, the facial expression will change during the sign WHY because a question is being asked, and then will revert to a sad facial expression again (fig. 5.6). This suggests that the facial expression is linked to the language, because if it was only outside the language it would not be interruptible.

Fig. 5.6 SAD ME WHY RABBIT DIE
'I'm sad because my rabbit died'

Fig. 5.7 I-REMEMBER

Facial expressions are also of different intensities in different social situations. They are less marked in formal linguistic settings, and more intense in casual, relaxed linguistic settings. If the facial expression were a simple emotional reflex, it would be the same in all contexts.

HEAD NODS

Head nods are used by both BSL signers and English speakers to mean 'yes'. In chapter 4, we saw that the head nod may be sufficient to signal 'yes' in BSL, without any manual sign at all. Although English speakers also use nods to mean 'yes' this is a conventionalised gesture that is outside English. However, English speakers do not just use them to mean 'yes'. One study of interviews on American television showed that one nod means 'I'm listening', two nods means 'tell me more' but three nods or more makes the speaker pause or change the subject.

In BSL, nodding is also an important part of feedback in conversation to show attention. This is a 'discourse feature'; it is not a part of the language, but it is used during sign conversation.

Nodding also has grammatical functions in BSL, apart from the topic marking that we have already discussed. The number of nods, and their speed and intensity is important.

(a) A head dip can be used to indicate first person ('I'). Instead of signing I REMEMBER, the signer can nod while signing REMEMBER (fig. 5.7).

(b) Fast head nods can be used when insisting on the truth of something. This is a bit like the use of *si* in French or *é* in Portuguese. For example:
rapid hn
CAT DOG CHASE

has the extra meaning of 'yes, the cat did definitely chase the dog, no matter what you may think'.

(c) A single small nod or two small nods can indicate that a comment upon a topic, or a given phrase, is complete. For example:

hn   hn

FLY LONDON ATHENS   AEROPLANE-LAND

Here, the first nod simply shows that the first piece of information is complete, and the second nod shows that the action of flying was complete.

In summary, then, we can say that head nods have a variety of functions in BSL: to say 'yes', for social feedback, and for grammatical marking.

HEAD SHAKES

We have already touched upon the use of head shakes and head turns in chapter 4. Here we will further describe the way these movements carry information in BSL.

(1) To respond 'no' to a Yes–No question.
   As with the head nod for 'yes', the head shake is sufficient for 'no' in BSL.

(2) negation
   In our previous discussion of negation in BSL we mentioned side-to-side head shakes, and half head turns. Head shakes can be used in the following ways:
   (a) to negate a rhetorical question

_____br ____hs

CLEVER Index$_3$
'Is she clever? No'

Note that there is no manual negation here, and that the negation does not start until after the question.
   (b) to negate the topic, e.g.

_____t _____hs

Index$_3$ GET MONEY Index$_3$
'It wasn't her who got the money'

Again there is no manual negation here, but the headshake suffices. Note, too, that the negation is marked only during the comment, not during the topic.
   (c) to negate the whole clause, e.g.

_____hs

Index$_3$ GET MONEY Index$_3$
'She didn't get the money'

(3) to express emotions such as regret, frustration, disbelief, or sorrow, e.g.
GROUP LEAVE NINE-O'CLOCK ARRIVE ME FIVE-PAST NINE
_____hs
GONE

'The group left at nine o'clock, and I arrived at five past nine, to find them gone'

Note that this headshake does not mean that the group had *not* gone. The 'disappointed' facial expression and the slower speed of the head shake indicate that.

In summary, head shakes can serve for 'no', and can also negate a rhetorical question, a topic or a whole clause. They can also indicate emotion during a sentence that is grammatically positive.

EYE GAZE

Eye-gaze has at least five important uses in BSL: at the phonological level for lexical distinctions; in conjunction with the location and movement of referents in space; to show 'role shift'; to contrast pseudo-questions (rhetorical and echo) with genuine questions; and for marking time.

Lexical distinction (i.e. the eye gaze is part of the sign)

In some signs, eye gaze is obligatory, e.g. GOD, HEAVEN, PATRONISE, JAVELIN. The signs GOD and BOSS differ in eye gaze only (fig. 5.8). Without the required eye gaze, the sign has a different meaning or no meaning.

Fig. 5.8a GOD   Fig. 5.8b BOSS

In conjunction with the location and movement of referents in signing space

We can point to locations in signing space that have been assigned to referents, but it is also grammatical just to look at the locations.

Eye gaze is also important for indicating the difference between the second person ('you') and the third person ('he' or 'she') (see chapter 3). YOU is signed with the eye gaze at the conversational partner, so that the eyes look to where the hand is pointing. HE/SHE may be signed in the same location in signing space as YOU, but eye gaze is not towards the location of the third person.

Eye gaze can also be used to follow movements traced by the hands. For example if locations for a ball and goal have been established in signing space, then the eyes follow the path of movement of the sign in (BALL)-FLY-THROUGH-THE-AIR-TO-GOAL.

If the movement of the hand during a sign shows the motion of a referent (e.g. a car or person moving), then the movement path of the eye gaze follows it. If the movement does not represent the motion of something (e.g. in WORLD or MORNING) then gaze does not follow the hands.

To indicate role shift

Changes in gaze allow a signer to take different roles of different characters in a story. When a signer is shifting between narrator and character roles, the eye gaze shifts. When a signer is narrating, gaze is directed at the conversational partner; when role shifts to that of a character, gaze is towards whatever the character is looking at. We will discuss this in more detail in chapter 14.

For distinguishing pseudo-questions and genuine questions

If a question is not functionally a question (for example, 'rhetorical' or 'echo' questions – chapter 4) the signer does not look at the conversational partner, since looking directly at the conversational partner signals turn-taking (see below).

To invite someone else to sign

This is a discourse function (like nodding to show that we are paying attention). When a person is signing, direction of gaze changes frequently, but there are brief gazes at the conversational partner for feedback. The main signal for relinquishing a turn of signing is by gazing directly at the conversational partner and holding the gaze there.

For marking time

Looking to the side can indicate past, while looking directly ahead or down can indicate the present time, and looking up can indicate future time. These differences are often very slight and can be missed by non-fluent signers. We will discuss this again later in chapter 10 where we discuss the ways in which BSL indicates time reference.

Eye gaze is thus important at the lexical level, grammatically, and in discourse.

SUMMARY

Mouth patterns in BSL are derived from English and also come from BSL itself. Use of English spoken components is not the same as mouthing English during signing. There are many oral components in BSL that are an essential part of signs or provide extra grammatical information.

Non-manual features are an important part of BSL. All signs need to be described in terms of their non-manual features, even if these are 'neutral'.

Facial expression has many functions in BSL – to show emotion, lexical distinctions, and grammar. Head nods and head shakes have a range of forms and functions, and are important to the grammar and in conversation. Eye gaze has a range of lexical and grammatical functions, and also is important in role-shift, turn-taking and interaction.

EXERCISES FOR CHAPTER 5

1. Mouth and face
    (a) Find examples of signs for proper nouns (for example, in the *BSL/English dictionary*). Do they contain a spoken component? Why would this be?
    (b) Find at least five signs where the facial expression is a vital part of the sign. Distinguish signs which have a different meaning when the facial expression changes from signs which are incomplete without facial expression.
2. Spoken and oral components
    (a) Identify signs that are 'coincidental manual homonyms' which are differentiated by the spoken component, e.g. FINLAND and METAL.
    (b) Identify 'semantically related pairs' of signs that are manual homonyms, and which are differentiated by the spoken component, e.g. HUSBAND and WIFE.

    (c) Identify five examples of visually motivated oral components that are used lexically (i.e. as part of a sign e.g. BITE).

    (d) Using the following three verbs (CLIMB, WALK, and HAUL-A-ROPE) add different adverbial oral components to create different meanings that show how the action was done (e.g. CLIMB with a firm 'mm' mouth pattern shows climbing determinedly).

3. Watch a video clip of a fluent signer telling a story.
    (a) Identify fifteen examples of spoken components.
        (i)   Do the spoken components represent the full English word, or only a part (or can you not tell)?
        (ii)   Decide if the signs accompanied by each of these spoken components are names of people or places, other nouns, verbs, adjectives, or something else.
        (iii) Why might the signer have used these spoken components?
    (b) Identify ten examples of oral components.
        (i)   Describe the oral components you have chosen.
        (ii)   What is the meaning of these oral components?
        (iii) What is the overall meaning of the signs that they are part of?
        (iv) Classify them as one of the following:
            (a) visually motivated or emotional
            (b) lexical but not visually motivated
            (c) adverbial or adjectival modification
            (d) something else

4. Eye movement
    (a) Identify ten signs where the movement of the hands represents the movement of the referent (e.g. a frog jumping across a pond). In all these signs, do the eyes follow the movement of the hands?
    (b) Identify ten signs where the movement of the hands does not represent the movement of the referent (e.g. MORNING). In all these signs, do the eyes follow the movement of the hands?

5. Watch a video clip of a fluent signer telling a story.
    (a) Go through the clip and identify use of facial expression. Why does the signer use these facial expressions?
        (i)   Is the signer showing emotion?
        (ii)   Is the emotion of the narrator or a character in the story? How do you know?
        (iii) Is the facial expression being used for grammatical purposes (e.g. asking a question or negating)?
    (b) Observe any head movements.
        (i)   Why are head nods used?
        (ii)   Are the nods small or large?

(iii)   Are they repeated or single nods?
(iv)   Why is head-shaking used?
(v)   Does the head shake from side to side, or make only a half turn?

FURTHER READING FOR CHAPTER 5

Ebbinghaus, H., and Hessman, J. 1996, 'Signs and words: accounting for spoken language elements in German Sign Language', in W. Edmondson and R. Wilbur
(eds.), *International review of sign linguistics, Vol. I.* Hillsdale, NJ: Lawrence
Erlbaum Associates, 23–56.
Engberg-Pedersen, E. 1990, 'Pragmatics of nonmanual behaviour in Danish Sign
Language', in W. Edmondson and F. Karlsson (eds.), *SLR '87: Papers from the
fourth international symposium on sign language research,* Hamburg: Signum Press,
121–8.
McIntire, M., and Reilly, J. 1988, 'Non-manual behaviours in L1 and L2 learners of
American Sign Language', *Sign Language Studies* 61, 351–76.
Pimiä, P. 1990, 'Semantic features of some mouth patterns in Finnish Sign Language',
in S. Prillwitz and T. Vollhaber (eds.), *Current trends in European sign language
research,* Hamburg: Signum Press, 115–18.
Vogt-Svendsen, M. 1990, 'Eye-gaze in Norwegian Sign Language interrogatives', in
W. Edmondson and F. Karlsson (eds.), *SLR '87: Papers from the fourth interna-
tional symposium on sign language research,* Hamburg: Signum Press, 153–62.

Chapter six

Morphology and morphemes in BSL

In this chapter we discuss the idea of 'units of meaning' in BSL. Morphology is the area of linguistics concerned with the meaning of words and signs and their structure.

WHAT IS A MORPHEME?

A morpheme is the smallest unit of meaning in a word or sign. If we break words or signs into smaller and smaller units, eventually they no longer have any meaning. In BSL, morphemes can be combined to make a sign that has several meaningful parts to it, but which is still a single sign.

Sometimes one morpheme is exactly one sign, and one sign is exactly one morpheme. This occurs where the sign only has one unit of meaning. In some languages, almost all words contain only one morpheme. This means there is only one unit of meaning in every word. The Chinese language is one example. There are many BSL signs and English words that only contain one unit of meaning. English and BSL (and many other languages) also have words and signs containing more than one morpheme. These are called 'poly-morphemic' words or signs from the Greek *poly* ('many') and *morph* ('form').

The following signs cannot be broken down into smaller meaningful units, so they are single morphemes ('monomorphemic' signs): TRUE, SAY, MOUSE, RED, KITCHEN, HAPPY, AEROPLANE.

The following signs are all single signs that have at least two meaningful units, so they are polymorphemic: PROMISE (made up from SAY +TRUE), BELIEVE (made up from THINK + TRUE), SPACE-SHUTTLE, MINICOM, YOU-TEASE-ME, DRIVE-CASUALLY, CHECK (made up from SEE + MAYBE), ANIMAL-JUMP-OVER-WALL (fig. 6.1).

These signs can be split into units of meaning. SPACE-SHUTTLE has the separate meanings 'aeroplane' and 'rocket', but they are combined to give the meaning 'space-shuttle'. The telephone used by deaf people, MINICOM, is made up from TELEPHONE and TYPEWRITER (see fig. 6.2 below). In

Fig. 6.1a DRIVE-CASUALLY   Fig. 6.1b ANIMAL-JUMP-OVER-
                                WALL

Fig. 6.1c SPACE-SHUTTLE

YOU-TEASE-ME, there are three bits of information in the one sign: 'you', 'tease', and 'me' (see also I-ASK-YOU in fig. 3.10a).

The number of movements or handshapes is not necessarily a good guide to the number of morphemes in the sign. We might think that shorter signs have one morpheme and longer ones have two. However, RED and TRUE both have one morpheme and one movement, but MAGIC has one morpheme and two movements. On the other hand, although PROMISE, CHECK and BELIEVE all have two parts to them and have two morphemes, SPACE-SHUTTLE, MINICOM, and DRIVE-CASUALLY only have one movement and have two morphemes.

It is important to be clear that when we discuss morphemes we are talking about the way that meaning is represented; we are not discussing what the sign looks like.

The same is true for English. Consider these words: *bath, picture, tape, run, jump, small, happy*. Each only has one unit of meaning. We cannot break the word up and get two smaller meanings. But think of these English words: *bathroom, picture-frame, tape-recorder, rat-run, high-jump, jumping, smaller,* and *happily*.

Each of these can be broken up into meaningful parts, e.g. *bath* and *room*, or *light* and *house*. Some of these may seem a bit strange, for example, *small* and *-er. Small* has meaning, and *-er* has meaning in a way because, in specific contexts, it means 'in comparison'. We will discuss these morphemes that do not have their own independent meaning in the next section.

A morpheme in English is not always one syllable long. The length of a word is not necessarily linked to the number of morphemes. *Dog, table, antelope,* and *avocado* all have different numbers of syllables, but each contains one morpheme, because they all contain only one unit of meaning and cannot be broken into smaller meaningful units. Words can also have one syllable but still contain more than one morpheme. For example, *man* has one morpheme but *men* has two morphemes (one meaning 'man' and another to show there is more than one man). *Sing* has one morpheme but *sang* has two morphemes (one meaning 'sing' and another to show it is in the past).

Different languages differ in relation to morphemes just as they differ in grammar. For example *bedroom* in English can be split into two meaningful parts 'bed' and 'room', but BEDROOM only has one morpheme in BSL. In English we need three separate words to say 'I ask you', and each of these words is monomorphemic. In BSL we use one sign, and it is polymorphemic.

BOUND AND FREE MORPHEMES

There are two types of morpheme:

(1) 'Free' – These can stand alone, for example *kitchen, bath,* and *room,* or RED, TRUE, and SAY. A word or sign can be a free morpheme.

(2) 'Bound' – These have meaning, but cannot stand alone. They must be combined with at least one other morpheme (e.g. the *-er* of *smaller,* or the 'CASUALLY' of DRIVE-CASUALLY).

BSL sign morphology may be schematised like this:

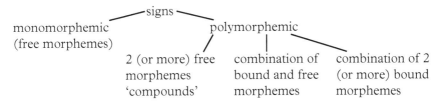

We will return to a discussion of bound morphemes later.

Two free morphemes can be brought together to make a compound. A compound is a combination of two free morphemes that form a new sign/word with a different (but related) meaning. There is often a change of stress in the way the sign or word is made. Although a compound is a combination of two free morphemes, it functions like a single sign.

Compounding is a common way in many languages to make new words or signs (that is, it is very 'productive'). We see this in English, for example: *high-jump* from *high jump; inner-tube* from *inner tube; tracksuit* from *track* and *suit*.

Many compounds in BSL are direct loans from English, so they have the same compound form, e.g. GUINEA-PIG, or BALANCE-SHEET.

Other compounds are not English loans. BLOOD (RED + FLOW), PEOPLE (MAN + WOMAN), MINICOM (TELEPHONE + TYPE-WRITER) and CHECK (SEE + MAYBE) are all compounds in BSL, but not compounds in English. (Note that not all signs with the same meaning have the same morphology. There are several BSL signs glossed as PEOPLE, but some are monomorphemic even though there is also a compound sign.)

Linguists once thought a sign compound was just formed by putting two signs together. However, consistent changes take place in the form of the two signs when they are brought together. The linguists Edward Klima and Ursula Bellugi have studied this in detail in ASL, as has Lars Wallin in Swedish Sign Language.

Compounds take less time to articulate than two separate signs. The length of a compound is similar to the length of a non-compound sign. This is because of blending, smoothing, elimination of transition, loss of repetition, and compression of the first sign in the compound.

The rhythm of the signs changes when a compound is produced:

- the initial hold of the first sign is lost;
- any repeated movement in the second sign is lost;
- the base hand of second sign is established at the point in time when the first sign starts;
- there is rapid transition between the first and second sign;
- the first sign is noticeably shorter than the second.

Reduction occurs in both the first and second sign: the first sign loses stress and repetition and the second sign loses repetition but retains stress.

Loss of movement is common. The sign PARENTS is a compound of MOTHER (-m-m-) and FATHER (-f-f-) which should produce -m-m-f-f- but one segment or even two are lost. So we get -m-f- or -m-m-f- or -m-f-f-, but not -m-m-f-f-.

In BELIEVE, the signs combined are THINK and TRUE. In the sign THINK, the hand moves in an outwards direction, but in BELIEVE it moves

Fig. 6.2 MINICOM

straight down. Also THINK is made with one hand, but in BELIEVE the base hand for TRUE is in place when THINK begins.

MINICOM is a compound of TELEPHONE and TYPEWRITER but often in conversation both hands take the TELEPHONE handshape or the TYPEWRITER handshape (fig. 6.2).

In CHECK the handshape of SEE is combined with the handshape of MAYBE (fig. 6.3).

Sign linguists often distinguish two different types of compounds: 'simultaneous' and 'sequential'. In simultaneous compounds, both elements occur at the same time, for example MINICOM and SPACE-SHUTTLE. In sequential compounds, the two elements occur one after the other, for example, BELIEVE, PROMISE, and PARENTS.

All the morphemes in compounds are 'free' morphemes because they can stand alone as meaningful units. 'Bound' morphemes are different. They cannot be independent but can be joined to a free morpheme or to another bound morpheme. Many bound morphemes in both BSL and English contain grammatical information.

BSL bound morphemes cannot stand alone. While they do have meaning they are not independent signs. One bound morpheme may be the location or movement, while the handshape may be another bound morpheme. For example, in the signs: THREE-£ (pounds), THREE-YEARS-OLD, I-ASK-YOU-YOU, YOU-ASK-ME, DRIVE-CASUALLY, each is a single sign, but there are bound morphemes in each one. In THREE-£ and THREE-YEARS-OLD the handshape is a morpheme meaning 'three'. But the morphemes meaning £ or YEARS-OLD cannot be signed separately, because these morphemes can only occur in combination with the location and move-

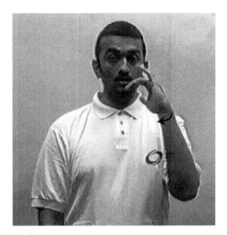

Fig. 6.3a CHECK

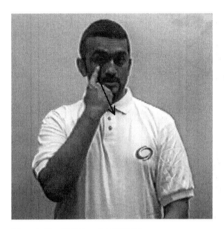

Fig. 6.3b SEE + MAYBE

ment of the handshape. 'Hand at the chin' or 'hand at the nose' means £ or YEARS-OLD in some abstract way, but we cannot sign them without using a handshape to say how many pounds or years-old there are (fig. 6.4).

In YOU-ASK-ME and I-ASK-YOU, one morpheme is the handshape meaning ASK, but I and YOU are not signed separately. They consist of locations and movements which cannot stand alone without a handshape, so they are bound.

In DRIVE-CASUALLY, DRIVE has location, movement and handshape, but CASUALLY only consists of a non-manual element which needs to be combined with it. The non-manual element cannot stand on its own to mean 'casually'.

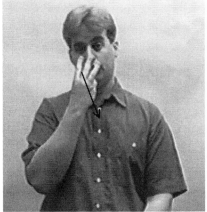

Fig. 6.4a £3   Fig. 6.4b 3-YEARS-OLD

PLURAL MORPHEMES

We will now focus upon one special morpheme, the 'plural'. The 'plural' indicates that here is more than one of something. Information about plurals can be attached to nouns and verbs with bound morphemes. It can also be provided by separate, free morphemes.

Plurals in English are made by adding a plural morpheme to a noun. The plural morpheme in English is bound because it cannot stand alone. The morpheme may have different surface forms, but it always has the same meaning. In English we have the following forms: in *cat* + *s* – [s] is the form of the plural morpheme; in *dog* + *s* – [z] is the form of the plural morpheme; in *horse* + *s* [iz] is the form of the plural morpheme; in *ox* + *en* [en] is the form of the plural morpheme (similarly with *children*) and *mouse* becomes *mice* and *goose* becomes *geese* (in these, the whole word changes because the vowel in the middle has changed to show the plural morpheme). All these have different surface forms, but all mean 'more than one', so we say they are all different ways of showing the plural morpheme.

Some English words have a 'zero' plural. In *sheep*, since the form is the same for one *sheep* and two *sheep*, linguists say that the plural has a zero form. However, separate morphemes, such as *one, two, ten, many*, and so on indicate how many sheep there are.

We should note that /s/ at the end of a word is not always a plural morpheme. In the sentence *James buys his clocks from Argos*, only the -*s* at the end of *clocks* can really be counted as a plural.

In summary, we can say that as a basic rule, English makes nouns plural by adding an /s/ to the end. BSL plurals are different. There is no regular

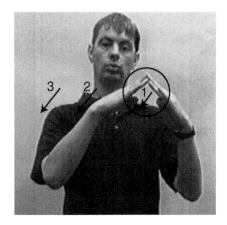 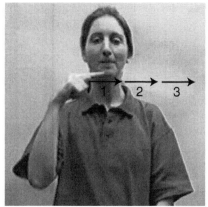

Fig. 6.5a HOUSES   Fig. 6.5b *BOYS (ungrammatical)

addition at the end of the sign. Instead, there are several different ways of making a noun plural in BSL. In some cases, the whole sign changes in some way by adding a bound plural morpheme; in others the plural precedes or follows the noun using separate free morphemes.

Some plurals are made by repeating the sign, with each repetition distributed in a different location, e.g. CHILDREN. The sign CHILD is a free morpheme, but the extra movement to show the plural is bound to CHILD. VIDEO-CAMERAS, STUDENTS (or PERSONS), and HOUSES are other examples (fig. 6.5a). The movement is usually repeated three times, but this does not mean that there are three of something. The same movement is seen whether there are three children or ten. Only signs that are not body-anchored can pluralise in this way. For example, *BOYS is ungrammatical (fig. 6.5b).

Any noun with repeated movement in the singular (e.g. INTERPRETER) cannot take this distributive bound plural morpheme. Instead, like *sheep* in English, plural is indicated by the presence of quantifiers such as ONE, TWO, TEN THOUSAND, FEW, MANY, etc.

Quantifier signs usually come before the noun, e.g. HE BUY TWO CAKE. There can also be 'quantifier copying' before and after the noun, e.g. HE BUY TEN CAKE TEN.

The number can actually be part of the sign, as we saw when we discussed bound morphemes before. In THREE-£, the handshape is the morpheme meaning 'three' and the location and movement comprise the morpheme 'pounds'. This again is a bound morpheme that marks plural.

Another very important way of marking number in BSL involves the use of proforms. Signs that are body-anchored (and therefore cannot take a distributive plural) can be represented by a proform which can take a distribu-

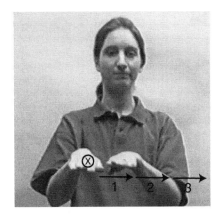

Fig. 6.6 BEDS

tive plural, e.g. BED pro-2D +++. If the proform is repeated distinctly in different locations, it means there are that number of beds in those locations. However, if it is performed with a sweeping movement, there are many of them, and the distribution is just a formal grammatical device (fig. 6.6).

It is also possible to combine the use of quantifiers and distributives, e.g. if we wanted to say there were five beds in a row, we could sign FIVE BEDS pro-2D-IN-A-ROW. Just as with the simple distributive, the proform is repeated three times; the number information is in the '5'-hand quantifier, and the proform indicates the distributive.

BSL also uses pronouns to show plural (e.g. THOSE-TWO, or ALL-OF-THEM). CAT THEM or MINISTER THEM can be seen as equivalent to *cats* or *ministers* (fig. 6.7). It is important to remember that in these examples,

Fig. 6.7 MINISTERS

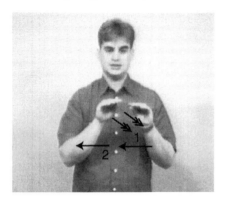
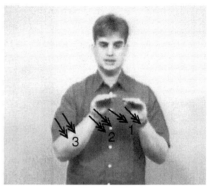

Fig. 6.8a I-TEACH-THEM-ALL   Fig. 6.8b I-TEACH-EACH-OF-
                                     THEM

there is often more than just an idea of 'one' vs. 'more than one'. There is also information about where the referents are, and/or how they are arranged.

VERB MORPHOLOGY

There is information about number in verbs, too. BSL verbs give information about whether an action is performed more than once, or if more than one person is involved in the action. In the verb I-TEACH-THEM-ALL, the sweeping movement of the verb TEACH indicates that a group receives the single action of a single person. In the verb I-TEACH-EACH-OF-THEM, the repeated and distributive movement indicates that a number of individuals each receives the single action of a single person (fig. 6.8). This contrasts with the absence of distributive movement in I-TEACH-HIM. It should be noted that repetition of movement in a verb can have different meanings depending on the rest of the sentence. Repetition of GO, for example, without distributed movement can mean either that one individual goes repeatedly, or that many individuals go. In chapter 8 we will discuss in more depth the information provided by verbs in BSL.

GRAMMATICAL CLASS: NOUNS, VERBS, AND ADJECTIVES IN BSL

Nouns, verbs, and adjectives can all contain complex morphological information in BSL. The form of the information and its meaning depend on the grammatical class of a sign.

At one time it was thought that nouns and verbs had identical forms in BSL. Now we know there are often differences in form as well as use (for

Fig. 6.9a FISH (verb)   Fig. 6.9b FISH (noun)

example, some morphemes combine with nouns and some with verbs). However, it is not unusual for languages to have nouns and verbs with identical surface forms. In English, there is often no difference between a noun and a verb in their basic forms (for example *a run* and *to run* or *an address* and *to address*). Some nouns and their associated verbs in BSL are very different, e.g. FISH (fig. 6.9). However, often the handshape and location of the noun and verb are identical and only the movements differ, e.g. BROOM vs. SWEEP or SERMON vs. PREACH-SERMON (fig. 6.10).

In these related forms, the underlying form of the noun is characterised by ending with a hold, while the verb ends with a change (see chapter 9). The surface form of the noun thus appears more restrained, and ends more

Fig. 6.10a SERMON   Fig. 6.10b PREACH-SERMON

abruptly. In addition, the verb often contains extra information to show where the action is taking place, or the manner of the action. Even in the 'citation form' (i.e. the base form, before any extra grammatical information has been added) verbs often use a conventionalised meaningful location.

Adjectives

Adjectives, too, can contain extra morphological information. Adjectives express some feature or quality of a noun (or pronoun). There are two kinds of adjectives:

(1) 'Attributive adjectives' – These occur in the noun phrase. In English the adjective comes before a noun when it is attributive, for example, *a big book, a tall man*. In BSL an attributive adjective can come before a noun (as we saw earlier, in chapter 3, with the example of HOT FOOD), after a noun (SHIRT WHITE), or can be incorporated into a noun (for example in LARGE-HOOP-EARRINGS, SHORT-LIST, SMALL-SPOTS) but in all cases it occurs within the noun phrase (see SMALL-BOX in fig. 3.8a).

(2) 'Predicative adjectives' – These act like a verb and occur in the verb phrase, e.g. MAN Index₃ TALL ('the man is tall').

A predicative adjective makes a predicate and the sentence is complete with it. With an attributive adjective, the sentence is not complete, e.g. *The big book* . . . or *The tall man* . . ..

There has been little research on BSL adjectives. It has been said that there are fewer adjectives in BSL than in English, and adjectives do appear to be used less often in BSL. There may be several reasons for this.

(1) There are often no separate adjectives, since some adjectives can be incorporated into the noun, with the size of the sign indicating the size of the referent, or the handshape indicating the size and shape of the referent, e.g. long, short, narrow, round, curved, flat, etc.

  However, separate adjectives have to be used with some signs, because changing the size of the sign does not always mean size change in the whole referent. If we make the signs BIRD, ELEPHANT, or PRIEST bigger, the meaning is 'big beaks', 'big trunks', and 'big collars', rather than 'big birds', 'big elephants', or 'big priests'.

(2) It has been argued that BSL predicate adjectives do not work like English predicate adjectives. BSL does not have the verb 'to be' so we cannot sign 'the man *is* big' in BSL – the equivalent sign sentence is MAN BIG. This means that the predicate adjective can equally as well be seen as a sort of verb.

More evidence for this is that many signs that would be called adjectives in English can be modified in a way similar to that of verbs (see chapter 8) suggesting that they are more like verbs (e.g. DRUNK or ILL). However, they cannot always inflect to show frequency, e.g. '*I'm regularly red' or '*I'm often tall', in the way that verbs can. If there is a frequency inflection on an adjective, it means it is characteristic of a person or that the person shows a disposition to this trait. For example, a person can be frequently ill or regularly ill, or ill for a long time, or ill again and again and again.

The American sign linguists Edward Klima and Ursula Bellugi have described the changes in movement that can be made to some ASL predicative adjectives. They suggest that the ASL predicative adjective ILL can be inflected to show: 'characteristically ill'; 'easily ill', 'often ill for a long time'; 'be ill over and over again'; 'be ill for an uninterrupted length of time'; 'be ill all the time'; 'be very ill'; and 'be totally ill'. These are shown by changes in movement (see chapter 7 for a discussion of similar inflection in verbs).

Adjectives in BSL can also be modified to show intensity.

(a) A premodifier, e.g. VERY or QUITE, can be added. There is a similar structure in English. Some signers consider this use of a premodifier to be an influence from English.

(b) A different sign can be substituted, e.g. SCARED or TERRIFIED; SMALL or TINY; TIRED or EXHAUSTED (fig. 6.11).

(c) In English *very* can be placed in front of adjectives, e.g. *very big, very tall* etc., but only if the adjective can be graded. A **very nuclear family* would not be acceptable. In English, degree can also be marked by using *more*

 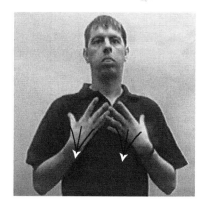

Fig. 6.11a TIRED   Fig. 6.11b EXHAUSTED

 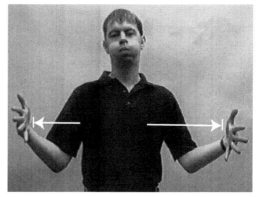

Fig. 6.12a LONG   Fig. 6.12b VERY-LONG

and *most* or *-er* and *-est,* e.g. *red, redder,* and *reddest* or *beautiful, more beautiful,* and *most beautiful.*

BSL Adjectives can be inflected to indicate intensity. That is, they take an extra bound morpheme. This has the form of a long, tense, initial hold, followed by a very rapid release to a final hold, e.g. HOT vs. VERY-HOT and LONG vs. VERY-LONG (fig. 6.12).

It should be noted that the form is independent of the meaning. For example, VERY-SHORT has a long hold, just as VERY-LONG does.

(d) Non-manual features can also be used to indicate intensity, as we saw in chapter 5.

SUMMARY

In this chapter we have introduced morphemes. A morpheme is a single unit of meaning in a language. Compounds are created by combining two free morphemes. Compounds are different in systematic ways from the signs that comprise them. We have also discussed bound morphemes, discovering how they cannot stand alone but only in combination with other morphemes. We have described one example of bound morphemes, plurals in BSL, looking at how BSL marks nouns and verbs to indicate that there is more than one referent involved. Not all of the information about plurals in BSL is given by adding bound morphemes to free morphemes. There are also free-standing plural morphemes in BSL, and combinations of bound morphemes, for example, bound plural morphemes and proforms.

We have also discussed grammatical categories of signs: nouns, verbs, and adjectives. There are small consistent differences between the forms of some related nouns and verbs and they are used quite differently, so there is rarely any doubt in context if a sign is a noun or verb. We have seen, too, that adjectives can be modified by adding extra morphemes, and that it is not always clear whether a sign is an adjective or a verb.

EXERCISES FOR CHAPTER 6

1. What are the differences between SONG/SING, AEROPLANE/FLY, CAR/DRIVE, BROOM/SWEEP, LECTURE/GIVE-LECTURE, KEY/LOCK, PEN/WRITE, CIGARETTE/SMOKE, BOOK/READ, FOOD/EAT? If these signs are used in the context of a sentence, how do they differ from their citation form?

2. Units within signs
   (a) Try breaking the following signs down into smaller parts. You should find that you cannot break them down into smaller units that have any meaning in the context of this sign.
      (i) TRUE, SAY, MOUSE, FLOWER, RED, KITCHEN, BEDROOM, HAPPY, AEROPLANE, CAR
   (b) Try splitting the following signs into smaller units. You should find that you can split them into smaller units with meaning.
      (i) PROMISE, BELIEVE, SPACE-SHUTTLE, MINICOM, I-ASK-YOU, DRIVE-CASUALLY, PEOPLE, BLOOD, CHECK, ANIMAL-JUMP-OVER-WALL, VERY-FAT

3. Compounds
   (a) Find examples of ten English compounds.
   (b) GUINEA-PIG, BALANCE-SHEET, and CHRISTMAS-TREE are compounds borrowed from English into BSL. Find five more of these.
   (c) BLOOD, PEOPLE, MINICOM, and CHECK are all compounds in BSL, but not compounds borrowed from English. Think of five more of these.
   (d) For each of your examples of compounds above, consider the individual signs that make up the compound. Say
      (i)   what the two free morphemes are
      (ii) if the compound is simultaneous or sequential
      (iii) what differences there are between the compound and the two separate signs.

4. Free and bound morphemes
   (a) Find examples of ten signs that only contain one morpheme each.
   (b) Find examples of ten signs that contain at least one free morpheme and one bound morpheme.
   (c) For each sign, say
      (i) what the free morpheme is
      (ii) what the bound morpheme means and how it is articulated.

5. Using a video clip of a fluent BSL signer, identify examples of ways in which BSL shows that there is more than one of something.
   (a) For each example, say if a noun or a verb is showing the information (or if you are not sure).
   (b) For each example, say how the plural is made (e.g. by repetition and distribution, by a separate quantifier like LOTS, by a separate proform, or by a combination, etc.).
6. Adjectives
   (a) Take the adjective 'long': the signs for 'hair', 'wait', 'sleeves', 'list' and 'story' will change depending on the length. Think how these would vary with the adjective 'short'.
   (b) Think about the adjective 'thick' and then think how this could be incorporated into a 'thick' 'sandwich', 'coat', 'pillow', or 'porridge'.
   (c) Make up ten sentences containing different adjectives that occur as predicates.
   (d) Change the intensity of these adjectives (e.g. 'not very tired', 'quite tired', 'tired', 'very tired', 'exhausted'). You might use a separate sign as the intensifier; a different sign for the adjective; change the movement of the sign or change the facial expression. Make a note of the changes that occur as you make the adjective more or less intense.

FURTHER READING FOR CHAPTER 6

Bergman, B. 1983, 'Verbs and adjectives: some morphological processes in Swedish Language', in J. G. Kyle and B. Woll (eds.), *Language in sign*, London: Croom Helm, 3–9.

Klima, E. S., and Bellugi, U. 1979, *The signs of language*, Harvard University Press.

Kyle, J. G. and Woll, B. 1985, *Sign language: the study of deaf people and their language*, Cambridge University Press.

Liddell, S. 1985, 'Compound formation rules in American Sign Language', in W. Stokoe and V. Volterra (eds.), *SLR 83*, Silver Spring, MD: Linstok Press, 144–51.

Wallin, L. 1983, 'Compounds in Swedish Sign Language', in J. G. Kyle and B. Woll (eds.), *Language in sign*, London: Croom Helm, 56–68.

Chapter seven

Aspect, manner, and mood

In the previous chapter we introduced the basic idea of morphemes, and then considered some of the ways that morphemes are used in BSL. We looked in some detail at nouns and adjectives. This chapter will focus on the morphological information that can be found in BSL verbs.

BSL verbs contain a considerable amount of morphological information, and very much more than English verbs do. The three types of information featured here (aspect, manner, and mood) are usually provided in English through the use of separate adverbs; in BSL the information is often incorporated into the verb itself. Before we consider these three inflections, however, it is worth discussing tense. BSL does not use tense, while English does.

TENSE

Tense is one way of locating events in time. It means showing time by adding morphemes to verbs to provide information such as 'past', 'present' and 'future'. Some languages have tenses indicating 'distant past' and 'distant future' too. Tense is deictic; that is, it needs a specific reference point for it to have any real meaning. Using a reference point of 'the present', English verbs show when an event occurs by adding this information morphologically. There is little evidence so far that BSL uses tense, but it is a feature worth discussing because so many other languages do, including English.

In English, there are only two basic tenses: present and past. English does not have a future tense. In the present tense, in English, a regular verb such as *walk* either has no ending (for first and second person singular, and for all plurals) or it has an -*s* added for third person singular (e.g. *I walk, you walk, they walk, he walks*). In the past tense, a final -*ed* is added (e.g. *I walked, you walked, he walked, they walked*).

English refers to the future by using expressions of intent (such as *will* or *going to*), or lexical time markers (such as *tomorrow*) combined with the

Fig. 7.1a WIN   Fig. 7.1b WON

present tense. *Will* is probably more rightly categorised as part of mood, rather than tense. We will discuss mood later in this chapter. The English verbs used with these other markers of future time may have a final *-ing*, or the present tense *-s*, or no added suffix at all (e.g. *We will walk to London, Tomorrow he walks to London, I am walking to London on Monday*, or *I am going to walk to London on Monday*).

Like English, BSL uses base verb forms with other separate lexical time markers (manual and non-manual) to refer to the future. It uses expressions of intent, such as WILL, and lexical markers, such as TOMORROW, just as English does. It uses similar devices to refer to the present and the past.

French has a rich tense system, including a future tense (e.g. *il sautait – he jumped, il saute – he jumps, il sautera – he will jump*). A French speaker might claim that French is better than English, on the grounds that English is such a poor language it does not even have proper tenses, and needs to rely on something as unsophisticated as a separate lexical time marker to indicate the future. Native users of English would disagree with such an interpretation, and yet it has been suggested that BSL is somehow a poorer language than English because English has a tense system and BSL does not. Use of a tense system does not make a language better, just different.

Some verbs in some BSL dialects differ depending on whether the action is in the past or present e.g. WIN/WON, SEE/SAW, GO/WENT, but it is probably better to say we have different lexical items, rather than saying there is systematic alteration for tense (fig. 7.1).

William Stokoe and Lynn Jacobowitz have claimed that future tense in American Sign Language is shown by an extension of the wrist, elbow, shoulder, or neck, and past tense by flexion of the same joints. No formal research has been done in Britain, but signers do not appear to be using this system of tense marking in BSL.

Fig. 7.2a 'Are you going to Liverpool?'   Fig. 7.2b 'Have you been to Liverpool?'

It is possible that moving the head forward or back may show some of this information. A forward movement of the head and shoulders may be used by some signers to show the future, and a backward movement of head and shoulders may be used in the same way to show the past. This is a possible line of inquiry. Certainly sentences in BSL that would be translated as *Are you going to Liverpool?* and *Have you been to Liverpool?* may well be distinguished solely by different head and body movements. However, this cannot be seen as a true tense system because whole phrases and sentences are covered by these non-manual markers, not only verbs (fig. 7.2) (also see chapter 5).

Finally, it is worth noting that pragmatics (common sense) can be used to show if an event is in the past or not. If someone with an obviously short, neat haircut is discussing something happening at the barber's, it is likely the event took place in the past. If someone's hand is in a bandage and they are talking about an accident in which their hand was hurt, it must be in the past. This is also the case if people are talking about an action of someone who is dead (e.g. Queen Victoria or Alexander Graham Bell). If someone is signing about the end of the universe, it is certain that they are talking about the future.

It is important to emphasise that it does not matter if there is no evidence of tense in BSL. A lack of a tense system does not make BSL worse than English (any more than a lack of future tense in English makes English worse than French); it simply shows that languages are different and use different methods of marking the time events take place other than tense. We will consider ways that BSL does talk about time in chapter 10.

BSL verbs, then, do not contain morphological information to locate an event in time relative to the present, and it does not really make sense to talk of tense in BSL. However, BSL verbs do contain a good deal of other morphological information, most notably for aspect, manner, and mood.

ASPECT

Aspect allows a signer to describe the internal timing of events. Aspect focuses on when something happened relative to another event, so that it shows how long the event went on for, whether it is complete or still in progress, and so on. Aspect may be shown in many ways, including verb inflection, separate lexical markers, and word or sign order.

BSL verbs inflect to show a great deal of information about aspect, and English verbs show very little (the converse to tense where English uses it and BSL does not). Russian verbs inflect for both tense and aspect. However, all languages can provide the same information about aspect somehow.

BSL frequently marks aspect within the verb. A signed sentence glossed as *LOOK LONG TIME is not considered by many signers to be grammatical in BSL (fig. 7.3b). Use of the separate signs LONG and TIME would be considered a part of Signed English. The BSL construction would be a single sign: LOOK-FOR-A-LONG-TIME, where LOOK has been inflected for aspect by repeating the sign LOOK, with a short circular movement, or by holding the sign for a longer period than normal, with an increased tension (fig. 7.3a).

Inflections for aspect

Mary Brennan has detailed several of the changes in movement that may occur as a part of inflecting for aspect in BSL. Some of the important ways that BSL verbs can change to show different features of aspect are as follows: repetition (slow or fast); a change from straight to arcing movement; a sudden hold at the end of a sign; an initial hold of the sign; a hold for a longer period; moving the sign bit by bit; and moving the sign slowly. BSL aspectual

Fig. 7.3a LOOK-FOR-A-LONG-TIME

Fig. 7.3b *LOOK LONG TIME

inflections are frequently visually motivated. If an action is interrupted suddenly, the sign reflects this in a sudden interruption of the movement. If an action happens smoothly, the sign movement of the verb is smooth. If the action continues for a noticeably long time, the sign may be held for a noticeably long time. We will now consider each of these aspectual inflections described by Brennan in more detail.

Repetition of movement in a sign can show aspectual information. For some verbs (e.g. WAIT, WALK) the repetition shows how long the action lasted. Short, fast repetition of the sign WAIT would be translated into English as *wait for a long time*. Slower repetition of the sign WAIT, with even larger movement, would be translated into English as *wait for an extremely long time*.

For other verbs (e.g. KNOCK, GO) short, fast repetition either indicates that the action is always performed or that it occurred very quickly. Short, fast repetition of the sign KNOCK could be translated into English as either *always knock* or *knock rapidly*. Context will disambiguate these two meanings.

For these verbs, the slow repetition can be translated as *to do something again and again*. Slow repetition of the sign KNOCK would be translated into English as *knock again and again*. Note, then, that the same movement can have different meanings depending on the type of action in the verb.

For the following inflections, the movement of the hand reflects the timing of the action. End marking is signed by pausing at the end of the movement of a sign. This inflection is used to show that an action came to an abrupt halt (cessive inflection). Abrupt halts would be seen in 'I was sauntering through the forest, when suddenly I stopped as I came to a wide river' or 'I thought and thought and thought about it and suddenly, I understood.' In these examples, the signs SAUNTER and THINK come to a sharp, abrupt halt to show that the action was suddenly interrupted.

The use of an initial hold shows that an event is about to happen but does not. This is sometimes referred to as 'inceptive aspect'. The sign may finish with this initial hold or it may continue after the hold, if the interruption is only temporary. In the sentences that carry the meanings 'I was about to cross the road when a car came rushing past' or 'I was about to eat my dinner when the doorbell flashed', the signs CROSS-ROAD and EAT-DINNER would have an initial hold.

The sign may be held for much longer than normal. This serves the same purpose as repetition for some verbs (i.e. that something went on for a long time) but is particularly used with signs that have no movement in them. LOOK held for a long time would be translated in English as *look for ages*. A similar meaning would be given to the sign HOLD held for a long time. Extra muscular tension in the sign may also be important here.

The movement of a sign may not be smooth but more 'stop-start'. This shows that something happened bit by bit (and is sometimes called 'incremental aspect'). Examples include WIND-UP-BY-DEGREES and GET-WEALTHIER-BY-DEGREES.

It is also possible for a signer to change the speed of the movement of a verb sign. If the sign slows down, it suggests something happened gradually, but not in the jumps suggested by incremental aspect. Examples include GRADUALLY-COME-TO-UNDERSTAND and GRADUALLY-APPROACH.

Separate aspect markers

Although BSL signs change movement to show aspect, there are also separate signs for some aspect marking. The idea of completion of an action is also part of aspect, and is shown in BSL by an extra sign, rather than by a change in the verb sign. Aspect shows whether an event is finished (or complete) or is still in progress.

BSL uses signs that can be glossed as FINISH or BEEN to show completion. These signs may be used at the end of a clause to show that the action is now finished and complete. BEEN can also be used at the beginning of the clause to show that the action about to be mentioned is completed. It is also possible to use BEEN together with another verb itself, if it is one-handed, e.g. SEE BEEN or EAT BEEN (that is, 'already seen' and 'already eaten'). For this reason, some people see this BEEN marker as a marker for tense, perhaps even as a suffix. In many cases, it may be the only marker to show that an event took place in the past. However, it can only be used for completion. It would be ungrammatical to sign *BEEN EAT+++ to mean 'I was eating'.

As well as aspectual inflections on verbs, signers may also use adverbs like OFTEN, ALWAYS, FREQUENTLY, NORMALLY for indicating aspect. English may have influenced BSL here. Sometimes, the separate adverb and the inflection can both be used to refer to the same action.

Simultaneous signing to show aspect

BSL signers can also represent aspect in respect of two events happening relative to each other, by showing the two events on two different hands, or one event on the hands and one on the face. If a train passenger was reading while the person beside them talked, we can show this in BSL with the information about the 'reading' on one hand, and the 'talking' on the other (fig. 7.4). There are many examples of this device being used in BSL: 'I held the baby while I picked up the bag'; 'She gripped the steering wheel as she sounded the horn'; ' Holding the flag in one hand, he saluted smartly'; 'Putting his arm around the little girl, he asked if she felt OK', and so on. In each example, one action

Fig. 7.4 READ-WHILE-SOMEONE-TALKS

is shown on each hand. We will discuss this idea of 'simultaneous signs' in chapter 11 in more detail. However, this is a very good example of the very different ways that BSL can make good use of both hands and space to show quite complex grammatical information.

Stative and dynamic verbs

Verbs have some idea of aspect built into them, because of their underlying meaning, and we can divide them into two main groups: stative verbs and dynamic verbs.

Stative verbs describe states or processes that have no obvious action, e.g. 'be', 'have', and 'know'. They do not indicate aspect, because the 'event' cannot be said to happen at any one time. If we consider the idea 'I have two sisters', it does not really make sense to say that 'I keep having two sisters' or that 'I gradually had two sisters'. Consequently, we can say that these stative verbs do not readily show aspect. Of course, it is always possible to find exceptions, but normally these constructions would not make sense.

English has a class of predicates which are formed by the verb *to be* with predicate adjectives. These can be considered as stative verbs, since they describe the state of the subject. In BSL, it has been argued that there is no difference between a predicative adjective and stative verbs.

In the sentences MAN TALL and MAN GROW, the predicate is essentially the same sign, while in English, the two predicates are different (*is tall* and *grows*) (fig. 7.5).

Dynamic verbs describe something happening, rather than just being or existing. They are verbs that allow us to talk about the internal timing of an event and to show how the action happened relative to other events, so these are the verbs that can show aspect. Dynamic verbs are of two types, which again affect the way they may show aspect: 'durative' and 'punctual'.

Durative actions can go on for any length of time. The actions referred to

Fig. 7.5a TALL   Fig. 7.5b GROW

in WALK, ANALYSE, THINK, SWIM, TALK, READ, and WRITE are all capable of going on indefinitely.

Punctual verbs only happen in a moment, at one point in time. The actions described in the verbs KNOCK, BLINK, NOD, TAP, and HIT all happen in a single instant. Some mark a transition so that there is only one moment when an event happens before circumstances change, e.g. ARRIVE, SCORE-A-GOAL, and LEAVE. Anyone may be working towards arriving, scoring a goal, or leaving for quite a while. However, when the event of arrival, scoring or leaving happens, it happens in an instant. After this moment, the person has arrived, scored, or left.

This distinction between durative and punctual verbs is not always clear, and there are times when the verb could be either. Consider, for example, SHOUT. It is not really durative because it does not go on indefinitely (in the end, we would run out of breath), but it is not punctual either, because it does not happen only at one point in time. However, as the shouting *can* go on for a while, the verb is considered durative.

JUMP is also difficult to classify. If we jump up and down, the verb looks like it is punctual, because the jump happens in a moment. But if we jump a long way (e.g. over a cliff in an action film), the jump could go on for a long time. This may be a problem of semantics, however. Perhaps there is one verb JUMP for leaving the surface, and then the rest of the action is actually 'travelling through space and then descending' rather than 'jumping'. We might also describe the signs glossed as JUMP in English as actually two very different signs in BSL. Perhaps a better gloss would be JUMP-ON-THE-SPOT and JUMP-THROUGH-SPACE, so that the former is punctual and the latter is durative.

In durative verbs, if we sign WAIT+++ TEN MINUTES, the action of waiting would continue for 10 minutes. In punctual verbs, if we sign NOD+++ TEN MINUTES, the action of nodding would continue over and over again over a period of 10 minutes. In both cases, it is possible to stop and start the activity but one goes on continuously, whereas the other occurs repeatedly.

Aspect in English

We have seen then, that BSL indicates aspect mainly through verb inflection, although it may also use separate signs. We may compare this with English. In English, verbs will show if something is still in progress (progressive) or if it is complete (perfect). Perfect in English uses *have* with a verb with *-en*. For example, *I have written my love a letter*, means that I have finished the letter. Completion does not need to be in the past: it could be a prediction, as in *By next Sunday morning, I will have written my love a letter*.

Progressive in English uses *be* with *-ing* on the end of the verb. For example, *I am writing my love a letter* or *I was writing my love a letter*. The first example is set in the present (or even in the future if the context is *Next Sunday morning I am writing my love a letter*) and the second example is set in the past, but in neither case have I finished the letter to my love.

The progressive and perfect are shown by changing the verbs in English, but for most information about aspect, English uses many other words and phrases in place of the BSL inflections. Examples of English include: *I had **only started** writing my love a letter **when...**; I was **about to** write my love a letter **when...**; I **had been** writing my love a letter for nearly ten minutes **when suddenly...**; I **have been** writing my love a letter for hours; I write my love a letter **regularly** every Sunday*; and *I **often** write my love a letter.*

These separate words (shown in bold italics in the above examples), are usually called 'adverbs of time' in English, and that is how we most commonly show aspect in English. In English, these adverbs are usually separate words. In BSL they are frequently built into the verb as bound morphemes.

In summary, aspect tells us when an event happened relative to another event, how long for and how often. English often uses other words to show aspect (mainly adverbs), but BSL often changes the movement of the verb, or articulates two verbs simultaneously.

MANNER

Manner tells us how an action was done. Examples of manner in English would be *slyly, cheerfully, lightly, humorously, like a Frenchman, in the style of a great Diva, sweetly, confidently,* and *drunkenly.*

In some cases, there may appear to be an overlap between adverbs of manner and aspect, if there is an element of time in the way something was done. For example we might have adverbs of manner like *slowly, quickly,* or *gradually,* although this is usually considered a part of aspect, because they contain some element of meaning of timing.

Most of the time, however, manner is clearly separate from aspect. In BSL manner may be shown using separate signs that are adverbs like SLOWLY, CONFIDENTLY, CAREFULLY, or LIKE FRENCH (i.e. the way a French person does something), etc. In English, adverbs are used a great deal to show manner (e.g. *slowly, quickly, easily, happily, miserably*).

Information about manner can also be conveyed by using a different word or sign. This is because manner can be a part of the semantics of a word or sign. For example, the basic verb WALK can be replaced by related signs depending on the way that a person or animal walked. English also does this. Different manners of walking are implied in words such as *scuttle, trot, saunter, jog, mince, hobble, stride, swagger, stagger, limp,* and *teeter.*

BSL also uses facial expression (and especially oral components) to give information about manner. In fact, we may describe all verbs as having an accompanying facial expression which gives information about the manner in which an action occurred (although often that manner is 'neutral' or 'unmarked'). We discussed adverbials on the face (for example 'mm', 'th', and 'ee') when we discussed mouth patterns in chapter 5. Other facial expressions may give information about the emotions linked to the manner of the action (such as a relieved facial expression accompanying the meaning 'I handed her the baby with relief' or a sad facial expression when signing 'I told her, sadly, that the train had left').

It is not always easy when watching a signer to make the distinction between the manner in which something occurred and the feelings of the signer. In many cases, they are the same. Translations into BSL of *I was happy when I walked through the forest* and *I walked through the forest happily* would use a similar facial expression. Thus, a facial expression that gives information about emotion may be considered information about manner too, when it is used in conjunction with verbs.

However, there are times when the emotions of the person referred to in the sentence are not the same as the signer's. This occurs when the signer is registering an emotional reaction to the event described. For example, in the BSL sentence meaning 'He did not answer me – he just walked off!', the signer's facial expression may well be one of indignation, but the manner in which the man walked off is left unstated by the face. More information about the way the person walked off may be found in the movement of the sign itself or in an extra sign.

Change in movement is another important way in which information about manner is given in BSL verbs. If we consider intensity (how much effort something is) we can see how changes in movement to the verb can show this. We can consider intensity as small (not very intense) and large (intense). Where intensity is small, the strength of the signing and size of the signing often decrease. Where it is large, strength and size often increase.

In summary, how the action is carried out may be shown by adding an adverb of manner, changing the verb completely, using facial expression or by changing the movement of the verb. In English this information is provided either by an adverb or by using a different verb.

MOOD

Mood is the third of the traditional three-way split in linguistics for information that verbs can show: tense, aspect, and mood.

Mood tells us about the speaker's attitude to the information in the sentence. For example the speaker may show uncertainty, possibility, or definiteness. Mood distinguishes commands, statements, and things we are not completely sure about (subjunctive). In English mood is shown by modal auxiliaries like *may, can, shall,* and *must.*

In BSL, there has been little formal research, but there are at least two manual ways of showing mood, as well as non-manual ways. The first manual way is to use modal auxiliaries, just as English does. Thus, BSL uses signs such as SHOULD, CAN, MUST, and WILL either before or after the verb (or both before and after). The second manual way to show mood is to vary the tenseness, strength, and size of the verb sign. SHOULD-ASK is smaller and less tense and strong than MUST-ASK, but larger, tenser, and stronger than COULD-ASK. A third way to show mood is to use non-manual features, such as expressions of doubt or determination. These are obligatorily used with manual marking. These three markers of mood are often all used together.

SUMMARY

In this chapter, we have seen that BSL verbs contain information about the timing of events and the way in which an action was performed or occurred. This information about aspect and manner may be shown by adverbs (as it usually is in English), but is more frequently shown by changes in the movement of verb signs or by non-manual information.

EXERCISES FOR CHAPTER 7

1. Read the following passage from '*Body of Evidence*' by Patricia Cornwell (1993) London: Little, Brown (pp. 282–3). Identify as many examples of aspect as you can find.

   Parking in the gravel lot designated for visitors, I went into the lobby of Victorian fur-nishings, Oriental rugs, and heavy draperies with ornate cornices well along their way to being threadbare. I was about to announce myself to the receptionist when I heard someone behind me speak.

   'Dr Scarpetta?'

   I turned to face a tall, slender black man dressed in a European-cut navy suit. His hair was a sandy sprinkle, his cheekbones and forehead aristocratically high.

   'I'm Warner Masterson,' he said, and smiling broadly, he offered his hand.

   I was about to wonder if I had forgotten him from some former encounter when he explained that he recognised me from pictures he had seen in the papers and on the tele-vision news, reminders I could do without.

   'We'll go back to my office,' he added pleasantly. 'I trust your drive wasn't too tiring? May I offer you something? Coffee? A soda?'

   All this as he continued to walk, and I did my best to keep up with his long strides. A significant proportion of the human race has no idea what it is like to be attached to short legs, and I am forever finding myself indignantly pumping along like a handcar in a world of express trains. Dr Masterson was at the other end of a long, carpeted corridor when he finally had the presence of mind to look around. Pausing at a doorway, he waited until I caught up with him, then he ushered me inside. I helped myself to a chair while he took his position behind his desk and automatically began tamping tobacco into an expensive briar pipe.

'Needless to say, Dr Scarpetta,' Dr. Masterson began in his slow, precise way as he opened a thick file folder, 'I am dismayed by Al Hunt's death.'

'Are you surprised by it?' I asked.

'Not entirely.'

'I'd like to review his case as we talk,' I said.

He hesitated long enough for me to consider reminding him of my statutory rights to the record. Then he smiled again and said, 'Certainly,' as he handed it over.

I opened the manila folder and began to peruse its contents as blue pipe smoke drifted over me like aromatic woodshavings.

2. Give examples of five BSL verbs inflected to show the following aspectual information:
   (a) the action continues for a long time
   (b) the action continues for a very long time
   (c) the action regularly happens
   (d) the action is repeated slowly
   (e) the action is repeated fast
   (f) the action continues and is suddenly interrupted
   (g) the action is about to happen but is interrupted
   (h) the action happens bit by bit, gradually
   (i) the action happens smoothly
   (j) two actions happen simultaneously (one shown on each hand)
   (k) two actions happen simultaneously (one shown on the hands, one non-manual)
   (l) three actions happen simultaneously

3. Manner
   (a) Think about how to sign different ways of walking. You should try to use several different handshapes and movements. Your body movement and facial expression should also vary.
   (b) Vary the intensity of the effort of the actions in the verbs EAT, and RUN. Do this by changing the size, strength, and speed of the movement in the verb. Translate these into English.

4. Watch a video clip of a fluent signer.
   (a) Identify any verbs where movement change shows aspect, (e.g. by repetition, steps, change in speed, or change in tension of the sign).
   (b) Decide if these verbs are durative (the activity could go on for a while) or punctual (the activity can only happen for a moment), or is it not easy to decide?

5. Watch a video clip of a fluent signer. Identify examples of changes in signs to show manner (the way the action was done, e.g. 'happily', 'carefully', 'like a horse', etc.). Is the manner shown by the face, or the hands, or both?

FURTHER READING FOR CHAPTER 7

Bergman, B. 1983, 'Verbs and adjectives: Some morphological processes in Swedish Sign Language', in J. G. Kyle and B. Woll (eds.), *Language in sign*, London: Croom Helm, 3–9.

Brennan, M. 1992, 'The visual world of BSL: an introduction'. In *The dictionary of British Sign Language/English*, London: Faber & Faber, 1–134.

Engberg-Pedersen, E. 1993, *Space in Danish Sign Language*, Hamburg: Signum Press.

Klima, E. S., and Bellugi, U. 1979, *The signs of language*, Harvard University Press.

Kyle, J. G., and Woll, B. 1985, *Sign language: the study of deaf people and their language*, Cambridge University Press.

Liddell, S. 1980, *American Sign Language syntax*, The Hague: Mouton.

Padden, C. 1989, 'The relation between space and grammar in ASL verb morphology', in C. Lucas (ed.), *Sign language research: theoretical issues*, Washington, DC: Gallaudet University Press, 118–32.

Chapter eight

Space types and verb types in BSL

In this chapter we will be considering the different uses of space in BSL, and the way this influences the use of verbs in BSL. We will discuss the difference between syntactic space and topographic space, using evidence from brain-damaged deaf people as well as evidence from experiments with healthy deaf people. We will then think about the way these two types of space are used by the three groups of verbs that can be identified in BSL; namely plain verbs, agreement verbs, and spatial verbs. The division of these verbs is based upon the grammatical information they include. The use of space is one of the most important characteristics of BSL verbs and needs describing before we can talk about verb types any further.

SYNTACTIC AND TOPOGRAPHIC SPACE

Some linguists have claimed that there are two different types of space that are used in sign languages. Physically, the signing space is exactly the same, but the space is used in two very different ways by the language.

Topographic space recreates a map of the real world. It is a spatial layout in signing space of representations of things as they really are. For example, when we describe a local shopping area to someone in BSL, we place things in our signing space according to where these things really are in relation to other things. If the church is opposite the fruit shop, and the fruit shop is next to the post office, then we place them that way in signing space. If we place the signs anywhere else, or if we do not attempt to place these signs (or their proforms) at all, then it is ungrammatical.

English does not need spatial information from its speakers, in the normal course of events. A speaker could simply say that there was a fruit shop, a post office, and a church without needing to say where these are. Of course speakers of English can and do describe where things are, if they need to; however, this is not done by changing the words, but rather by adding words. This, again, highlights the many differences between BSL and English.

While topographic space reflects the layout of things in the real world, syntactic space is created from within the language and may not map onto the real world. As an example, we may consider how we might express that some deaf Asians in Britain find themselves torn between two strong cultures: the British Deaf community and the British Asian community. Perhaps a signer wants to sign that it is difficult being Asian and deaf in Britain because she does not fit into either group. The signer might place a sign referring to ASIAN on the left side of her signing space and a sign referring to DEAF on the right. There are actually no Asian people on her left, and no deaf people on the right. The placing of the two groups is just created from within the language to allow the signer to refer to them in space. It would be equally possible to place two totally abstract concepts in signing space, so that a sign representing HONESTY could be placed in one area, and a sign for WEALTH in another, to allow the signer to discuss the relative merits of the two.

Syntactic space uses grammatical structures which move in space between grammatically defined points. For example, in 'I gave my aunt a book' (AUNT Index$_3$ Index$_1$ BOOK$_1$ GIVE-BOOK$_3$) the real aunt in the real world does not have to be where the signer placed her for this sentence. The signer could even have posted it to her from London to Tokyo, but the grammatical location of the aunt is the same and that is where the book is directed.

We can compare topographic and syntactic space. In topographic space, the referent is at the location (e.g. where we place the sign for the church relative to where we place the sign for the post office represents their real location in the world), whereas in syntactic space the referent is the location – and the location is the referent – (so the arbitrary location we give to British Asians and British deaf people is used to mean them).

This idea of dividing space like this is not accepted by all linguists. Some people (e.g. Trevor Johnston in Australia and Scott Liddell in America) have argued that there is no difference between these two. Certainly there are some examples where there seems to be overlap, and the debate is not yet resolved. Despite this, the distinction is helpful for someone learning about BSL, and there is strong experimental evidence that there is a real difference between the two uses of linguistic space.

Evidence from brain-damaged deaf people

The brain is divided into left and right hemispheres: the left is known to be more important for language and the right is more important for spatial skills. Even though sign languages are visual languages, they are still primarily located in the left hemisphere. Much of the research into the relationship between the brain and signing has been done by Howard Poizner and Ursula Bellugi in America.

Damage to the left hemisphere of any person – whether they are a signer or speaker – can create very serious language problems but still leave them with spatial skills (e.g. they can match shapes, or look at two different layouts of an area they know and indicate which is correct). Some deaf people with left hemisphere damage can manage a few simple signs and can place some of those correctly. They may also be able to indicate if someone is describing a layout wrongly.

Damage to the right hemisphere can have relatively little effect on a person's signing, in relation to both lexicon and grammar, except for the effects on use of topographic space. A right-hemisphere-damaged signer asked to describe a zoo might describe it with clear signs, but each sign would be placed in the same location, creating a visual image of animals being stacked higgledy-piggledy in one part of the 'zoo'.

This distinction provides evidence that syntactic and topographic space in sign languages are treated differently in the brain, so we may expect them to function differently in signing.

Evidence from healthy signers

Evidence for two different uses of space in sign languages also comes from experiments conducted with healthy deaf people. An American researcher, Karen Emmorey, together with colleagues did work with two types of scenarios; one involving topographic space, and one using syntactic space (fig. 8.1). She provided signers with two different types of sentences signed in ASL, and asked people to make a decision about a probe sign that did or did not occur in the sentence. The idea behind this experiment is that when people are in some way uncomfortable with what they have just seen, their decision-making processes will be slowed down. Thus, if subjects showed significant differences in speed of reaction to different types of probes in different sentences, this could be taken as evidence that they were thinking in different ways.

In an example of a sentence using topographic space, she described her dressing-table as a terrible mess. 'My blusher case (right) is broken. My nail polish (centre) is spilled. My perfume (left) is empty.' This description uses topographic space because it recreates a map of the dressing table and everything is laid out as it is in the real world.

In an example of a sentence using syntactic space, she described the problems of her parents' house. 'It is so expensive to run. It uses a lot of gas (right), electricity (centre) and water (left).' The space used here is syntactic because the three utilities are not located anywhere specifically in the real world, in her

Layout in topographic space

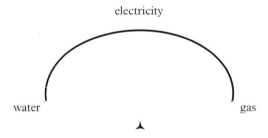

Layout in syntactic space

Fig. 8.1a Emmorey's two types of scenario

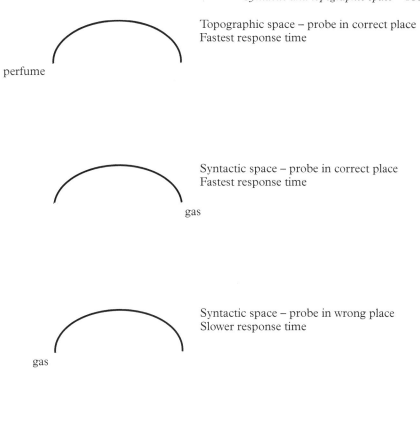

perfume

Topographic space – probe in correct place
Fastest response time

Syntactic space – probe in correct place
Fastest response time

gas

Syntactic space – probe in wrong place
Slower response time

gas

Topographic space – probe in wrong place
Slowest response time

perfume

Fig. 8.1b   Reaction times to probes in Emmorey's scenarios

parents' house, and certainly not necessarily to be found at the right, centre, and left of the house.

After each sentence she gave a 'probe sign' and asked the volunteers in her experiment if that probe was in the sentence. The volunteers had to decide quickly. For example, she might give the probe OIL or HAIRBRUSH, and they would be expected to respond 'no', because these were not in the previous sentence. If she gave the probe GAS or PERFUME, they would be expected to respond 'yes', because these *were* in the previous sentence.

The 'correct' probe was sometimes given at the correct location and sometimes not. For example, GAS_L (which is the wrong location) or GAS_R (the correct location); $PERFUME_L$ (correct location) or $PERFUME_R$ (wrong location). In both cases they were slower at responding 'yes' to the correct probe when it was in the wrong place, and quicker when it was in the correct place. This shows that when a sign is placed in the wrong part of space, signers are made to feel uncomfortable in some way. We can confirm from this that placement in space is important for building up a signer's linguistic understanding.

However, more importantly, the volunteers were quicker to recognise the probe for GAS at the wrong location than they were to recognise the probe for PERFUME at the wrong location. They were quicker for GAS because no topographic image had been created. It took them longer to respond 'yes' for PERFUME when it was a probe in the wrong place because a topographic image had been created. This, again, suggests that the two types of space are treated differently in the brain.

BSL VERB TYPES

Now that we have seen that space is used for different functions in sign language, we can think about the way that verbs in BSL use these two different types of space. This is part of a larger consideration of the sort of information that a verb in BSL can include.

We have already seen in chapter 7 that very few, if any, verbs show information about tense (or, if they do, they do not use space to show this information). Most verbs include information about aspect, but a few are very limited in the sorts of information they can include. These are the stative verbs we discussed in the previous chapter. They have also been called invariant verbs, although even these can include a small amount of morphological information, e.g. the verbs KNOW and HAVE can include information about the signer's attitude ('definitely know', 'sorry to have', etc.).

There are some verbs that carry aspectual information about events by changing their movement, but they carry no more regular grammatical information than that. (Some can carry information about the direct object, as part of the handshape, and that will be discussed later.)

A great many other BSL verbs use movement through space to show information about the subject and object (both direct and indirect). Many other BSL verbs use movement and location in space to show the movement and location of the object during the action of the verb.

SPACE AND VERBS

The difference in use of space is very important when we consider verbs. In some verbs, we have an image of a layout and the verbs move with their related objects through this image. That is, they use topographic space. In other verbs the location is part of the verb, and not part of any pre-existing layout.

For the rest of this chapter we will look at the way verbs use space in BSL. We will consider how verbs show the subject and object (direct and indirect) and the location of referents involved in the action.

When we consider different groups of verbs, we need to think about information that will tell us who is doing the action (the agent or, grammatically, the subject) and who or what is receiving the action (the goal or, grammatically, the object). For both the subject and object, we need to know if the person involved is the signer or someone else, and how many people or things are involved. We mentioned this earlier in chapter 3 when we compared personal pronouns in BSL and English. We saw that English pronouns can only tell us if one person or more than one person is being referred to. BSL pronouns can tell us if one, two, three, four, many or each of several are being referred to. This same information can be shown in some BSL verbs.

With a clear idea of manner, aspect, person, and number, we can now discuss the different verb types in BSL. There are three basic classes of verbs in BSL, depending on what information they carry:

plain verbs – they can be modified to show manner, aspect and class of direct object;

agreement verbs – they can be modified to show manner, aspect, person, number, and class of direct object; and

spatial verbs – they can be modified to show manner, aspect and location, movement, and related noun.

PLAIN VERBS

Examples of plain verbs are RIDE-A-BICYCLE, LOVE, RESEARCH, RUN, SMOKE, THINK, and UNDERSTAND,

These plain verbs show relatively little modification and do not move through space to show grammatical information. Most can show information about aspect, although some do not (stative verbs like HAVE). Manner and

Fig. 8.2 THINK-HARD

aspect are marked in these verbs by speed of the repetition of the verb and presence of non-manual features. For example, THINK-HARD is made by a small circling repetition of the sign, with a 'effortful' facial expression (fig. 8.2). RIDE-A-BICYCLE-CASUALLY is made using a relaxed facial expression with the loose 'mm' oral component described in chapter 5. RESEARCH-FOR-AGES is made by a repeating arcing movement of the sign RESEARCH (as we saw when we discussed aspect in chapter 7) (see also figure 7.3a).

Many plain verbs are made using the body as the location (sometimes called 'body-anchored'), which may, at first glance, appear to be a good reason for them to be plain verbs. After all, if a verb gives information about subject and object person and number by moving through space, then a body anchored verb will not be able to do this. Examples of body-anchored plain verbs include LIKE, LOVE, THINK, KNOW, SMOKE, UNDERSTAND, FEEL, SWEAR, and WANT. However, this is only a generalisation because there are other verbs that are not body anchored and are still plain (e.g. SWIM, RIDE-A-BICYCLE, RUN, and RESEARCH).

Any information about 'person' and 'number' in plain verbs needs to be given separately, by pronouns. Plain verbs cannot move through space to show this information. '(I) like him' is signed LIKE Index$_3$, not *ME-LIKE-HIM (fig. 8.3).

Some information about the features of the direct object can also be included in plain verbs. This can be shown by the handshape, or movement. For example, in the verb SMOKE, the base form of SMOKE is usually given as the sign more accurately glossed as SMOKE-CIGARETTE but the hand-shape can also be changed to show SMOKE-PIPE, SMOKE-JOINT, SMOKE-CIGAR, SMOKE-HOOKAH, and so on (see the discussion in

Fig. 8.3a 'I like him'

Fig. 8.3b Ungrammatical form of '*I like him'

chapters 3 and 11) (see also figs. 3.11 and 3.12). This topic has also been researched in Israeli Sign Language by Anat Stavans.

The main point here is that plain verbs include information about manner and aspect, and sometimes direct object, but other information about person and number is given in separate signs.

AGREEMENT VERBS

Examples of agreement verbs are ASK, GIVE, TELL, TELEPHONE, TEASE, CRITICISE, BLAME, FILM, and SAY-NO.

Agreement verbs allow the inclusion of information about person and number of the subject and object. This is accomplished by moving the verb in syntactic space. That is, information about who is carrying out the action, and who or what is affected by the action is shown by changes in movement and orientation of the verb. Information about manner and aspect can also be given by changing the movement of the verb and by adding non-manual features, just as with plain verbs. Some agreement verbs also identify the direct object through the handshape.

This group of verbs includes verbs that are sometimes called 'directional' verbs. However, 'directional' focuses on the form of the verb (e.g. where it moves). Calling them 'agreement' verbs focuses on the morphological information in the verb. We can say that the information about where the verb moves 'agrees' with the person and number of the subject and/or the object.

Agreement verbs may agree with first, second, and third person. For the first person, the verb is directed to, or located at, where the signer is. For the second person, the verb is directed to or located at the conversational partner. The third person may be marked with an index (or a proform) or the noun may be located at that position with the agreement marker moving between the locations. In theory, BSL allows as many third person agreement markers to be operating in the signing space as the signer chooses, but in practice there are very rarely more than three in any one turn.

Usually, the starting point of these verbs is the location of the subject. Usually, too, the end point is where the object is. That is, in an agreement verb, there is a start point (subject agreement marker) then a linear movement (verb stem) and then an end point (object agreement marker). This means, for example, that the verb I-ASK-YOU starts at the place in space that is used to refer to the subject 'I' (a place near the signer), and finishes at the place in space that is used to refer to the object 'you' (a place at the far side of the signing space, in the direction of the conversational partner).

The exceptions to this are a few verbs with 'backwards agreement' where the start point marks the object and the end point marks the subject. Examples include TAKE-FROM, INVITE, CHOOSE, BORROW, and INTRODUCE. The verb I-INVITE-YOU starts at the place in space used to refer to the object 'you' and moves towards the space used to refer to the subject 'I' (fig. 8.4) (see also fig. 8.5 and fig. 3.10).

Number agreement in agreement verbs is quite complex and verbs differ in how they show different information about number for the subject and the object. In some instances, all the information about number in the subject and the object is shown by movement of the verb; in other instances a pronoun is used for some of this information, too. Number agreement may be for singular, collective plural, dual, triple, and exhaustive.

(1) Singular is marked by a single simple movement from the subject marker towards the object marker (e.g. I-ASK-YOU or YOU-TELL-HER or SHE-GIVES-ME).

Fig. 8.4 I-INVITE-YOU

(2) Collective plural of the object is shown by a sweeping movement of the verb across an arc that refers to the plural object. The verb is not repeated, but rather, it is displaced. This sweeping movement to show collective plural is for object agreement only, for example in I-ASK-YOU-ALL or HE-ASKS-THEM. It is not used to show collective plural for subject agreement, so that the verb form *WE-ALL-ASK-HIM is unacceptable. For plural subjects, the signer uses a sweeping proform, for example, in WE-ALL ASK-HIM or THEY-ALL ASK-US (fig. 8.5).

Some signers do not use sweeping movement to show the plural object if the basic verb already has repeated movement (e.g. SHARE, TEASE). These signers use a sweeping proform for the plural object, as well as for the plural subject.

(3) Dual agreement is marked in various ways. If the object is dual (i.e. 'I ask the two of you'), we can show the information in one of three ways (in the following examples, SISTER and BROTHER have been located on the right side and left side of signing space respectively):

(a) we can make the verb movement twice with the end point of the second movement at the location of the second object. If we take the example 'I asked my sister and brother', this may be written as:

$$\overline{\hspace{5cm}}^{t}$$
SISTER Index$_{R}$ BROTHER Index$_{L}$ $_{1}$ASK$_{R}$ $_{1}$ASK$_{L}$

SISTER is placed at location 'R' by an index, and BROTHER is placed at location 'L' by another index. The verb moves from the first person ('1' – close to the signer) to the location 'R' and then repeats the movement from the first person, but to location 'L' (fig. 8.6a).

(b) if the verb is one-handed (for example ASK, TELL, or TELE-PHONE) we can also double the verb stem to a two-handed form

Fig. 8.5a I-ASK-YOU-ALL

Fig. 8.5b Ungrammatical form of
*WE-ALL-ASK-HIM

Fig. 8.5c Grammatical form of WE-ALL ASK-HIM

and move both hands simultaneously, or one after the other. The same idea 'I asked my sister and brother' may be written like this:

$$\frac{\qquad\qquad\qquad\qquad\qquad\text{t}}{\text{SISTER Index}_R\ \text{BROTHER Index}_L\ \text{(right hand) }_1\text{ASK}_R\text{\rule{1cm}{0.4pt}}}$$
$$\text{(left hand) }\quad_1\text{ASK}_L$$

Again, SISTER and BROTHER are placed at locations 'R' and 'L', but this time both hands make the handshape for ASK, and the right hand moves from the first person location ('1') to location 'R', at the same time as the left hand moves from the first person to location 'L'. Alternatively, the right hand can move to 'R' and be held there, while the left hand moves to 'L' (fig. 8.6b).

If the verb is two-handed (e.g. BLAME or TEASE) this doubling of the verb is not a possible option.

Fig. 8.6a ASK-TWO-OF-THEM: one hand moves to each object location

Fig. 8.6b ASK-TWO-OF-THEM: each hand moves to an object location

Fig. 8.6c ASK TWO-OF-THEM: separate pronoun shows the object

(c) a third option is to use a single movement towards one of the objects, and then use pronouns like TWO-OF-THEM. Once again, with 'I asked my sister and brother', we may write this as:

_____t
SISTER Index_R BROTHER Index_{L 1}ASK₃ TWO-OF-THEM

$$\overline{\hspace{4cm}}t$$
SISTER Index$_R$ BROTHER Index$_{L\ 1}$ASK$_3$ TWO-OF-THEM

Here SISTER and BROTHER are again located at 'R' and 'L', and the verb ASK is moved simply from first person to a third person location near 'R' and 'L'. The signer then signs the pronoun TWO-OF-THEM referring to 'R' and 'L' (fig. 8.6c).

This third option is often the preferred choice for the verb when the subject is dual, for example, as in 'My sister and brother both asked me at the same time.'

Moving the verb between dual subjects located at 'R' and 'L' and then moving it towards the object (the first option here for dual objects) is not

 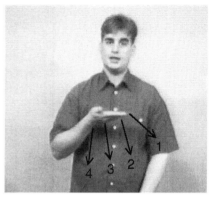

Fig. 8.7a I-GIVE-TO-EACH-OF-THEM

Fig. 8.7b I-GIVE-TO-HER-AND-HER-AND-HER-AND-HER

grammatical. The American sign linguist Carol Padden has claimed that the second option (doubling the verb so that the two verb signs move from subjects at 'R' and 'L' towards the object simultaneously) also works in ASL when the subject is dual, but not all BSL signers agree on its acceptability in BSL.

(4) Triple agreement works in a similar way to dual agreement marking, but uses a triple end point to the verb stem or uses both hands to duplicate the verb sign. It is anatomically impossible to use three hands for this, so both hands are used, and one hand repeats the end point. Again, another option is to use the pronoun THREE-OF-THEM with the basic third person movement.

(5) Exhaustive agreement (i.e. each of more than three) is shown by repeating the verb stem at least three times, with the end point moved. Three is the conventional number of repetitions. If a kind uncle gives ten children presents, we only need to make the exhaustive movement three times, so long as the number 'ten' is specified. We could write this as TEN CHILDREN PRESENTS GIVE-EACH-OF-THEM.

Carol Padden has observed that this is not the same as verbs being repeated in a series of clauses where the subject happens to be the same. She has pointed out that there is a difference between 'I give one to each of them' and 'I give one to her, and to her, and to her' (fig. 8.7).

In 'give one to each of them' there is repetition of only the verb stem, with a moving end point. In 'give one to her, and give one to her, and give one to her', the whole verb is repeated.

Padden has suggested that all the modifications occurring in agreement verbs are in the horizontal plane. (This may not seem very important for now, but we will see that spatial verbs can have movement in other planes too.) The

Fig. 8.8 TELL in 'The master tells his dog'

exception to this, however, is that it is possible to move agreement verbs through an inclined plane, if there is a perceived height difference between subject and object. If telling a story in which a small child asked a question of a tall adult then I-ASK-YOU would move away from the subject and up towards the object. In a story where a master told his dog something, the verb would move out from the subject and down towards the object (fig. 8.8). It is still true, though, that agreement verbs are limited in the angles along which they can move (whereas spatial verbs, as we will see, are not).

We have been describing agreement verbs as they move through syntactic signing space. However, some agreement verbs do not change direction of movement to show agreement, but instead they change orientation of the fingers. For example I-LOOK-AT-YOU does not move from the subject to the object, but instead the fingers point from the subject ('I') towards the object ('you'). In the verb YOU-LOOK-AT-ME, the hand is simply turned round so that the fingers point from the subject ('you') to the object ('me') (fig. 8.9). Other agreement verbs like this include FILM, TEASE, and SAY-NO-TO.

A third group of agreement verbs change direction of movement to show agreement, but do not change orientation of fingers, such as ANSWER and (in some dialects) SUPERVISE (fig. 8.10).

Many agreement verbs simply agree with subject and object. This is the 'classic' agreement verb. I-TELEPHONE-YOU has syntactic locations for the subject and the object.

Some verbs can agree with *two* subjects, where the action is reciprocal. The BSL verbs meaning 'they exchanged papers with each other' and 'they changed places with each other' use both hands, so that the two subjects are signed at the same time.

Fig. 8.9a I-LOOK-AT-YOU

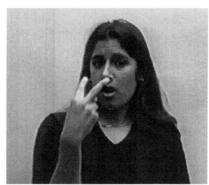

Fig. 8.9b YOU-LOOK-AT-ME

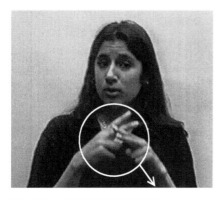

Fig. 8.10a I-SUPERVISE-YOU

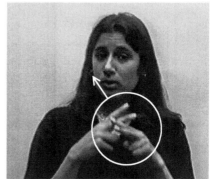

Fig. 8.10b YOU-SUPERVISE-ME

Some verbs can agree with two objects. In the BSL verb in 'I separated two dogs fighting' 'I' is a single subject but there are two dogs in the object, and again, the signer uses both hands, one for each object.

Agreement verbs do not only show information by using syntactic space. Information about the direct object can be shown in the handshape. In I-THROW-YOU-BALL, the direct object (the ball) can be incorporated into the handshape during THROW and the movement shows the subject and indirect object. The handshape would be different in I-THROW-YOU-BRICK and I-THROW-YOU-CHAIR, because the handshapes reflect the way we handle bricks and chairs when we throw them. Verbs like THROW have a very large number of potential handshapes, depending upon what exactly is thrown. They are still agreement verbs, however, because the starting and finishing points relate to grammatical roles like subject and not to topographic locations in space.

In summary, agreement verbs move through syntactic space to show information about subject and object, and use a variety of devices to show number for the object. They can also be modified to indicate manner and aspect. Some can also show information about a direct object in the hand-shape, although not all agreement verbs can include all this information.

SPATIAL VERBS

These verbs use topographic space, not syntactic space. They may inflect to show manner and aspect, but they do not inflect for person or number. They can give information about the path, trajectory and speed of movement of the action described by the verb and about the location of the action. The movement and location of these spatial verbs are 'isomorphic' with the real world. By this we mean that whatever the movement or location of the referent, the verb moves in the same way. They can also, in many cases, give some limited information about the class of noun of either the subject or the object. The linguist Ted Supalla has called these 'verbs of motion and location', and other linguists have called them 'classifier verbs'. However, we will continue to call them spatial verbs. Spatial verbs include RUN-DOWNSTAIRS, GO-TO, DRIVE-TO, PUNCH-(someone), SHAVE-(somewhere), CARRY-BY-HAND, or PUT-(somewhere).

There is not always a clear difference between agreement verbs and spatial verbs. Verbs that appear to behave as agreement verbs also behave as spatial verbs. For example LOOK-AT appears to act as an agreement verb, with forms such as I-LOOK-AT-YOU, THEY-ALL-LOOK-AT-ME, and WE-TWO-LOOK-AT-HER. However, I-LOOK-AT-MY-ARM or I-LOOK-AT-THE-FLOOR act as spatial verbs because they tell us the location of the looking (fig. 8.11).

It is possible to resolve this problem in some cases by saying that spatial verbs have movements and positions that may look exactly the same as agree-

Fig. 8.11 I-LOOK-AT-MY-ARM

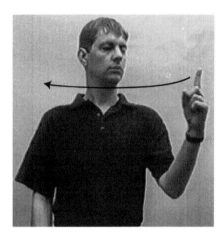

Fig. 8.12a WALK-FROM-LEFT-
TO-RIGHT'

Fig. 8.12b WALK-FROM-RIGHT-
TO-LEFT

ment verbs, but the movements and positions mean different things HE-
GIVES-HER and IT-MOVES-FROM-A-TO-B may look exactly the same,
but the difference is that in the first sentence we use syntactic space and in
the second sentence we use topographic space.

In 'I walked over there' the spatial verb sign can start anywhere, not just at
a location near the signer's body. If the location is near the signer, it just
means that the area in question is placed near the signer in the signer's
mental map. It does not contain any information that the signer (i.e. the first
person) walked from that location. The verb would look exactly the same for
'I walked over there' or 'You walked over there' or 'She walked over there',
because it is the location that is included, not the person. Similarly, 'I walked
from left to right' and 'I walked from right to left' would have very different
movements and starting locations, even though both involve the first person
(fig. 8.12).

Spatial verbs can move in a vertical plane (e.g. 'slide a small object
upwards', or 'haul down on a rope') or, indeed, in any plane (e.g. 'bore a
tunnel ahead uphill at 45 degrees, then to the left, then ahead again, and then
downhill at a 20 degree angle'). The movement is not limited to the horizontal plane in the way that agreement verbs are. In the verb PUT the movement
can vary to show that we can put things high up or low down, e.g. on shelves,
in pigeon holes, under tables, and so on. We cannot GIVE the same things up
or down, unless we are reflecting a difference in heights, as discussed earlier,
such as an instance of a child handing something to her mother. Any variation from the horizontal plane for agreement verbs still requires movement to
referents at syntactic locations. Movement in spatial verbs can be anywhere
within the signing space.

Fig. 8.13 PUT-IT-UP-THERE

Fig. 8.14a CARRY-BAG   Fig. 8.14b CARRY-BABY

There are different types of spatial verbs.

(a) Some have the location and movement included in the verb, but no information about what is acting or being acted on in the verb. Examples are COPY, BREAK, and PUT. In verbs expressing the ideas 'put it there' or 'put it up here' the handshape does not change to show the class of the object although we move the handshape isomorphically with the real action (fig. 8.13).

(b) Other spatial verbs have information about the location of the noun in the action and also show the shape of the object or the way that it is handled. In the verb CARRY, the handshape varies according to what is being carried (e.g. CARRY-BAG, CARRY-BABY, or CARRY-BOX) (fig. 8.14). Other examples include DROP, OPEN, and SCREW. In the

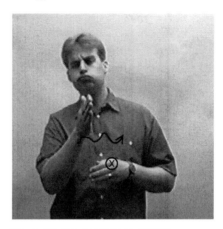

Fig. 8.15 BOAT-BUMP-OVER-
ROUGH-SEA

case of SCREW, the handshape would differ for verbs meaning 'screw in
with a screwdriver', 'screw on a lid', or 'screw in a light bulb'.

(c) An important group of spatial verbs contain information about location
and have semantic classifiers (or a proform, such as we considered in
chapter 3). Examples include CAR-TURN-LEFT, TWO-MEN-
WALK-INTO-EACH-OTHER, MAN-STAND-UNDER-BRIDGE,
BOAT-BUMP-OVER-ROUGH-SEA (fig. 8.15). In each of these examples we know where something is, where it moves from and to, how fast
it moves, and what semantic class it belongs to. Other examples include
FOLLOW, MEET, and GO-UPSTAIRS.

(d) In another group of spatial verbs, the meaning involves an action using a
part of the body, and the location of the verb is on the body itself.
Examples include HIT-(a part of the body), PAINT-(a part of the body),
SCRATCH-(a part of the body), and WASH-(a part of the body) (fig.
8.16).

There are also some spatial verbs that Carol Padden has called 'locative
verbs'. Like the spatial verbs mentioned above, these also represent location,
by using a location in real space. However, the handshape does not tell us anything about the object. For example, OPERATE-(on some part of the body)
and HURT/ACHE-(in some part of the body) are made on the appropriate
location on the body, but the handshape remains the same.

For signs where the action is directed at a fairly large area of the body, such
as the trunk, the legs, or the head, the location of the verb does not have to be
on the signer's body, but can be on an 'imaginary mannequin' placed in front

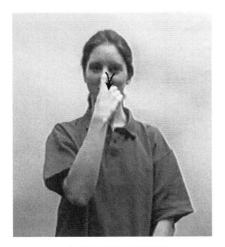

Fig. 8.16a SCRATCH-NOSE

Fig. 8.16b SCRATCH-TUMMY

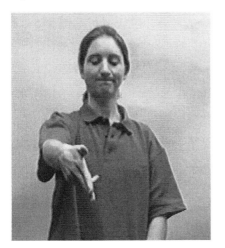

Fig. 8.17a POINT-GUN-AT-
PERSON'S-FEET

Fig. 8.17b POINT-GUN-AT-
PERSON'S-HEAD

of the signer. Examples include POINT-GUN-AT-PERSON'S-FEET or POINT-GUN-AT-PERSON'S HEAD (fig. 8.17).

Spatial verbs can also contain information about manner and aspect, e.g. BRUSH-HAIR-FURIOUSLY and CARRY-BABY-WITH-EFFORT-FOR-AGES. As with plain and agreement verbs, this information is shown by change in movement of the verb, and by changes in non-manual features.

In all these examples, though, there is no information in the verb to show who points the gun, who drives in the car that turns left, who screws in the light bulb, or who carries the bag or puts something somewhere. This extra information about the subject must be shown separately.

The main point arising from this discussion is that spatial verbs include information about the location and movement of the object within the verb. They frequently also show information about the object as part of the hand-shape.

VERB SANDWICHES AND SERIAL VERBS

Some verbs in BSL have so much information to carry that it cannot all be carried in one sign. When this happens, we may get 'verb sandwiches', where the same verb is repeated, but with different information. Sometimes the verb is first given with little or no extra information, and then signed with the morphological information. Other times, there is different morphological information in each verb. For example, we may sign DRIVE as a brief, uninflected sign, with the spoken component 'drive'. This may be followed by DRIVE-CASUALLY-FOR-A-LONG-TIME, with information about manner and aspect shown by the facial expression and small, fast repetition of the sign. Another sign could then follow which would show where the car moved, and how fast, while it was being driven.

Serial verbs are similar to verb sandwiches. In serial verbs, the verb occurs in two parts, with one part carrying the aspectual information. However, while in verb sandwiches the same verb appears both inflected and uninflected, in serial verbs, the two parts differ. For example, the verb POUR-WATER-ON-SOMEONE'S-HEAD occurs in two parts: POUR, and POUR-ON-SOMEONE'S-HEAD. If we wanted to sign 'He poured water on many people's heads', we would inflect POUR, and not POUR-ON-SOMEONE'S-HEAD (fig. 8.18).

SUMMARY

Verbs in BSL may be classified as plain, agreement, or spatial according to the amount and type of information they can include. Most verbs include information about manner and aspect. Plain verbs contain the least informa-tion. Information about subject and object and movement and location are shown lexically where relevant, or by using a different form of the verb. Agreement verbs contain considerable information about the subject and object and they do this usually by movement through syntactic space, or at least by the orientation of the hand.

Spatial verbs do not mark subject and object by their movement and there-fore this information must be provided lexically. Spatial verbs, however, do

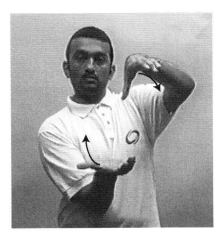

Fig. 8.18a POUR-WATER

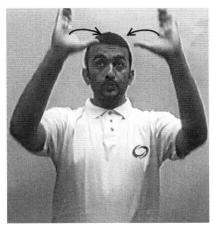

Fig. 8.18b POUR-WATER-ON-
SOMEONE'S-HEAD

Fig. 8.18c POUR-WATER-ON-
MANY-PEOPLE'S-HEADS

include information about movement and location of the object, and frequently contain information about the class of subject.

EXERCISES FOR CHAPTER 8

1. Plain and agreement verbs
   (a) Find examples of ten plain verbs. Five of the verbs should be body-
   anchored and five should not.

(i)   Can you include information about the direct object in some of the verbs you have chosen (e.g. EAT-APPLE or EAT-SWEET-CORN)?

(ii)   Make up some sentences using these plain verbs but using subjects and objects, e.g. 'I like all of you' or 'We all smoke a lot of cigarettes.' Note that these verbs need separate pronoun markers to give information about person and number.

(iii)   Inflect these plain verbs for different types of manner, e.g. 'easily', 'cheerfully', or 'carefully'.

(iv)   Inflect them for different types of aspect, e.g. 'for a long time', or 'often', or 'to be about to'.

(b) Find examples of ten agreement verbs.

(i)   Make up some sentences using these agreement verbs with subjects and objects, e.g. 'I tell all of you' or 'we all give presents to the children'. When do you need a separate pronoun and when can you show this information by inflecting the verb?

(ii)   Inflect these agreement verbs for different types of manner, e.g. 'easily', 'cheerfully', or 'carefully'.

(iii)   Inflect them for different types of aspect, e.g. 'for a long time', 'often', or 'to be about to'.

2. Decide which of the verbs given here are plain verbs and which are agreement verbs.

(a) ASK
(b) BLAME
(c) CHEER
(d) CHOOSE
(e) CRITICISE
(f) CYCLE
(g) EAT
(h) FEEL
(i) FILM
(j) GIVE
(k) KNIT
(l) KNOW
(m) LIKE
(n) LOOK-AT
(o) PATRONISE
(p) SMOKE
(q) SUPERVISE
(r) SUSPECT
(s) SWIM
(t) THROW

3. Translate the following sentences into BSL. You will need to consider using spatial verbs located on the body, as well as located on a 'mannequin'. You may wish to use 'serial verbs' here, too.
   (a) *Freda held a gun to Ivan's head.*
   (b) *The nurse gave Linda an injection in her bottom.*
   (c) *A fight broke out at the Last Gulch Saloon. When the sheriff arrived, the barman was holding a gun to the piano-player's head and the piano-player was punching a cowboy on the nose.*

4. Spatial verbs
   (a) Identify three spatial verbs in which the handshape varies according to how the object is held.
   (b) Identify three spatial verbs that contain a proform.
   (c) Identify three spatial verbs that use the body as a location.
   (d) Identify three spatial verbs that can use a 'mannequin' as a location.

FURTHER READING FOR CHAPTER 8

Emmorey, K., Corina, D., and Bellugi, U. 1995, 'Differential processing of topographic and referential functions of space', in K. Emmorey and J. Reilly (eds.), *Language, gesture and space*, Hillsdale, NJ: Lawrence Erlbaum Associates, 43–62.

Padden, C. 1989, 'The relation between space and grammar in ASL verb morphology', in C. Lucas (ed.), *Sign language research: theoretical issues*, Washington, DC: Gallaudet University Press, 118–32.

Poizner, H., Klima, E. S., and Bellugi, U. 1987, *What the hands reveal about the brain*, Cambridge, MA: MIT Press.

Chapter nine

The structure of gestures and signs

In previous chapters we have discussed the ways signs are combined and changed in BSL grammar. Here we explore the basic 'building-blocks' of single signs. Signs, like any use of the body for communication, can be called gestures, but they form only a small set of the possible gestures that can be made, and they differ in specific ways from most gestures. We will begin by describing the elements which combine to form the signs of BSL and then discuss the relationship between gestures which are part of the language and gestures which are not.

In chapter 1 we discussed the design features of human language. One of those features is duality. A small set of basic meaningless features can be used to build up a large set of meaningful signs. The study of how these small units combine to create larger units is called phonology. An important principle of phonology is that it is not concerned with little variations which do not contribute to differences in meaning. For example, middle-aged female learners of BSL often keep their fingers together where other signers spread them, as in SIGN, but such variation is not 'contrastive', and therefore is not the concern of phonology (fig. 9.1). However, if SIGN was articulated with 'A' handshapes, it would no longer mean SIGN, it would mean ENGINE. So we can say that 'A' contrasts with '5' and is therefore part of BSL phonology, as phonology is the study of the smallest contrastive units of language.

The term 'phonology' may seem odd in the context of sign linguistics, since the word has as its root *phon* – the Greek word for 'sound'. In earlier research on sign languages the term 'cherology' (from the Greek *cheir* – hand) was used. However, sign linguists now prefer the term phonology to emphasise that the same level of structure exists in sign language and spoken language, despite the differences in modality.

The study of sign phonology began with the work of William Stokoe, the American founder of sign linguistics. Instead of regarding signs as unanalysable gestures, he identified and described regular patterns of contrasts in elements within signs. He identified three basic sign 'parameters' or parts:

Fig. 9.1a SIGN (with fingers together)   Fig. 9.1b SIGN (with fingers spread)

handshape, location, and movement. Later researchers suggested the addition of two other parts: orientation (the direction in which the palm and fingers face) and facial expression.

Signs can share one or more parts. For example, the signs NAME (fig. 9.2a) and AFTERNOON (fig. 9.2b) have identical handshape, movement, orientation, and facial expression, but differ in location. The signs MORNING (fig. 9.3a) and SOLDIER (fig. 9.3b) have identical location, handshape, movement, and facial expression, but differ in hand orientation. The signs LIKE (fig. 9.4a) and MY (fig. 9.4b) have identical location, movement, orientation and facial expression, but differ in handshape. The signs

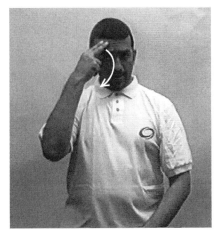

Fig. 9.2a NAME   Fig. 9.2b AFTERNOON

Fig. 9.3a MORNING

Fig. 9.3b SOLDIER

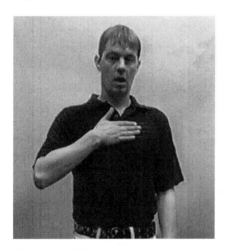

Fig. 9.4a LIKE

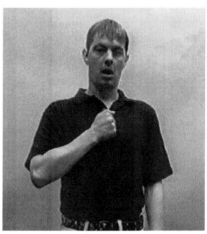

Fig. 9.4b MY

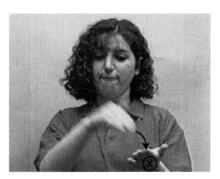

Fig. 9.5a ARRIVE

Fig. 9.5b JAM

Fig. 9.6a CHEW   Fig. 9.6b WASH

ARRIVE (fig. 9.5a) and JAM (fig. 9.5b) have identical location, handshape, orientation, and facial expression, but different movements. The signs CHEW (fig. 9.6a) and WASH (fig. 9.6b) are identical in all parts except facial expression.

Since a difference in only one part results in a difference in meaning, we know that these are important elements in the structure of signs. When we analyse the phonology of signs by comparing pairs of signs, we are concerned with which part of the sign is responsible for a difference in meaning. Pairs of signs which differ in only one part and have different meanings are called 'minimal pairs'.

As discussed in chapter 1, there are only a limited set of elements for each part. If we look at location, for example, we can see that signing is confined to a specific signing space, and that not all possible locations within that space are used in BSL: there are no signs located on the underside of the upper arms, on the top of the ears, etc. If we look at handshape, we can see that not all possible handshapes are used in BSL.

It is important to remember that phonology is about contrasts in meaning, not necessarily contrasts in appearance. Two handshapes may be rather different in appearance, but still not contrast with each other in terms of sign meaning. For example, the handshapes 'F' and 'bO' look quite different, but the choice of one or the other does not result in a contrast in meaning. For example, the sign FLOWER may have either handshape (fig. 9.7). In ASL, the handshapes illustrated are contrastive.

There are only a small number of contrasting handshapes in BSL, but they can be used at different locations with different movements, so that many different signs can be made. An important point about the phonological level is that we look at elements such as location and handshape from the point of

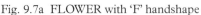

Fig. 9.7a FLOWER with 'F' handshape   Fig. 9.7b FLOWER with bO
                                           handshape

view of their having no meaning in themselves. Of course, elements with the
same surface form may have meaning at the morphological level. The same
is true of English. In English, /s/ is both a phoneme (without meaning, for
example in the word *sit*) and a morpheme (as in plural *-s*, or third person singular *-s*). In BSL, the handshape 'B' is a phonological element with no
meaning (as in PROOF (fig. 9.8)) and a morpheme (with meaning) as in the
proform 'B' for vehicles (see fig. 3.3 and fig. 3.5b).

SIMULTANEOUS AND SEQUENTIAL CONTRASTS

Stokoe developed a notation system for writing ASL which was adapted and
used by linguists researching many other sign languages. A variant of Stokoe
notation is used in the *BSL/English Dictionary*, and the labels for the handshapes he devised are also used in this book. However, later researchers

Fig. 9.8 PROOF

Fig. 9.9a COPY   Fig. 9.9b SEND

identified a number of problems with Stokoe's descriptions. Some of these are fairly minor – for example, Stokoe allowed for only one location in the space in front of the body (neutral space), but the signs HEAVEN and HILL (both in 'neutral space') are in very different locations.

A more serious problem with Stokoe's analysis relates to his view of the underlying structure of the sign. In English, there are both sequential and simultaneous contrasts between elements. The sounds in words are combined in sequence, over time, and the order of the combination can result in differences in meaning, although the elements themselves are the same. The words *pat* and *tap* have the same elements, but in different order. It is also possible to consider the elements or 'phonemes' of English as consisting of simultaneous bundles of features. For example, /m/ uses voice, is articulated at the lips, and the air flows steadily through the nose ('nasal'), whereas /b/ uses voice, is articulated at the lips, but the air flow is stopped and then released. Words like *bat* and *mat*, therefore, do not contrast in the sequence of their elements. In their first element, however, the bundle of simultaneous features differs in one particular way. This parallels the way in which we have described the make-up of signs.

Stokoe had claimed that sign languages differed from spoken languages in that sign languages had only simultaneous structure. He believed that in words, the elements which make up a word were only combined in a linear order, whereas in sign languages, the elements formed a simultaneous bundle. In a sign like WOMAN, the handshape, location, motion, orientation, and non-manual features all occur simultaneously. However, there are many signs in which contrast is better described as sequential. For example, in Stokoe notation, the signs COPY and SEND appear very different. COPY has a 'B̂' handshape, while SEND has 'Ô'. COPY has a closing motion, and SEND has an opening motion. However, it is more economical to regard them as identical but the reverse of each other (fig. 9.9).

CHANGES AND HOLDS

Another problem with Stokoe's original system was that all signs were described as having one or more movements. When Margaret Deuchar began researching BSL in 1977, she realised that there were many signs which did not move during their articulation. Signs such as GOOD and the numerals (e.g. ONE, TWO, THREE, FOUR, etc.) have movement to get the hand to the required location, but once in that location, the hand is held still. This observation was independently made some time later by the American researchers Scott Liddell and Robert Johnson. They went on to develop an alternative phonological description of ASL. Their basic claim is that signs consist of 'hold' and 'movement' segments which are produced sequentially. We will use the term 'change' rather than 'movement' to avoid confusion with Stokoe's use of the word. During holds, all parts of the sign are held in a steady state; during changes, some aspect of the articulation changes. This may be a change of handshape, a change of location, a change of orientation, or a combination of these. The Liddell and Johnson model solves many of the descriptive problems found in the Stokoe system. Their model sees sequence as a basic feature of sign languages, just as it is a basic feature of spoken languages. This model also provides a straightforward description of some of the morphological features of BSL. For example, the citation form of THINK can be described as consisting of change (C) + hold (H) (CH). In the compound BELIEVE (see chapter 6), however, THINK consists of a hold (H). When THINK is inflected for durative aspect ('think for a long time') it consists of a change (C). Related nouns and verbs can also be described in this way: AEROPLANE has the form CH, while FLY has the form C.

SIGN TYPES

Signs can be classified in terms of their form. Type 1 are those signs made with one hand only, articulated without touching or being near to any specific body part: WHAT, SALT (fig. 9.10a), etc. Type 2 are one-handed signs which make contact with, or are close to, a body part other than the non-dominant hand: WOMAN, LIVE (fig. 9.10b), etc. Type 3 are two-handed signs where both hands are the same shape, are active and perform identical or symmetrical actions without touching each other or the body: SIGN, BICYCLE (fig. 9.10c), etc. Type 4 are signs where two hands with identical handshapes perform identical actions and contact each other: AGREE, TALK (fig. 9.10d), etc. Type 5 are two-handed signs where both hands are active, have the same handshape, perform identical actions and contact the body: INTERESTING, COW (fig. 9.10e), etc. Type 6 are two-handed signs where

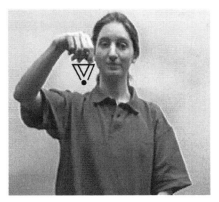

Fig. 9.10a SALT (Type 1)

Fig. 9.10b LIVE (Type 2)

Fig. 9.10c BICYCLE (Type 3)

Fig. 9.10d TALK (Type 4)

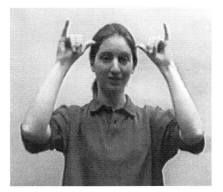

Fig. 9.10e COW (Type 5)

Fig. 9.10f WRONG (Type 6)

the dominant hand is active, and the non-dominant hand serves as the location for the movement; they may have the same or different shapes: BUTTER, WRONG (fig. 9.10f), etc.

UNMARKED HANDSHAPES

If we examine the frequency of occurrence of particular handshapes, we find that a relatively small number of handshapes dominate in BSL, with just four handshapes, 'B', '5', 'G', and 'A', accounting for 50 per cent of all signs. These four are interesting for a number of reasons. They are the most contrasting handshapes in all sign languages. They contrast in terms of their geometric properties: A is maximally compact; B is a simple flat surface; 5 is the most extended and spread; and G is a narrow linear form. These properties are actively used in proforms (see chapter 3). These handshapes can also be described in terms of specific features: B has fingers extended and together; 5 has fingers extended and spread, etc. These four handshapes are among the first handshapes mastered by children acquiring BSL and other sign languages as a first language. They are also found in all known sign languages.

These very common handshapes have also been described, in linguistic terms, as 'unmarked', that is, they are the most basic handshapes. The concept of 'unmarked' handshape can also be seen in the shapes of the location hand in Type 6 signs. In half of the Type 6 signs, active and location hands have the same handshape (e.g. MAKE, BETTER, etc.); in the remaining Type 6 signs the active and location hands have different shapes. However, for these signs, only a small number of handshapes can occur in the location hand, and most of these are the unmarked handshapes. In BSL only the following handshapes appear in these location hands: A, B, 5, G (e.g. LEMONADE, TOWN, CENTRE, and TEASE respectively) and a small number with Å, I, O, and V (e.g. FIRST, END, POISON, and THROUGH respectively).

CONSTRAINTS ON SIGN FORM

We have already discussed constraints on sign form, for example, the restriction of signing to a specific space, and the limitations on location handshapes. Two other constraints have been proposed as universal restrictions on sign form, which limit sign complexity. Robin Battison, in an early study of ASL, was the first to identify these phonological constraints on the form of signs. He called these the Dominance and Symmetry constraints. We have already touched on the Dominance constraint in our discussion of location handshapes.

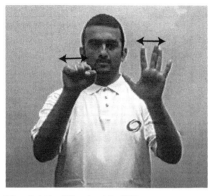

Fig. 9.11a 'Sign' violating the
Dominance constraint

Fig. 9.11b 'Sign' with different
handshapes violating the Symmetry
constraint

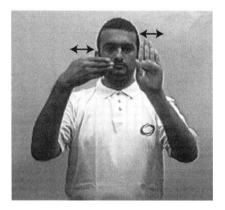

Fig. 9.11c 'Sign' with different orientations
violating the Symmetry constraint

The Dominance constraint states: if the hands in a two-handed sign have different handshapes, then one hand must be the location of the sign, and the location shape is restricted to one of the unmarked handshapes. The example in figure 9.11a is not a possible BSL sign because it violates the Dominance constraint.

The Symmetry constraint states: if both hands of a sign move independently during its articulation, then both hands must have the same location, the same handshape, the same movement (either simultaneous or alternating) and orientation must be symmetrical. The examples in figures 9.11b and c are not possible BSL signs because they violate the Symmetry constraint.

These two constraints clearly serve to limit the complexity of signs. Put very informally, if signs could have two completely different handshapes with two completely different movements, in two different locations, with two different orientations, it would be much harder to understand a signer, and at the same time the sign would be much harder for a signer to articulate. It is interesting to note that BSL does allow the two hands to have different hand-shapes, locations, and movements, but this only occurs at the phrase or sentence level. For example, in the phrase BORN DEAF, in which two different signs are produced at the same time, the two hands have different shapes, they are in different locations, and they make different movements (see also chapter 11).

THE SOURCE OF SIGNS

In the remainder of this and in the next four chapters, we will look at the relationship between signs and what they represent, and discuss visual motivation in BSL in relation to creating signs. The role of gesture in providing a source for signs will be explored. We will also think about the role that metaphor plays in sign creation and about 'productive' signs which are not part of the BSL lexicon but are made up by the signer on the spot. Later on we will consider the ways in which signs can be produced simultaneously to provide new meanings. We will also discuss how signs are borrowed from other languages.

We will seek to explain the source of most signs that are used in BSL. They are mostly (but not exclusively) based on some visual representation of the referent, or borrowed from another language. Some are borrowed from other sign languages, and some are derived in some way from English.

In spoken languages most words have a recognisable source. Exceptions in English include some trade-names, e.g. *Kodak*, and words from fiction, e.g. *Dalek* and *Klingon*. One word that has been made up from nothing is *googol-plex* which means 'one, with one million noughts after it'. Otherwise, most English words are known to have developed from other English words or to have been borrowed from other languages.

Here, we will think about the relationship between signs and what they represent. In other words, we will think about 'iconicity' and will consider ideas of gestures, arbitrariness, and visual motivation.

In chapter 1 we learned that a feature of languages is that the symbols they use are conventional (we are all agreed that they have a specific meaning), and can be arbitrary (there is no link between their form and their meaning), although BSL has many signs that have a visually motivated link with their referents. This is natural for signs in a visual language. It is less natural for spoken words to have a sound-based link with their referents because fewer things make a noise.

Arbitrariness and onomatopoeia in spoken languages

Most of the words of English are totally arbitrary and conventional. If they were not, words would be the same in all languages. For example, the chemical compound H_2O (the wet stuff we drink and where fish live) would be *water* in all languages, rather than *water, dwr, eau, mayim, agua, shui,* and so on.

The converse is also, of course, true. The same sound combination has different meanings in different languages, e.g. the word that sounds like *mit* means 'with' in German, and 'glove' in English. The word that sounds like *gatto* means 'cake' in French and 'cat' in Portuguese. If sounds were all linked to meaning by some natural rule of the universe, a word would have the same meaning in all languages.

But the relationship is not always so removed. There is some link between the object and the word, even in spoken languages. Spoken languages are capable of incorporating the sounds, and even the movements made by certain referents into their words.

There are words that are based on the sound that the referent makes. This is termed 'onomatopoeia', and is an attempt at direct imitation of the sound. There are a few such words in all languages and many of them are animal noises, e.g. *moo, woof,* and *cock-a-doodle-doo.* Others are a bit less imitative, e.g. *swish,* or *dash,* but the form of the words is still an attempt to show how the sound/movement occurred. It is hard to think of a word in English to describe a sound that is not onomatopoeic (e.g. *whisper, murmur, crash, squeak, giggle, pop,* etc.).

This is really the only opportunity that spoken languages have to use their modality (sound) to represent objects. However, it is rather limited because not many objects or events make noises. After all, what noise does a cake make? Or a glove?

Even words whose sounds represent their referents' sounds are still governed by language rules. Even when words may be based on the sounds that the referents make, the words are not the same in all languages. If we took a pig to the UN and it grunted, an English speaker would say it went *oink,* a Welsh speaker *och,* and Japanese *bu.* An English hen says *cluck* but a Welsh hen says *clochdan.* So even here there is no pure reflection of the sound. Most importantly, none of these words make a sound exactly like a pig or chicken. We are capable of imitating the sound of a pig or a hen using our voice but it sounds nothing like *oink* or *cluck* because we are using sounds not only outside English, but also outside speech.

Arbitrariness and visual motivation in signed languages

Linguists used to focus disproportionately on the fact that sign languages could use arbitrary signs. The existence of visually motivated signs suggested that sign languages were not real languages, as the lexicon was not totally arbitrary. Now we know that symbols do not have to be arbitrary to be part of a language. They are mostly arbitrary in spoken languages because spoken languages are not designed to represent visual forms in the real world. They are able to reflect some sounds, but the names of sounds are only a small part of any language's lexicon, so most symbols are arbitrary. Sign languages do not need to rely so heavily on arbitrary symbols because they use the visual modality and many objects and actions have an obvious visual form. It would be unnatural for sign languages not to use visual symbols. The fact that all meanings are conventionalised is now considered more important than issues of arbitrariness.

We know that there are some signs that are totally arbitrary and cannot be guessed by anyone who does not know BSL. Examples include WANT and ELEVEN (see fig. 2.3).

However, because non-arbitrary signs are such an important part of BSL we will focus here on signs that are not totally arbitrary and will ask where they come from.

GESTURES

One issue that needs addressing is the relationship of signs and gestures. Some people have argued that sign language is just a set of gestures, because they think, wrongly, that sign meanings are obvious. This implies that gestures themselves are immediately transparent and understood by everyone. However, this is often not true. Gestures can be arbitrary, and their meaning is only arrived at by convention.

We might think that some gestures (sometimes called 'emblems') are completely natural and that their meaning is obvious to anyone, but in fact gestures are often specific to certain cultures. Many gestures are used outside language, but with language. This use of gesture outside a language is sometimes termed 'extra-linguistic' gesture.

(1) If we tap our cheek below the eye in Britain, it means 'watch out for' or 'wait and see'. In parts of central Africa it means 'nothing at all' (fig. 9.12a).

(2) If we make the thumbs-up gesture in British culture, we mean to say that something is good. In some cultures, this is a very rude gesture.

(3) The rudest possible gesture a person can make in Russia is a gesture that means 'good luck' in Brazil. In Britain this gesture means nothing at all (fig. 9.12b).

(4) We all know in Britain that if we mean 'yes' we nod our head, and if we mean 'no', we shake it. We think of these as two gestures that are quite natural. However, in some cultures, a head shake means 'yes', and in others a sort of head nod means 'no'.

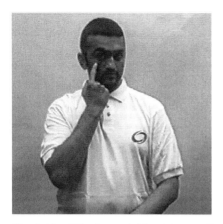 

Fig. 9.12a 'Watch out for'/'nothing at all'   Fig. 9.12b 'Good luck'/obscene gesture

So even these emblematic gestures have some conventional meaning. But they are spread across many cultures, among users of many languages.

Emblematic gestures that are part of British culture are used both by English speakers and by BSL signers.

In English, it is fairly easy to distinguish between gestures (which are outside English) and words (which are part of the language) because they exist in two different modalities. It is not so easy in BSL, where signs can look just like extra-linguistic gestures on the surface. Sign linguists have tried to describe the differences between emblematic gestures and signs in BSL, to demonstrate that BSL is more than just a collection of gestures and is a real language.

In the broadest sense, just as words are 'audible gestures', signs are visible gestures with conventional form and meaning and which obey specific formational rules. Just as speakers may make sounds outside spoken language, some pantomimic signing may move signs out of signing space, so it is hard to know where to draw the line between signs and gestures. An additional difficulty is that some signs were probably once emblematic gestures but have now become BSL signs.

There is some debate among sign linguists about the use of gestures in sign languages. Is the sign GOOD an emblematic gesture borrowed from hearing culture and used within a language, or a sign in its own right? Is RUN a gesture?

There are some strong arguments for distinguishing between extra-linguistic gestures and signs:

(1) Signs are part of BSL when there is no other sign that they replace or add to. If an English speaker nods her head, it is in place of saying *yes* or occurs while saying *yes*. In BSL it means YES.

(2) Signs are part of BSL when they are affected by the morphology of BSL. The sign RUN may look like a gesture, but it has a number of different forms, governed by the rules of BSL.

(3) It is possible that BSL has taken forms that are 'only' gestures in English users' conversation, and made them a part of the language. In other words, they have been borrowed. We will see in a later chapter that borrowing is common in all languages. BSL can borrow from anywhere, so long as the form is visual.

4) Signs can be joined together into sentences, according to the grammatical rules of BSL. Gestures cannot be combined into grammatical sentences.

In the final analysis, the distinction may not matter. BSL signers use these forms as part of BSL discourse. So, no matter where signs may have come from originally, they are part of BSL now.

VISUAL MOTIVATION

'Visual motivation' means there is a link between an object or action and the form of a sign (e.g. it has the same shape or movement). 'Visually motivated' is a better term than the frequently-used term 'iconic', as the latter has a rather narrow meaning. 'Icon' just means 'picture'. Many hearing people still think that BSL is iconic and that all signs are just pictures or mimes, and that all deaf can communicate anywhere in the world. This is not true. Even if this were true it would still be impossible to communicate using gestures around the world because the gestures differ too. This is because the meanings of gestures are based upon cultural norms, and these vary. For example, British people may understand a gesture referring to fishing with a rod and line because that is how British people fish; in other cultures one fishes with a spear: in Britain we eat with a knife and fork and could gesture accordingly, but a culture that uses chopsticks would gesture the idea of 'eating' very differently.

Cross-cultural issues

Research by Elena Pizzuto and Virginia Volterra in Italy aimed to find out just how many signs and gestures could be understood by people from other cultures and using other languages. They showed forty signs from LIS (Italian Sign Language) to hearing non-signers and deaf signers in Italy and in six other European countries. A few signs were understood by the majority of non-Italian volunteers (deaf and hearing alike). This shows that there are some features of signs that have a 'transparent' meaning for people in any lan-

Fig. 9.13a HEAR (transparent in many countries)

Fig. 9.13b MIRROR (transparent to deaf signers in many countries)

Fig. 9.13c HUNGER (transparent to Italians – deaf and hearing)

guage or culture (e.g. HEAR, fig. 9.13a). The non-Italian deaf signers understood many more of the visually motivated LIS signs than the non-Italian hearing volunteers (e.g. MIRROR, fig. 9.13b). Pizzuto and Volterra concluded from this that signers have some general skills that come from using a visual language, which enable them to extract meaning from visually motivated signs. The final interesting finding was that some LIS signs were understood by hearing, non-signing Italian volunteers, but not by the hearing volunteers in the other countries. These LIS signs were felt by the Italians to be rooted in Italian culture, and this highlights the importance of culture in the meaning of many gestures (e.g. HUNGER, fig. 9.13c).

The continuum of visual motivation

Signs may be more or less visually motivated. Where a meaning is not at all visually motivated, it must come completely from convention. Following Mandel, the signs in fig. 9.14 are arranged in order from most strongly visually motivated to most arbitrary. It is worth noting that fingerspelled signs (as in fig. 9.14d) are all arbitrary (and, thus, conventional) because they are based on hand arrangements that reflect English letters. The forms of English letters bear only an arbitrary relationship to the referent.

Fig. 9.14a I-LOOK-AT-MY ARM

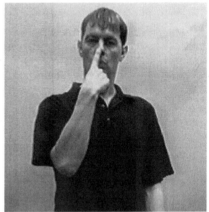

Fig. 9.14b NOSE

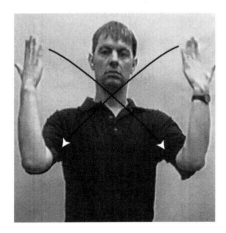

Fig. 9.14c DARK

Fig. 9.14d MOTHER

Fig. 9.15a COFFEE (ASL)   Fig. 9.15b COFFEE (BSL)

All signs are conventional to some extent. The question is how much they are arbitrary. A sign can be visually motivated but also arbitrary in some ways. For example, CAT is visually motivated if the sign reflects brushing the whiskers or if it reflects stroking the fur, but which aspect of the referent is focused on (e.g. whiskers or fur) is arbitrary. The sign glossed as COFFEE is visually motivated in both ASL and BSL, but BSL focuses on drinking and ASL on grinding the beans (fig. 9.15). If all signs were completely non-arbitrary, all signs in all languages would be the same. However, we saw in chapter 1 that sign languages have signs that look exactly the same and have different meanings (e.g. the BSL sign RABBIT is the same as the ASL sign HORSE).

SUMMARY

In this chapter we have seen that all signs in BSL are built up from combinations of a limited set of elements. BSL is a visual language, and draws constantly on visual sources. The use of visual sources does not mean that all signs can be universally understood, any more than non-linguistic gestures can be understood in different cultures. Each language and culture have their own conventional symbols, even where the source of the sign or gesture is visually motivated.

EXERCISES FOR CHAPTER 9

1. Sign formation
   (a) Find three pairs of signs that use the same handshape but are made at different locations (e.g. MY:STUPID, or SCHOOL: AFTERNOON).
   (b) Find three pairs of signs that use the same location but are made using different handshapes (e.g. THINK:KNOW or MORNING: DOCTOR).

2. Describe the handshapes of the following signs, using the names of letters of the American manual alphabet. (You will find the handshapes listed in the Conventions section.) You may find that you know several different signs for the same gloss, so you should choose a handshape that describes each one.
   (a) ILL
   (b) PUNCH
   (c) NEXT-WEEK
   (d) SCHOOL
   (e) HOPE
   (f) DEAF
   (g) HEARING
   (h) NOTHING
   (i) TEMPT
   (j) JUMP
   (k) AEROPLANE
   (l) SNAIL

3. Collect examples of gestures used by hearing people in Britain.
   (a) How many of these gestures have a conventional meaning?
   (b) How many of these gestures are also used as signs in BSL?

4. Visually motivated signs
   (a) Show the following signs to a person who knows no BSL. How many can they guess correctly?
   WHAT, GREEN, WALES, OLD, MOTHER, BREAD, FRIDGE, LIGHT, TEE-SHIRT, KNIFE, BOOK, CAR, TEA, CAT, TRAIN, BIRD, TREE, LOOK, PUNCH, SIT
   (b) Can you explain why some are guessed more easily than others?

5. Find five examples each of:
   (a) Type 1 signs
   (b) Type 2 signs
   (c) Type 3 signs
   (d) Type 4 signs
   (e) Type 5 signs
   (f) Type 6 signs

FURTHER READING FOR CHAPTER 9

Brennan, M. 1990, 'Productive morphology in British Sign Language', in S. Prillwitz and T. Vollhaber (eds.), *Current trends in European sign language research*, Hamburg: Signum Press, 205–30.

Brennan, M., Colville, M., and Lawson, L. 1984, *Words in hand: a structural analysis of the signs of British Sign Language*, Edinburgh: Moray House College of Education.

Liddell, S. and Johnson, R. 1989, 'American Sign Language: the phonological base', *Sign Language Studies* 64, 195–277.

Mandel, M. 1977, 'Iconic devices in ASL', in L. Friedman (ed.), *On the other hand*, New York: Academic Press, 57–108.

Schroeder, O. 1985, 'A problem in phonological description', in W. Stokoe and V. Volterra (eds.), *SLR '83*, Silver Spring, MD: Linstok Press, 194–201.

Stokoe, W., Casterline, D., and Croneberg, C. 1965, *A dictionary of American Sign Language on linguistic principles*, Washington, DC: Gallaudet College Press.

Chapter ten

Visual motivation and metaphor

This chapter continues the discussion of the sources of signs, focusing in the first section on how handshapes are used in visually motivated signs. In the second section, we consider the role of metaphor in the creation of the BSL lexicon.

All signers use visually motivated signs, but most of the time they use these signs automatically without thinking about why they are made that way or what information is included. Understanding how signs show different degrees of visual motivation, and in different ways, is very important when it comes to understanding how to create new signs. We will talk about this more in chapter 11. For now, we can say that it is important to understand how BSL can reflect the visual nature of an object or an action.

CLASSES OF VISUALLY MOTIVATED SIGNS

In the 1970s, the American sign linguist Mark Mandel classified visually motivated signs into different groups:

(a) those that show an image of the referent or action itself (these are 'presentation' signs, because we present the referent or action in some way); and

(b) those that make a picture of the referent, either by drawing it or by making the shape of it with the hands (these are 'depiction' signs because they make a picture).

Presentable objects

These can be pointed to, because they are present. There is no specific sign because the referent is in the environment, so simply pointing will give all the information needed.

Pronouns like I, YOU, WE, and YOU-ALL come into this group. Parts of

Fig. 10.1 DRUM

the body can also be pointed to, e.g. NOSE, EAR, FINGERS, and EYES. A flat hand can be used for pointing to a larger area, e.g. CHEST, BREAST, BODY, and HEAD. Pointing may also represent more abstract ideas. For example MIND and TIME are made by pointing to the forehead and the wrist, which represent the concepts by association.

Presentable actions

These involve using the body to perform the action that is being referred to. Examples include STROKE, SCRATCH, HEAD-BUTT, RAISE-ONE'S-HAND, and SWIM. These are sometimes called 'imitative actions'.

There are also actions that are carried out with the handshapes showing how an object is held. Examples of signs like these are many and varied. They include WRITE, ELECTRIC-PLUG, COOK, DRUM (or TO-DRUM), BROOM (or SWEEP), DRIVE (or CAR), INJECTION, CURTAINS, FISHING, and so on (fig. 10.1).

Virtual depiction

In this type of visually motivated sign, the hands act like a pencil, drawing the outline or marking out the area of the object. In all the examples given in figure 10.2 the hand leaves behind an imaginary trace of the shape of the object in discussion.

The most common handshape for these signs is the 'G' hand, used for tracing a fine line. Examples include WINDOW, CIRCLE, UNIVERSITY, and LIGHTNING (fig. 10.2a).

It is also possible to sketch broader outlines using the 'H' hand, for example in PARIS and HOUSE, and the 'C' hand is used for some signs such as COLUMN and ELEPHANT, to show a wide, curved outline (fig. 10.2b and c).

Fig. 10.2a LIGHTNING

Fig. 10.2b HOUSE

Fig. 10.2c ELEPHANT

Fig. 10.2d TABLE

The 'B' hand is used for showing the surface area of an object, for example in WALL, FIELD, or TABLE (fig. 10.2d).

Substitutive depiction

Another way of showing a referent is to make the handshape become the referent. The signer no longer draws the outline but creates an image of the referent with the hands, by substituting their hands for the object. Examples include AEROPLANE, BIRD, TREE, BUTTERFLY, SNAIL, and TELE-PHONE (fig. 10.3a. See also fig. 2.1).

Actions can also be performed using the hands as 'tools'. For example in DINNER (or RESTAURANT), the hands 'become' the knife and fork, and the arms act out their use (fig. 10.3b). In KNIT, the hands 'become' the knitting needles and then the signer uses these to show the action of knitting.

We might also say that the proforms discussed in chapter 3 (e.g. with the

Fig. 10.3a SNAIL   Fig. 10.3b DINNER

'G' hand, the 'B' hand, and the '5' hand) are examples of substitutive depiction, because the proform has in some sense become the referent (e.g. the person, or the vehicle).

Some signs can be varied to show variations in the referent. A very high wall or a very long table could be represented by increasing the distance that the hands move. However, if someone drives a large car, this would not be shown by signing a larger steering wheel. Similarly, a large hospital would not be signed by making a larger cross on one's arm. We will talk about this more in chapter 11.

Visual motivation in use of space

So far we have been talking about the visual motivation shown in handshapes. However, we have seen in chapter 8 that BSL uses space to reflect real space in the real world. There is a great deal of visual motivation in the use of space in BSL. For this reason we should note that spatial verbs are highly visually motivated when it comes to movement, even if handshapes are not necessarily very visually motivated.

METAPHOR IN BSL

We have seen that the forms of many signs in BSL are based upon the appearance of their referents. This is an important way of creating signs in the BSL lexicon. Another way of expanding a language is to use metaphor. By stretching and extending the meaning of a sign or word, new meanings can be expressed. We will now consider the ways that BSL uses metaphor.

There are two different types of language: 'literal' and 'figurative'. In literal language, we mean exactly what we say, for example 'I love my dog', or

'London is the capital city of England.' In figurative language, our language is not meant to be understood for its obvious meaning, but with another level of meaning. This is often extended in some way from the literal meaning.

For example, in BSL we can sign: MAN Index₃ JUMP-UP-AND-DOWN. Literally, it means 'The man is jumping up and down.' However, it also has the figurative meaning 'The man is very happy.' In this case, the man is not really jumping up and down but he is so happy that he could be jumping up and down.

English uses a great deal of figurative language. Many spoken languages do the same and the same idea can often be phrased metaphorically in different ways in different languages. In English we say *I wouldn't like to be in his shoes* but the Finns say *I wouldn't like to be in his trousers*. Both are figurative phrases to show that the speaker does not envy another person. English speakers say *That's nothing to write home about* and the Swedes say *You wouldn't hang that on your Christmas tree*, but both mean literally that the speaker is unimpressed by something. Some researchers say that as much as two-thirds of all English discourse is figurative. That figure may be a bit high, but certainly English is very figurative. So is BSL.

METAPHOR

One important part of figurative language is 'metaphor'. In metaphor, something is referred to as if it was something else. The focus is on a certain feature, and that feature is used to refer to something else that is related in some way. Importantly, the conversational partner must be able to make the link between the literal meaning and the metaphorical one. If a man says that from his experience girl friends are like buses or bananas, we need to be able to work out why he says that. He does not think that they transport shoppers around town, nor that they are yellow and curved. Rather he thinks that he waits for a girlfriend for ages (just like buses), and that they always come along in bunches (just like bananas). If the conversational partner does not know this or cannot work this out, the meaning is lost.

The same is true in BSL. If we are very hungry, we can sign that we have got little fish swimming around in our stomach eating all the food in there (fig. 10.4). Obviously there are no fish there, but the metaphorical understanding is that it feels as if there are fish in one's stomach. However, if the conversational partner has not made the link that the fish are related to our hunger, then they would not understand this metaphor.

Metaphor has been described by many linguists and philosophers. The ancient Greeks thought it was very important. Poets and writers have also thought about it a great deal. More recently, George Lakoff and Mark Johnson changed the way we consider metaphor in language, by the publica-

Fig. 10.4 RAVENOUSLY-HUNGRY

tion of their work in the 1970s. Metaphor has also been considered by sign linguists. Mary Brennan has done especially important work in the field of metaphor in BSL.

Some further examples of metaphor in BSL will now be discussed, in order to give a more detailed idea of metaphorical signs.

In BSL, if a signer is starting to panic, she might sign something like 'hanging on to the face of a cliff'. She is not actually hanging on a cliff-face, but there is something similar in how she might feel.

If we are fed up with something, we sign FED-UP as though we were full of something. We are not physically full up to the chin, but feel as if we were.

When someone has done something really stupid, and been put in their place, they might sign something like HEAD-DUCK-BEHIND-WALL. They are not really ducking behind a wall, but feel as though they would like to.

In 'put me in my place', the signer feels like a dog would feel when she puts

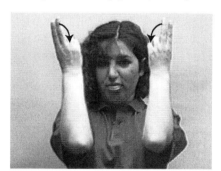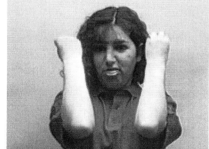

Fig. 10.5 'Put me in my place'

Fig. 10.6 (Christmas) came up
suddenly'

her ears down, but otherwise there is nothing similar between the signer and a dog (fig. 10.5).

Other examples include 'take it from your head and pop it in a drawer', meaning that we want to forget something bothersome; or 'opening up the mind, taking things in, and closing the mind at the end', meaning we are ready to learn new ideas.

If a signer wants to say that 'Christmas came up suddenly', it can be signed as though Christmas is a solid object. The sign is similar to a sign that means 'to come face to face with something as solid as a door'. However, we know metaphorically, that we have come face to face with Christmas (fig. 10.6).

Metaphors can be created on the spot and allow highly creative signing, for example, saying that 'someone's signing is wearing a bow tie', because it is so formal. Fluent signers can produce many, often very humorous, metaphors. Other metaphors have become a very central part of the language and everyone uses them, often not even thinking that they are metaphors.

Metaphor in time

We mentioned in chapter 1 that it is one of the features of human languages that they can all refer to the past and the future. All languages have to resort to metaphor to talk about time, and BSL is no exception. This means we talk about time as though it were something real that occupies space that we can see and touch, even though it is just an abstract concept.

We can talk about 'Universe' time, in English and BSL. We think of it as some sort of line that starts from the moment of 'The Big Bang' or the words *Let there be light* (or however people think time began) and goes on until 'The Big Crunch' or 'the final trumpet call' (or however people believe time will end). We can measure this 'universe time' in seconds, hours, days, seasons, centuries, and so on.

In our Western European culture, we imagine a line running from the start of time to the end, and place events on that line as they happen, relative to now. We should note that other cultures do not see time as a line, but as a circle or a spiral. (In English we also talk about some time as though it were circular, for example in the phrases *his birthday comes around so fast* and *the years go rolling by*.)

We can imagine time as proceeding linearly and that we are now at some point along that line of time. Some people imagine that we stand still, and time passes us by, or that time does not move, but that we move through it. Either way, the end effect is the same.

There are events that have already happened and events that have not happened yet. Our culture and language treat these with spatial metaphors; past events that have already happened are metaphorically 'behind' us (further towards the starting point of the line), and future events that have not yet happened are metaphorically 'ahead' of us (further towards the finishing point of the line). Both BSL and English use this spatial metaphor. However, this is only a cultural construction. The Urubu-Kaapor in Brazil (a Brazilian Indian people who use a sign language as well as a spoken language) believe that the future is metaphorically behind because we cannot see it, and the past is metaphorically ahead because we can see it. We will see that construction of the metaphor of time influences the way that signs are used to show time.

We have seen that English sees time metaphorically, and, importantly, also uses spatial metaphors to describe it. We have phrases like *the days ahead*; *well, that's behind us now*; *I look forward to that*; and *when I look back on my life*. When English uses spatial metaphors to talk about time, it needs to use words to describe the space. BSL can use space directly to talk about time, as we will see.

We saw in chapter 7 that our discussion of time is 'deictic'. That is, it needs a reference point. Usually the reference point is now. When we talk about the future and the past, it is relative to the present. At lunch-time, breakfast is in the past and tea is in the future, but by teatime, lunch is also in the past, and teatime has become the present because the reference point has shifted. We can also use other reference points, such as 'before I was born' or 'after 2022'.

The way that languages express time varies. Some languages use words – either singly or in phrases, and some use verb inflections (i.e. tense). Many languages use both. We have seen in chapter 7 that BSL does not use tense in the way that English does. Instead it uses separate signs which may be moved through space to describe time metaphorically. The area towards and at the signer's shoulder is used for time in the past, and the area in front of the signer refers to the future. Similarly, movements are metaphorically determined, so that moving the hands forwards implies time passing towards the future, while moving the hands backwards implies time in the past.

BSL uses lexical items that simply locate an event in time as well as lexical items that express the location of an event in time and also have some more specific meaning. BSL has manual signs that mean 'now', 'in the future', 'in the past', 'way in the future', 'way in the past', or 'recently in the past'. More specific signs and phrases include TOMORROW, YESTERDAY, TODAY, SOON, RECENTLY, LAST MONDAY, and 26 JANUARY 1847.

We have already seen in chapter 7 that some languages can refer to events located in Universe time by using tense. As well as past and future tense, some languages have tenses indicating distant past and distant future too. We can understand the reasons why BSL does not use tense when we consider the use of literal and metaphorical space in BSL.

We know that BSL uses space to show time metaphorically and that the movement and locations of the hands in signing space represents past, present, and future time. In theory there would be nothing to prevent verb signs from moving backwards towards the signer to represent past tense and forwards away from the signer for future tense. The sign ASK, for example, could move from centre-space to the signer's chest to mean *ASKED and from centre-space away from the chest to mean *WILL-ASK. However, this is not possible because this movement is already used for other functions: to represent the grammatical relations between first, second, and third person in the subject and object, or for topographic space. A sign does not use the same movement through the same part of space to mean both YOU-ASK-ME and *ASKED.

Because of this, BSL adds a separate sign, using space metaphorically to locate an event in time, in conjunction with verbs that inflect using space for other information.

Non-manual features also use space to show time in BSL. We mentioned this in our earlier discussion of non-manual features in chapter 5. Reference to time can also be made by the 'c–s' head movement (cheek to shoulder), with the head moving backwards to give information about the past. Body movement can also be used in conjunction with other signs to show time. For example the only difference between MORNING and EARLIER-THIS-MORNING may be in the movement of the body. In EARLIER-THIS-MORNING the body hunches slightly and the head moves slightly back (fig. 10.7). The same is true for EARLIER-THIS-AFTERNOON. These non-manual markers are easily missed by learners of BSL, who are more used to looking out for manual markers.

Eye-gaze is also very important, and uses the same spatial metaphor to refer to time. We saw in chapter 5 that BSL signers look to the side and slightly

Fig. 10.7a MORNING

Fig. 10.7b EARLIER-THIS-MORNING

downwards for past, and upwards when talking about the future. This again is using space as though time occupied space.

The use of metaphorical space in 'Time lines'

'Time lines' are probably the most frequently mentioned way of describing how BSL uses space to show time. A time line is a metaphorical representation of time. Some of the linguistics literature suggests that there are four of these lines, but this is not completely accurate.

Line A is said to be parallel to the floor from behind the body, across the shoulder to ahead up to an arm's length, on the signer's dominant side. It allows a signer to place the distant past, recent past, present, near future, and distant future. Roughly speaking, the shoulder and cheek mark the present; anything behind marks the past; and anything in front marks the future. Exact location is not actually relevant however, and direction, size of movement, and palm orientation along the line are more important. For example a signer can sign LONG-AGO starting well in front of the cheek and finishing near the cheek, so long as the sign moves in the right direction for the right distance. YESTERDAY can be signed with backward movement and backward-facing palm, or with forward movement and forward-facing palm (fig. 10.8a and b).

Line B is said to run from elbow to fingertips of the non-dominant arm, away from the signer. It is used for BEFORE and AFTER, as well as calendar units, especially WEEKS (fig. 10.8c).

Line C is said to run in front of the signer from left to right. It is used for continuity and duration, e.g. in the signs FOREVER and CONTINUOUS (fig. 10.8d).

Fig. 10.8a YESTERDAY (with backward movement)

Fig. 10.8b YESTERDAY (with forward movement)

Fig. 10.8c IN-TWO-WEEKS'-TIME

Fig. 10.8d CONTINUOUS

Line D is said to run from foot to head, by the signer's side on the dominant side. It incorporates growing up or maturing so that CHILD and ADULT are placed on the line, irrespective of the heights of the people (fig. 10.8e).

When we look at these lines, we see that the description is only partly satisfactory. For example, many signs often take a diagonal line across the signer's body, e.g. HAVEN'T-SEEN-YOU-FOR-AGES (fig. 10.8f). There also appears to be a 'time line' in the centre of the body, e.g. in POSTPONE, EVERY-WEDNESDAY or EVERY-MONTH (fig. 10.8g). Time line D is

Fig. 10.8e CHILD-GROWING-UP

Fig. 10.8f HAVEN'T-SEEN-YOU-
FOR-AGES

Fig. 10.8g EVERY-MONTH

perhaps the most unsatisfactory. It only has one use: to refer to the way that
humans grow over time. If a pregnant woman's tummy gets bigger over time,
the sign would move out from the stomach, in the centre of the body along
the same space as POSTPONE and EVERY-MONTH; if a vegetable
marrow grew over time, it would grow along the same space seen in time line
C; and if hair grew over time, it would grow along a line running from the
neck down to the navel. Thus the idea of growing over time may well be represented metaphorically, but not necessarily along any one line.

However, even if there is a dispute over the exact number and meaning of
time lines, it is clear that they all allow signers to use movement through space
to show the metaphorical passing of time.

IDIOMS

Another form of figurative language is the use of idioms. These are phrases that are specific to and an established part of one language. If the phrase is taken apart and each individual word is analysed, the meaning of each word would not be the same as when used in an idiom. English has many idioms. For example: *he passed with flying colours; she sees the world through rose-tinted spectacles; you're in hot water this time!; an old flame; never in a month of Sundays; a dog in the manger;* and *heads will roll*. Users of English know what *flying* means and what *colours* are, and also know that *flying colours* in this idiom does not mean colours that fly (as *flying birds* would) but 'very successfully'. Similarly, they know that the person need not wear spectacles at all to see the world through rose-tinted ones, because the idiom means that they never see the bad things in the world. We can see, then, that idioms have a literal and a figurative meaning. If someone takes a hot bath, they would literally be in hot water, but the idiom has another meaning, of 'being in trouble'.

One problem with discussing idioms in BSL is that they are not usually phrases of sequential signs in the way that they are sequences of words in English. Most BSL idioms are made up of a single sign, so it is not possible to break the meaning down into the component signs and see how the whole idiomatic meaning differs from the sum of the signs in a literal sense.

Some signs that have been called idioms in BSL have no figurative meaning. These include what have been called 'multi-channel signs' such as THERE-IS and COULD-HAVE-HAPPENED (fig. 10.9) (also discussed in chapter 5). These have been referred to as idioms because they are an estab-lished part of the language, they are specific to BSL and they have no ready translation into another language. However, this is only part of the meaning of idioms. Idioms usually have both a literal meaning and a figurative one, and signs such as THERE-IS and COULD-HAVE-HAPPENED only have a literal meaning. Therefore, these signs should not be called idioms. However, some 'multi-channel signs' do have both literal and figurative meanings, for example JAW-DROP. This is figurative because the jaw does not necessarily drop when a person is surprised. There is a literal meaning if the jaw really does drop, but the sign usually means 'being very surprised'.

Idioms are a subset of metaphors. If a metaphor has been used in the lan-guage often enough for everyone to know it, then it is also an idiom, because idioms are an established part of the language. If the metaphor has been created by someone on the spot, then it is not an idiom because it is not an established part of the language (yet).

BSL and English use many similar idioms. This might be because BSL has borrowed from English, or because the two cultures share the same view of the world, or for both these reasons.

Fig. 10.9 COULD-HAVE-
HAPPENED

Some BSL idioms are obviously borrowed from English, as part of a natural borrowing process (see chapter 12). Examples of borrowed idioms are BRAINWASH, HACKLES-UP, BROKEN-HEART, GRASS-ROOTS, and ROLL-SLEEVES-UP. Some are phrases translated from English, such as NOT MY CUP-OF-TEA or BACK-TO SQUARE ONE. Not all signers would use all of these, but they are all used by some BSL users (fig. 10.10).

Some BSL idioms are obviously created from within BSL. They have no link to English at all. For example, the idiom MAKE-ME-ITCH means 'great dislike of a person'. The idiom PUT-EARS-DOWN can be translated as 'put in one's place' (see fig. 10.5). Neither of these has any link with English.

Other idioms are similar to English ones but are not exactly the same. Examples include IN-ONE-EYE-AND-OUT-THE-OTHER (as opposed

Fig. 10.10a BRAINWASH   Fig. 10.10b GRASS-ROOTS

Fig. 10.11 'My hands are sealed'

to *in one ear and out the other*) and MY-HANDS-ARE-SEALED (as opposed to *my lips are sealed*) (fig. 10.11). The sign translated as *going over my head*, when a signer has not understood information, is an interesting example. Most people believe that the BSL sign is a direct translation of the English idiom, but it is not. In fact, in BSL it goes past the ears, not over the head.

Other English idioms do not find a ready equivalent in BSL with a similar meaning, e.g. *come hell or high water* or *once in a blue moon*. A signer could sign COME HELL -o-r- HIGH WATER or ONCE IN -a- BLUE MOON but these would be sign-for-word translations and would have no established meaning in BSL of 'determination' or 'rarity' respectively.

Metonymy and synecdoche

In 'synecdoche', a part of something is used to refer to the whole of it, for example, in the sign ELEPHANT. The sign represents the trunk of an elephant, but stands for the whole elephant. In 'metonymy', something associated with a referent stands for the referent, for example, SCOTLAND. The sign represents bagpipes, which are not a part of Scotland, but are closely associated with it.

English uses this figurative speech as a stylistic alternative to existing words. English has a word *monarchy* but also uses the term *the crown* as a metonym. In BSL the same sign often represents the referent, as well as something associated with the referent, and also part of the referent. The same sign is used to mean both CROWN and MONARCHY, and the sign SOMBRERO is also used to mean MEXICO. This is no cause for confusion, and signers know what is intended.

In BSL, the use of metonymy and synecdoche is very widespread, and is a major feature of signing. Visually motivated signs very often derive from a representation of one particularly noticeable part of an object (or action) to mean all of it. In the BSL sign COW, the horns are used to represent the whole cow, and in PRIEST the collar stands for the person who wears the collar. The sign BIRD only represents the beak, but it is used to mean the whole bird, not just its beak. To this extent we may want to say that figurative use of signs is very common in BSL.

Many referents that have no obvious visible form that can be generalised can still be represented by visually motivated signs because of metonymy and synecdoche. For example, a hospital has no obvious visible form, but in the sign HOSPITAL, the cross on the upper arm represents a red cross on the sleeve, and this feature, strongly associated with hospitals (at least in the past), stands for the complete concept of a hospital.

In BSL, metonymy and synecdoche are a central part of creating visually motivated signs. However, we should restrict the use of the term metaphor to those signs where there is clearly a figurative extension from a literal meaning. We would not want to say that GIRAFFE and ELEPHANT are metaphors, even though the signs were created by the process of synecdoche, as this would lead to all visually motivated signs being called metaphors, and this would weaken the idea of metaphor in other areas of BSL.

Metaphorical morphemes

The link between a whole sign and its meaning does not have to be complete. There can also be parts of signs (e.g. handshape, movement, or location) which have a meaning and signs sharing this particular part may share the meaning. In some signs, the meaning of one part relies upon extended meaning (metaphor). The term 'metaphorical morpheme' has been used for this.

Some signs with different locations and movements have handshapes that have a common meaning. For example the 'Å' handshape has the meaning 'good' within many signs: PROUD, HEALTH, BEST, RIGHT, and CONGRATULATE; and the 'I' handshape has the meaning 'bad': ILL, POISON, WORST, FAIL, and WRONG. There are other signs that use these handshapes and which do not have these meanings (e.g. DIFFICULT and SHEEP), but the shared meanings are widespread (fig. 10.12).

Other signs have a location with a shared extended meaning. For example, signs on the chest often are related to emotion like LOVE or ANGRY, (although there are other signs, e.g. ARMY that are nothing to do with emotion). Signs on the head are often linked with cognitive activities, e.g.

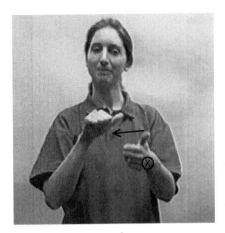

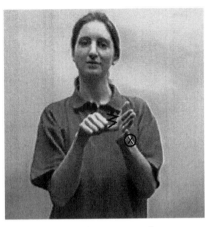

Fig. 10.12a BEST ('Å' carries 'good' meaning)

Fig. 10.12b DIFFICULT ('Å' does not carry 'good' meaning)

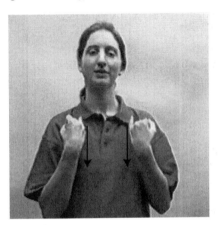

Fig. 10.12c ILL ('I' carries 'bad' meaning)

Fig. 10.12d SHEEP ('I' does not carry 'bad' meaning)

CLEVER, KNOW, THINK, INVENTION, and UNDERSTAND (but others are not, e.g. MOTHER (fig. 10.13)).

Something similar is found in English. It is termed 'sound symbolism'. If people are told the names of two couples: Bob and Deb, and Anne and Clive, and are asked to identify which is a tall and thin couple, and which is a short and plump couple, most English speakers will tell us that they think Bob and Deb are shorter and plumper, and Clive and Anne are taller and thinner. This is based entirely on the vowel sounds in their names. We associate the sounds 'o' (as in *Bob*) and 'e' (as in *Deb*) with short, round things and 'a' (as in *Anne*)

Fig. 10.13a LOVE (chest carries 'emotion' meaning)

Fig. 10.13b ARMY (chest does not carry 'emotion' meaning)

Fig. 10.13c UNDERSTAND (temple carries 'cognitive' meaning)

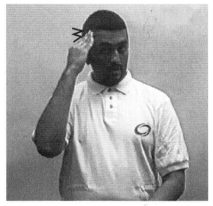

Fig. 10.13d MOTHER (temple does not carry 'cognitive' meaning)

and 'i' (as in *Clive*) with long, tall things. This shows that there is often some sort of generalisable, symbolic link between sounds and meanings in English.

The sounds 'ee' and 'i' are linked to small things in many languages (e.g. *teeny, weeny,* and *little*). The sound 'sk' occurs at the start of many words describing quick movement (e.g. *skip, scuttle, scoot,* and *scud*). At word ends, the sound 'ambl' is used for many unsteady movements (e.g. *scramble, shamble, amble,* and *ramble*).

In English verbs of motion, short vowels are linked to quick movement and long ones to slow movement. Words like *hop, skip,* and *jump* have short vowels and quick, short movements but words like *seep, creep, slide,* and *flow* have long

Fig. 10.14a SMELL   Fig. 10.14b THEORY

vowels and slow, long movements. We can see this in pairs of words too: *pull* is short but *draw* is long; *slip* is short but *slide* is long; *quick* is short but *slow* is long.

This is not always the case, e.g. the vowels in *house, mouse,* and *louse* do not refer to things that are very long and drawn out, and the 'sc' in *scone* has nothing to do with quick movement, but the pattern is nevertheless quite common in English. This shows that the idea of building meaningful ideas into parts of words and signs is very common in English as well as in BSL.

Handshape and movement as metaphorical morphemes

Mary Brennan has argued that we can describe handshape and movement as metaphors within signs. The '5' handshape (with the hand open and the fingers spread) is used to represent sets of long, thin things, such as grass, hair, or a fence. But the same handshape can also be used in the signs WATERFALL, BLOOD, SNORT, SMELL, and THEORY (fig. 10.14). We can also use the handshape to mean 'to spread rapidly', as with information, or a disease. In all these examples 'something' is seen to have some quality of long, thin lines, in a metaphorical way, and the fingers of the '5' hand show this. Brennan argues that these metaphorical uses of handshapes are important in the creation of signs in BSL.

Movement is also important in Mary Brennan's theory of metaphor and morphemes in BSL. She suggests that metaphors can be grouped into categories, such as:

(1) 'Emanate/emit' (flow out, give out). There are a group of signs in which something is represented as given out or sent out from a central source. Examples include SUN, MAGIC, and LIGHT. Brennan says these are metaphorical because nothing is actually given out. The metaphor is shown by the opening of the closed hand. The closed handshape repre-

Fig. 10.15 LIGHT

Fig. 10.16 CATCH-AN-ILLNESS

sents the source, opening the hand represents releasing the 'something', and the open hand represents the rays moving out (fig. 10.15).

(2) The opposite of 'emanate/emit' may be seen in 'copy/absorb', where the handshape closes. Signs like PHOTOCOPY involve the suggestion of something being taken in.

  Signs like LEARN, LISTEN, TAKE-IN-BY-SIGHT, ACQUISITION, and CATCH-AN-ILLNESS represent taking in abstract things, as if they were solid (fig. 10.16).

Relative location is also important in metaphors in BSL. 'Positional' or 'orientational' metaphors allow us to see abstract things as though they were set in space.

English uses these metaphors frequently. For example, we may talk about 'upper' and 'lower' class, suggesting that one class is higher than the other, although class as an idea is totally abstract. We also talk about being *up in the air* or *down in the dumps*, suggesting that being happy is somehow higher than being sad. The linguistic philosophers George Lakoff and Mark Johnson believe that we use metaphor like this because of the way we see the world. We see good things as being up, and bad things as being down. Heaven is said to be above us and hell to be below.

English uses these spatial metaphors a lot, but BSL is able to make even better use of them because it already uses space as a part of the language. (We saw something similar when we discussed the use of spatial metaphors for time in English and BSL.) When we talk about size or distance in BSL, we move the hands further apart to show increased size or distance. This may be for real objects in space, or for abstract concepts that are only placed in space because of metaphor. The hands can also be positioned to show different meanings using spatial metaphors, e.g.:

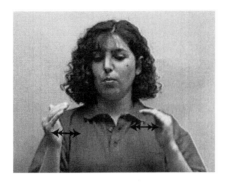

Fig. 10.17a WAR

Fig. 10.17b SUPERIOR

Fig. 10.17c MATCH

(a) opposition: ARGUE, FIGHT, CHALLENGE, COMPETITION, DEBATE, WAR (fig. 10.17a). Here the hands are set opposite each other, because the people involved in any of these concepts are metaphorically on 'different sides' in these situations. English uses similar metaphors in phrases like *different sides in the debate; meet the challenge;* or *face up to the competition.*

(b) status: EQUAL, COMMAND, INFERIOR, BOSS, SUPERIOR. Here, the hands are set at relative heights to each other, so that higher status referents are shown by hands higher in the signing space.

(c) separate/together: hands move apart or come together to show how abstract concepts may be seen as separate from or close to each other. In the signs DIVORCE, SPLIT, DIFFERENT, DISAGREE, and CONTRAST the hands move to show a metaphorical moving apart. In the signs AGREE, SIMULTANEOUS, SAME, and MATCH (e.g. match colours) the hands move together to show a metaphorical coming together (fig. 10.17c).

Note that these metaphorical morphemes also have literal meanings. In a sign meaning 'separating two dogs fighting', the movement of the two hands literally represents two objects being separated. Metaphor takes real, physical states, and uses them to talk about abstract concepts.

There are many other metaphorical morphemes like these in BSL, but it is worth remembering that English shares many of these spatial metaphors, using words, rather than real space, to express them.

SUMMARY

In this chapter we have looked at the ways that BSL can create signs. Visually motivated signs are formed by either 'presenting' (showing an example of) or 'representing' (depicting) the referent. We have also seen that the use of metaphor allows BSL to create even more signs with new meanings. We have seen that some metaphors are easily recognised as such; others are used regularly in BSL as idioms; still others are much less recognisable and are built into BSL at a very deep level. We called these metaphorical morphemes.

EXERCISES FOR CHAPTER 10

1. Arbitrariness and conventionality
   (a) Give three examples of visually motivated signs.
   (b) Give three examples of totally arbitrary signs.
   (c) Even visually motivated signs are conventional. Explain why the visually motivated signs you have given above are conventional.
   (d) Make a list of ten English words showing sound symbolism and beginning with the following sounds:
       (i) 'gl-' (meaning linked with light)
       (ii) 'sl-' (meaning linked with unpleasant things)

2. Metonymy and synecdoche
   (a) Find as many signs for animals as you can. How many of them could be called synecdoche?
   (b) Give ten examples of metonymic signs (e.g. SCOTLAND which uses bagpipes to stand for the country). Say why each one is a metonym.

3. Metaphorical morphemes
   (a) Identify some signs that have 'good' and 'bad' handshapes. What signs have the same handshape but do not contain the meaning 'good' or 'bad'?
   (b) Find examples of signs that are located on the chest and have some meaning linked to 'emotion' (e.g. LIKE).

(c) Find examples of signs that are located on the head and have some meaning linked to 'cognition' (e.g. DREAM).

(d) Find examples of signs that use metaphorical morphemes for the idea of 'opposition' or 'differing heights' (e.g. ARGUE or BOSS).

4. Give ten examples of signs or sign phrases that you think are metaphorical (e.g. 'panic' – hanging on the edge of a cliff, or 'feel stupid' – head behind a wall). For each one say what the literal meaning is, as well as the figurative meaning. Is there a similar expression in English?

5. Using a video clip of a fluent signer telling a story, identify as many signs as you can that can be categorised as:
   (a) totally arbitrary
   (b) a presentable object
   (c) a presentable action
   (d) a substitutive depiction
   (e) a virtual depiction

6. Metaphors of time
   (a) Find ten examples of signs that give an idea of time by moving along a straight line. How many different 'lines' can you think of?
   (b) Find four signs that give an idea of time by moving in a circle (possibly combined with a straight line, too, creating a spiral).

7. Time
   (a) Identify examples of the following:
       (i) five signs in BSL that place an event in time but give no other information
       (ii) ten signs in BSL that place an event in time, but also have some more specific meaning, e.g. YESTERDAY.
   (b) For each of the signs above say what information is contained in the sign (e.g. YESTERDAY tells you that it was in the past and the period of time is a day).
   (c) Identify five sentences in which 'common sense' from the context tells when the event occurred.

FURTHER READING FOR CHAPTER 10

Brennan, M. 1983, 'Marking time in BSL', in J. G. Kyle and B. Woll (eds.), *Language in sign*, London: Croom Helm, 10–31.
Schermer, T., and Koolhof, J. 1990, 'The reality of time lines: aspects of tense in Sign Language of the Netherlands', in S. Prillwitz and T. Vollhaber (eds.), *Current trends in European sign language research*, Hamburg: Signum Press, 295–306.
Wilbur, R. 1990, 'Metaphors in American Sign Language and English', in W. Edmondson and F. Karlsson (eds.), *SLR '87: Papers from the fourth international symposium on sign language research*, Hamburg: Signum Press, 163–70.

Chapter eleven

The established and productive lexicons

In this chapter we will continue our discussion of the origin of signs. We have already seen that they can be derived from a representation of the visual form of the referent, or created by metaphorical extension (often drawing on some visual metaphor). This chapter will consider several other mechanisms for creating signs in BSL, including new signs made by derivation. We will also consider signs that are not a permanent part of the BSL lexicon; they are created *ad hoc*, for the moment. We will also consider the use of simultaneous signs for creating new meanings.

The signs of BSL can be divided into those that are part of the 'established' lexicon, and those that are part of the 'productive' lexicon. Before we consider any more processes for creating signs, it is worth considering these two groups of signs.

English speakers have a large set of words to choose from, and they can combine these words together to make sentences. English creates new words by adding prefixes and suffixes, or by making compounds from two existing words, or by extending the meaning of a word to give it a new meaning. It can also borrow words from other languages. On the whole, though, these productive processes are not much used and English has a fairly large, fairly stable lexicon.

BSL is very different. In BSL, there are far fewer 'basic signs' fixed in the lexicon, but the process of using signs not in the established lexicon is much more important. The *BSL/English Dictionary* lists pictures of only 1,789 signs. Although in many cases a given form of a sign may have more than one meaning, and the dictionary does not list all core signs, there is no doubt that the core lexicon of BSL is relatively small when compared to English. People who do not understand how signs are formed in BSL may think that this means that BSL has a very small lexicon. In some respects this is true, and yet there are no limitations on signing. One way in which BSL expands is by borrowing, especially by using fingerspelling. We will discuss this process in the next chapter. Another way, though, is to create the sign that is needed, 'on the spot'. Many other languages which make extensive use of derivational processes also appear to have small core vocabularies.

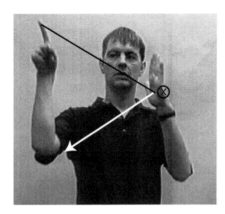

Fig. 11.1 SATELLITE

Signs in the established lexicon are those found in a dictionary, or in our 'mental lexicon' (the words or signs that we have stored in our brains as items of the language). These established signs are fairly easy to learn. Many of the signs in the established lexicon are nouns, and many of them can be easily translated into English words. Signs in the established lexicon can be visually motivated or can be totally arbitrary. They exist in citation form. That is, they can be understood when they stand alone, without any context to clarify the meaning, and can be cited in response to the question 'What's the sign for __?'

In contrast, the productive lexicon is created by signers from component parts that are combined to create a new meaning. A good image is that of shelves in our brains containing a range of basic components, like spare parts in a workshop. These components are: the range of permitted handshapes in BSL; the range of permitted movements; the range of permitted locations; the range of permitted orientations; and the range of permitted non-manual features.

To create a new sign, the signer must know the rules for the assembly of a sign using these basic components. The signer must know the rules for selection of a handshape (for example, to refer to the referent's semantic group – perhaps by focusing on the size and shape of the referent, or how it is handled); the rules for the movement of the sign; the rules for the orientation of the hand(s); the rules for the location (and location relative to the other hand, if necessary); and the rules for the selection of non-manual features, including mouth components and facial expression. The signer can then assemble these components into a new sign. The new sign always draws on visual motivation in some way. It cannot be arbitrary. This visual nature is central to the role that the productive lexicon plays in BSL.

In the recently created sign SATELLITE, the non-dominant hand ('B') represents the dish and the dominant hand represents signals travelling to and being reflected from the satellite (fig. 11.1).

Fig. 11.2 TALL-CHILD or SHORT-ADULT

However, this sign can be further modified, with infinite changes in the orientation of the non-dominant hand, and in the angle at which the dominant hand strikes the non-dominant, etc. These possible changes are infinite, because BSL maps representations of the real world directly into language by what is called the 'analogue' principle. Analogues are parallels of other things. For example, the sign TALL in BSL can vary depending on the height of the referent. In fact, there is no real contrast between TALL and SHORT, as the same form can be used depending on context: SHORT-ADULT vs. TALL-CHILD (fig. 11.2). In spoken languages, words are 'discrete'. That is, we cannot vary the word *tall* to indicate different heights.

The use of a productive lexicon makes the size of the lexicon in BSL very different from English. The visual basis of BSL allows the creation of signs from the productive lexicon for what might otherwise be core vocabulary. This is particularly true in BSL verbs which include noun information, e.g. PARADE-SLOWLY-CROSSES-FROM-RIGHT-TO-LEFT (fig. 11.3). It is also true for signs which contain information about nouns and their modifiers: TINY-BUTTONS-DOWN-THE-LEFT-SLEEVE (fig. 11.4).

Earlier, in our discussion of verb types in chapter 8 we discussed how handshapes can vary depending on the direct object. Signs for opening a door, a book, a window, a can of drink, or an umbrella will all be very different. Handing another person a trophy, a certificate, a jar of jam, a hot plate, or a set of keys would require different handshapes in BSL, because of the different ways we hold different objects.

The list of different possible forms of HAND and OPEN is extremely large. We would not want to say that all those signs are part of the established lexicon, and would not want to put them all in a dictionary of BSL, any more than we would enter phrases and sentences into an English dictionary. It is much more appropriate to say that there are basic verbs HAND-(something)

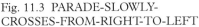

Fig. 11.3 PARADE-SLOWLY-   Fig. 11.4 TINY-BUTTONS-DOWN-
CROSSES-FROM-RIGHT-TO-LEFT   THE-LEFT-SLEEVE

and OPEN-(something), and that BSL rules allow the signer to select from the range of basic components for those verbs, to create new signs when necessary.

There are pairs of verbs, such as HAND-(something) and GIVE, and PICK-UP-(something) and CHOOSE which differ in their possibilities of including direct object information. GIVE and CHOOSE reflect change of ownership of the direct object, and therefore the handshape does not change. HAND-(something) and PICK-UP-(something) reflect change of location of the direct object, and therefore the handshape changes. This pairing of verbs representing change of ownership with verbs representing change of location is common in many spoken languages as well (fig. 11.5).

However, some of these forms may be used more often than others. For example, HAND-CARDS ('deal') is used more often than HAND-A-SIX-INCH-PIECE-OF-STRING. Both use a basic sign with the appropriate handshape, but the former intuitively feels more established than the latter. However, HAND-CARDS-TO-THREE-PEOPLE-SEATED-ON-THE-LEFT is clearly from the productive lexicon. This means that in our conversation about the established and productive lexicons, there is no clear dividing line between what is established and what is productive. One person might think they are creating a new sign, but the conversational partner might think that this is a part of the established lexicon. For some signers, the process of creating signs may be so natural that they are not even aware that they are doing it.

Use of the productive lexicon is particularly common in informal signing and story-telling but we can see its use at all levels of discourse. Signing that is more influenced by English makes less use of the productive lexicon.

Fig. 11.5a GIVE

Fig. 11.5b HAND-SOMEONE-A-BUNCH-OF-FLOWERS

Fig. 11.5c CHOOSE

Fig. 11.5d PICK-UP-APPLE

English-influenced signing is often seen in more formal contexts, so we may expect less use of the productive lexicon in formal settings.

Some signs from the productive lexicon end up being part of the established lexicon, if they are used often enough. This is the commonest way by which visually motivated signs enter the established lexicon, e.g. FAX, AUTOMATIC-DOORS, COMPUTER-MOUSE. We saw this process earlier with SATELLITE. These were all created *ad hoc* at one stage, and later became part of the lexicon, so that if someone asks 'What's the sign for -f-a-x-?' the signer can reply FAX.

INFLECTION FOR PERSON AND MANNER

In chapters 3 and 8 we noted that inflecting a word or sign changes some of the information in the sign, but that the basic sign stays the same. The citation form ASK, I-ASK-YOU, and HE-ASKS-YOU are all the sign ASK, but with different grammatical information. So much information can be added to a sign that signs with the same root can appear very different, and have very different meanings.

We know that plain verbs can be modified to show information about aspect and manner. We also know that agreement verbs can be further modified to show information about number and person. In all these examples, the inflectional morphology adds extra grammatical information.

It is difficult to say what is a new sign, and what is just a new form of a sign created through inflection. For example, in English, we would say that inflection does not create a new word (e.g. *running* and *ran* are really only two forms of the same word), but there is much more inflection in BSL, with verbs marked for aspect, manner, location, subject, and object. The sign glossed as RUN has a neutral facial expression, but if it has a 'mm' facial expression, it may be glossed as JOG. Because a different English gloss can be used, we may be tempted to say that a new BSL sign has been formed.

We have already considered the verb PICK-UP-(something). There are many ways to sign PICK-UP-(something), depending upon what is picked up, how it is picked up, and from where it is picked up.

Some of these should definitely be seen as forms of the same verb ('I pick up a bowl', or 'I pick up a match'), because they can be predicted from the rules of BSL. But what if a signer turns his head away while signing? For example: NAPPY Index$_A$ PICK-UP-NAPPY$_A$ (reluctantly/resentfully).

In this example, we need to decide if we have produced a standard sign with a manner inflection, or if this manner inflection is unusual enough to be classed as productive, or if this expression is outside the language (that is, 'gestural').

USING COMPONENTS TO SHOW SIZE AND SHAPE

The creative use of handshapes is a central part of using the productive lexicon, particularly the selection of handshapes to represent size and shape or the way an object is handled.

Consider a post or railing in a fence. Depending on the handshape, these posts can be represented as thicker or thinner. This makes them into different signs, even if they share the same basic meaning. English does not directly represent the size and shape of fence posts, and several very different-looking signs may all be glossed as FENCE-POST because of this. Again, the use of the English gloss may interfere with our understanding of what is a new sign, and what is a variant form of an existing sign.

The form of many BSL nouns includes information about the size or shape of a referent. In English, adjectives are used to describe the size and shape of

Fig. 11.6a WIDE-BELT   Fig. 11.6b NARROW-BELT

noun referents. For example, we could say that a belt was *wide* or *narrow*, or *thick* or *thin*. In BSL the sign itself is changed to show the size, using analogues of real size, so that rather than BELT, we get signs better glossed as WIDE-BELT or NARROW-BELT. There is an almost infinite number of possible thicknesses and widths of a belt. We certainly would not want to put all these signs in a dictionary (1-INCH-WIDE-BELT, HALF-INCH-WIDE-BELT, 2-INCH-WIDE-BELT, etc. (fig. 11.6)). The same could be said for the width of stripes, or the length of hair (not only HAIR, but SHORT-HAIR, LONG-HAIR, SHOULDER-LENGTH-HAIR, etc.).

SIMULTANEOUS SIGNS

There is also another way in which BSL can create new signs, by producing two signs simultaneously, one on each hand. We may want to say that such constructions are more like phrases or sentences, but there is no satisfactory distinction between signs which are single lexical items, and signs which are more complex constructions.

We will now consider the way that BSL uses simultaneous signs. In some cases, simultaneous signs are clearly single items of vocabulary. In others, the combination of two signs creates what many people would agree is a sentence.

SIMULTANEITY IN BSL

In chapter 3 we discussed word order and sign order. The underlying assumption in any discussion of order is that one sign follows another, just as words

The three of us doz-z-z-e

Fig. 11.7 'The poet, the dog and the bird all doze'

do in English. This is often true, but now we will focus on the way that signers can produce more than one sign at the same time in BSL.

It is only possible to have simultaneous production of signs because there is more than one major articulator. In spoken language, there is only one major articulator: the mouth. In BSL, each hand can act as an independent major articulator, as can the head and mouth, to a lesser extent. All simultaneous constructions are made by articulation in two or more channels, each channel carrying meaning units. In a poem by Dot Miles, 'Afternoon', the signer, her dog, and a bird all enjoy an afternoon doze together. She signs this by using both hands and her head, each as a separate articulator (fig. 11.7) (see chapter 14 for a further discussion of poetry in BSL).

In simultaneous signs, the information on the two hands is linked. Each hand does not produce content unrelated to the other hand. For example, the left hand does not sign about last night's film on television, while the right hand signs a cake recipe (although this can be done for humorous effect in jokes).

As we discussed in chapter 5, the head, face and mouth can all carry information, so they can provide channels for simultaneous signs. For example 'no hope' can be signed with HOPE on the hands and NONE using just the head and facial expression. In another case (as we also saw in chapter 5) it is possible to produce one sign on the hands but use a spoken component related to a different sign, and so give two pieces of information at the same time: for example, TYPING on the hands and 'finish?' on the face, or, following establishment of an appropriate context (e.g. a question about members of a signer's family) counting ONE, TWO, THREE on the hands and mouthing 'mother', 'father', and 'sister'.

Since much grammatical information (such as topic, questions, and negations) is provided on the face, we may want to say that this is also an example of simultaneous signing. However, here we are only going to look at what happens when the two hands give different, but related, information at the same time.

In this discussion, we will distinguish the dominant hand (the right hand in most right-handed signers) from the non-dominant hand (the left hand in most right-handed signers).

There is some debate about the functions of the dominant and non-dominant hands. Usually, where simultaneity occurs, the dominant hand provides the new, 'figure' or 'foreground' information, and the non-dominant hand provides old, 'peripheral', 'ground' or 'background' information, including indexes. (We know from the discussion in chapter 3 that indexes are old information because they refer to something already known.)

However, this rule is not fixed, and may depend on many factors, including signing fluency. Some signers (especially native signers) can easily alternate hand dominance.

We will now discuss some simultaneous signs. We must go beyond collecting examples, to arrive at a stage of being able to classify and group them, in order to explain why a person is using two hands in this way. The groups described below are not an exhaustive list but they help us to begin to understand the richness of BSL.

Some of these groupings come from the work of Chris Miller and his colleagues in Canada. Others are suggestions that have arisen as a result of observing signs in BSL. There are many others which have not yet been investigated.

To place referents in space

Two different signs may be produced at the same time in different locations but in the same field of view. This creates an overall picture of a spatial layout. (Note that this does not occur in English. Extra words must be used for

Fig. 11.8 MUG-ON-SAUCER

descriptions of spatial layout; in BSL signs can be placed in relation to each other.)

These can either be the full sign, if the sign can be produced with one hand, or alternatively a proform. Examples include MUG-ON-SAUCER or LIMPET-ON-SIDE-OF-SHIP (fig. 11.8). Here the signs represent the spatial relationship between the referents in the real world.

This process can produce an infinite number of constructions. 'There were two tables next to each other' could be signed using two 'B' hand proforms as TABLE TWO TABLE TWO-TABLES-NEXT-TO-EACH-OTHER-A-SHORT-DISTANCE-APART. However, depending on where the two 'B' proforms are placed, there are an infinite number of ways to represent the angles and distances. These simultaneous signs are best described as belonging to the productive lexicon.

To show how referents move in space

This is very closely linked to the previous group, but instead of describing where two referents are located, we say how they move. If two aeroplanes flew around in the sky, narrowly missing each other, each hand would represent one aeroplane, and their movements would show how the aeroplanes moved relative to each other. This type of construction is particularly common where proforms are used in verbs. The two hands can move in relation to each other, in order to show how and where the referents move, for example, BRIDGE CAR Veh-CL-UNDER-BRIDGE (see fig. 3.7).

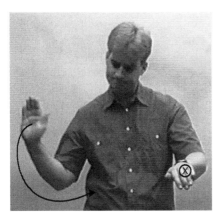
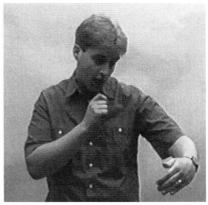

Fig. 11.9 'Hold a child over one's knee and smack its bottom'

Fig. 11.10 'Putting an arm around a child and asking: "Do you want ice-cream?"'

If we sign that two people meet each other, we would sign something that may be glossed as TWO-(people)-MEET. However, this sign can be varied, depending on the direction the two people come from, how they move and how long it takes them to meet. Thus, again, we have a potentially infinite number of productive signs, based on the potential of simultaneous signing.

In role shift

Another use of simultaneous signing occurs when a signer is using role shift. When a signer shifts into the role of someone (or something) else, they can use a sign that represents a presentable action. We saw this in chapter 7 when we discussed aspect. One hand could represent holding a naughty child over the knee while the other hand signs SMACK-ON-BOTTOM (fig. 11.9).

One hand can be used for the presentable action, showing what the character did, and the other can sign what the character said. For example, a character might have their arm around someone while asking another character if they want ice-cream (fig. 11.10).

To show the topic

Lynn Friedman, an ASL linguist, suggested in the 1970s that it is possible to maintain the topic of the sentence on the non-dominant hand while the

Fig. 11.11 'That man – I know him'

dominant hand signs the rest of the sentence. Margaret Deuchar observed this too for BSL in her discussion of the different ways of showing the topic in a sentence (as we saw in chapter 3). This maintenance of the topic on the non-dominant hand is a common use of simultaneous signing.

The non-dominant hand may show the full sign, or an index (usually pointing), or another sort of proform, e.g.:

CAR (d)   WE-LOOK-AT (directed to nd)
        (nd) Veh-Cl _____

'We looked at the car'

Other examples include 'That man – I know him', where the proform replacing MAN is maintained during the comment 'I know him' (fig. 11.11); and 'That woman over there is my sister', where the index locating the sister on the non-dominant hand is maintained during the comment (directed to the non-dominant hand).

To enumerate or establish a time frame

The non-dominant hand can be used to count things off, or to establish a time for the events on the dominant hand.

(d)   COLLEGE   GO-HOME STUDY ____ EAT
(nd) 2.00 _____ 4.00 _____ 6.00 ____ 7.00

'I'm at college from two o'clock, I go home at four o'clock and study until six. Then I eat at seven.'

(d)   LIFT-HANDSET   DIAL-NUMBER   LISTEN
(nd) ONE _____TWO _____ THREE _____

'First you lift the handset, then dial, then listen.

Fig. 11.12 'Those are deaf, those are deafened, and those are hearing'

To show a location or a pronoun

The non-dominant hand can be used to identify referents or locations associated with them, while information is presented with the dominant hand.

(d) DEAF   DEAFENED   HEARING

(nd) Index$_A$____Index$_B$_____Index$_C$__

'Those people are deaf, those are deafened and those are hearing' (fig. 11.12).

To emphasise a sign

An index can be directed towards the sign made with the dominant hand. Either the subject or the object can be indexed.

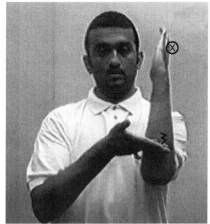

Fig. 11.13 '(Do you know) *HER*?'   Fig. 11.14 CUT-DOWN-TREE

(d)   Index₂ KNOW Index₃_____
(nd)   Index₃
'Do you know *her*?' (fig. 11.13)

This is much more emphatic than just using one hand and signing sequentially.

The index can be used to emphasise any sign. For example, in 'Of the deaf and hearing groups, we really need the deaf group', we can see that (DEAF) GROUP is emphasised.

(d) DEAF_____HEARING_____WE NEED   Index_L^++
(nd)   GROUP_L   GROUP_R   GROUP_L

To incorporate the object in the verb

The object is signed by the non-dominant hand, while the dominant hand signs the verb, to represent the object receiving the action of the verb.

(d)   CUT-DOWN-TREE
(nd) TREE_____
'Cut down the tree' (fig. 11.14)
(d)   HAMMER-NAIL
(nd) NAIL_____
'Hammer in the nail'

This can also be found in verbs where the two hands do not actually interact. For example GIVE or ASK can be directed towards a proform, e.g. a panel of four people could each be asked a question, with the sign ASK directed to each proform (fig. 11.15).

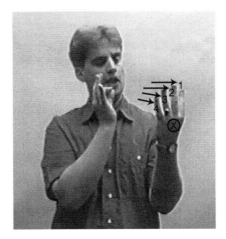

Fig. 11.15 ASK-EACH-OF-FOUR

In language play

The ASL researchers Edward Klima and Ursula Bellugi have discussed how two hands can be used in poetry and humour to set two separate ideas against each other, for example, signing HAPPY with one hand and DEPRESSED with the other. An example in BSL would be to sign YES and NO simultaneously, if the signer is unsure of something. As we will see in chapter 14, the use of simultaneous signs is an important poetic device in sign languages.

To maintain a topic and make a remark as an 'aside'

The non-dominant hand maintains the topic of the discourse, while the signer makes an 'aside', using the dominant hand. Then the signer returns to the topic, for example:

(d)   UNCLE DEAF_____MOTHER Index$_B$ HEARING Index$_A$
(nd)   Index$_A$_____
(d)   WENT DEAF SCHOOL
'(Her) deaf uncle ((her) mother is hearing) went to a deaf school.'

In simultaneous compounds

We discussed these in chapter 6. We mentioned signs like MINICOM and SPACE-SHUTTLE, where each hand represents different signs which are brought together to create a new sign with another meaning.

Simultaneous compounds derive from the productive processes which create simultaneous signs. But simultaneous compounds are lexicalised. They form a single sign in the established lexicon.

Established signs which use proforms or handshapes to represent how objects are handled, such as RIDE-A-HORSE, LOCK, WRITE, and TRAMPOLINE are best described as single signs rather than as two separate signs occurring simultaneously.

Signing two signs at the same time as part of a phrase

Jim Kyle and Bencie Woll have said that this is frequent in casual signing, e.g. 'born deaf' and 'small boy'. One hand signs one sign from the phrase, and the other hand signs the other sign. It is even more common for one sign to slightly precede the other, and then be held while the other is made, as we can see in the example below.

(d) BORN_____
(nd)   DEAF
      'born deaf'

We cannot always be sure if simultaneous signs are present or not. What may appear to be a 'simultaneous sign', may be an example of a sign remaining on the hand ('perseverating') for no reason other than that the signer has not dropped the hand. Often, in a two-handed sign, the dominant hand moves (to produce the next sign) while the non-dominant hand remains in its previous location. For example, in WRITE, the 'B' handshape of the non-dominant hand may be retained while the dominant hand articulates a new sign. Where this occurs, it may be difficult to distinguish from simultaneous signs.

Where the visual motivation of a sign is of two identical referents, one on each hand, we might argue either that we have a simple two-handed sign, or that each hand has its own meaning. For example, in RABBIT we have a simple two-handed sign, meaning 'rabbit', but this sign is derived from a representation of the two ears of an animal. This is clearly not simultaneous signing. However, we might produce a formally similar sign that refers to the ears separately (e.g. one ear might be straight up and one might flop over) (fig. 11.16). There are many examples which illuminate this. A useful convention is to say that in nouns, the two hands function as a single sign, but in verbs, the two hands may function more independently as simultaneous signs.

This convention may also solve the problem of how to classify signs created as presentable actions. If we 'mix something in a bowl', one hand represents the bowl and the other, the spoon. We may say that COOKING is a sign from the established lexicon, but DO-COOKING is potentially a simultaneous sign.

Simultaneous signs are very common in BSL, and may be seen as examples of the productive lexicon in action.

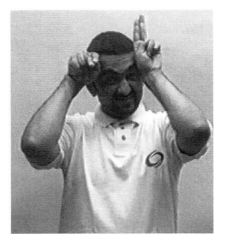

Fig. 11.16 'A rabbit with one floppy ear'

SUMMARY

This chapter has considered the creation of signs in BSL. We have seen that the established BSL lexicon is relatively small in comparison to the lexicon of English, but there are many devices for creating new lexical items in BSL. One way is through the creation of signs from component elements. We have seen that comparisons with English and especially translation of signs into English are frequently confusing when we consider new BSL signs. The two hands often present separate, but related, information, in order to create new simultaneous signs. We have also seen that there are times when a two-handed sign can be considered to be a single sign, and other times when the hands show different information, and should be considered as examples of simultaneous signs.

EXERCISES FOR CHAPTER 11

1. Signs from the productive lexicon
    (a) Think of fifteen different signs that could be glossed as PICK-UP-(something).
    (b) Think of fifteen different signs that could be glossed as OPEN-(something).
    (c) Think of fifteen different signs that could be glossed as (something)-FALL.
    (d) Think of fifteen different signs that could be glossed as CARRY-(something).

2. Using a video clip of a fluent signer telling a story, identify examples of signs from this story that you think are not a part of the established BSL lexicon.

   (a) List the signs that you have chosen, and say why you think they are from the productive lexicon. (Are they presentable actions? Are they using classifiers in a new way? Are they new simultaneous signs?)

   (b) There may well be some signs that you are not sure about. Include these, saying why you are not sure about them.

3. For each of the different functions of 'simultaneous signs' outlined in this chapter, think of three more examples for yourself.

4. BSL makes extensive use of productivity, but English is also productive.

   (a) Using a good English dictionary, find the meanings and origins of the parts that make up these words:

   (i)   *television*

   (ii)   *x-ray vision*

   (iii)   *telephone*

   (iv)   *xylophone*

   (v)   *alcoholic*

   (vi)   *shopaholic*

   (vii) *hamburger*

   (viii) *turkeyburger*

   (b) Find some new words that have come into English recently by adding prefixes or suffixes, by making compounds, or by extending the meaning of an existing word.

   c) In English we can *unscrew, untie, unknot, undress* and so on. We cannot, however, **unjump, *unhit, *unarrive* or **unblink*. Think of some more verbs that will accept this productive *un-* and some more that will not. Why can some verbs not be made using *un-*?

5. Watch a video clip of a fluent signer telling a story.

   (a) Identify examples of simultaneous signs that you can see in the story.

   (b) Describe the two signs made by the two hands, and say why the signer has used a simultaneous sign, instead of sequential signs.

   (c) If the simultaneous sign fits one of the categories discussed in the section on simultaneity in BSL, say which category that is, and why you think so. If it does not, try making a category of your own.

FURTHER READING FOR CHAPTER 11

Brennan, M. 1990, 'Productive morphology in British Sign Language', in S. Prillwitz and T. Vollhaber (eds.), *Current trends in European Sign Language research*, Hamburg: Signum Press, 205–30.

Brennan, M. 1994, 'Pragmatics and productivity', in I. Ahlgren, B. Bergman, and M. Brennan (eds.), *Perspectives on sign language usage*, Durham: ISLA, 371–90.

Deuchar, M. 1984, *British Sign Language*, London: Routledge & Kegan Paul.

Klima, E. S., and Bellugi, U. 1979, *The signs of language*, Harvard University Press.

Kyle, J. G., and Woll, B. 1985, *Sign language: the study of deaf people and their language*, Cambridge University Press.

Miller, C. 1994, 'Simultaneous constructions and complex signs in Quebec Sign Language', in I. Ahlgren, B. Bergman, and M. Brennan (eds.), *Perspectives on sign language usage*, Durham: ISLA, 131–48.

Chapter twelve

Borrowing and name signs

In the last chapter we discussed the productive and established lexicons and simultaneous signs. We said that signs in the productive lexicon are a very important part of signing BSL. In this chapter we will discuss another way for new signs to enter the language, through borrowing. As well as creating signs from within the language, BSL can borrow signs from other languages. It can borrow from other sign languages or it can borrow from English, either through the process of 'loan translation' or through fingerspelling.

As an illustration of these processes, we will also look at signs for brand names, people, and places. Personal name signs are particularly useful to study here because they show many different sign-formation processes. They provide a way to summarise some of the different ways that BSL adds to its lexicon.

BORROWING

BSL borrows from other languages. By this we mean that it uses signs that are derived from words or signs of other languages. English also borrows from other languages. There are a great many English words that can be traced to other languages and the process continues today. For example, *jihad* has recently come into English from Arabic, and *karaoke* has been borrowed from Japanese.

It is important to note that after a long time these words are often not recognised as foreign. *Potato, tobacco,* and *tomato* are not considered foreign words now, although both the referents and their names were, when they arrived 500 years ago.

We know that BSL borrows from other languages, and signers may not notice that such signs are 'foreign' either. For BSL, English is the major donor language, not other sign languages. This is because all languages borrow most from the language they have most contact with. British signers have most contact with English, so they borrow from English.

Fig. 12.1a AMERICA (old sign)   Fig. 12.1b AMERICA (new sign)

Loans into BSL from other sign languages

The number of loans from other sign languages is still small. It may well increase. For some British signers, many of their sign language loans are from American Sign Language, because ASL is a socially important sign language at the international level. It is the one that some British signers come across because of the influence of Gallaudet University in Washington, DC, America's liberal arts college for deaf students, which has many international students.

Nevertheless, loans do come from other sign languages. Other sign languages provide their signs for countries and major cities. For example, the old BSL sign AMERICA has been replaced by the ASL sign. This is becoming increasingly common as British deaf signers travel more and meet more foreign signers (fig. 12.1).

Signs such as AMERICA, FRANCE, CHINA, JAPAN, DENMARK, NORWAY, AUSTRIA, AUSTRALIA, and THAILAND, each borrowed from the respective sign language of those countries, are coming into increasing use in BSL (fig. 12.2). They are also now taught to learners of BSL, so we may say that they are now becoming part of a developing 'standard BSL'. Some of them are also listed in the *BSL/English Dictionary*, which helps to reinforce their acceptance. The names of cities such as COPENHAGEN, PARIS, LISBON, BRUSSELS, NEW-YORK, WASHINGTON, and ROME have also been borrowed from those countries' sign languages (fig. 12.3).

Many of these new signs replace – or are used alongside – signs that are

Fig. 12.2 THAILAND

Fig. 12.3a ROME (old sign)   Fig. 12.3b ROME (new sign)

already in use in BSL. This demonstrates that signs are not only borrowed where the language does not already have a sign. Loans can also replace (or exist alongside) old signs.

Technical terminology – especially linguistic terminology – has been borrowed from other sign languages. For example, two signs meaning LANGUAGE that are presently used in BSL were borrowed from Swedish Sign Language and ASL respectively (fig. 12.4). CLASSIFIER is a commonly cited example of a sign that has been borrowed from ASL, although the path of borrowing has been more complex. The BSL sign CLASSIFIER derives from the ASL classifier handshape for 'vehicle', with added movement (since classifiers themselves have no movement). Thus BSL has taken the form from ASL, but has given it a new meaning (fig. 12.5).

ATTITUDE is a loan from Danish Sign Language. The verb SAY-NO-

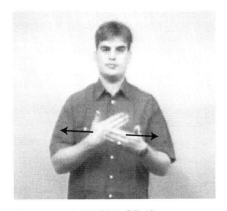

Fig. 12.4a LANGUAGE (from Swedish Sign Language)

Fig. 12.4b LANGUAGE (from ASL)

Fig. 12.5 CLASSIFIER

TO may have been borrowed from ASL, although some British deaf signers do not accept this. Other loan signs may include VIDEO from ASL.

It is worth making the point here that we often do not know where a sign came from. We cannot always be sure of a sign's history. Many Americans believe that an ASL sign glossed as NO-GOOD is borrowed from BSL, because the sign contains hand arrangements very similar to the British manual letters -n- and -g- (fig. 12.6). Unfortunately for this theory, BSL has no similar sign. People may have their own favourite theory about where a sign came from, but there is often no firm proof as to the source of a sign. Sometimes the etymology that is given is interesting in its own right, whether or not we can prove it.

Irish Sign Language is also a donor language for some dialects of BSL. This

Fig. 12.6 ASL sign NO-GOOD

Fig. 12.7 Irish Sign Language loan
BABY-DAUGHTER

is because these BSL dialects have close contact with Irish Sign Language. Dialects with Irish loans are found in Glasgow, Liverpool, and London where there are large communities of Roman Catholics and links to Ireland. Examples of signs borrowed from Irish Sign Language include YEAR and BABY-DAUGHTER (fig. 12.7).

Borrowing is not a one-way process; BSL is not a sponge that soaks up other signs without giving anything back. Other languages borrow from BSL, too. Many Irish signers use an increasing number of BSL signs. The Irish Deaf community has access to BSL through contacts with Northern Ireland, and also by watching BSL on British television programmes which can be seen in Ireland.

Loans into BSL from English

There are two different ways that BSL can borrow from English. Each sign can be translated, sign for sign or morpheme for morpheme from English to BSL, in a process called 'loan translation'. Alternatively, the letters from an English word can be represented in some way using the manual alphabet. Sometimes letters are used without any alteration, but on other occasions BSL adds extra information to loans made through fingerspelling.

We should remember, though, that loans are not only at the level of the sign lexicon. We discussed in chapter 5 that BSL can borrow at the phonological level (that is, part of a sign), for example by adding spoken components in signs such as FINISH or HUSBAND. It can borrow from English at the morphological level (as we saw in chapter 7 (fig. 7.3)), for example by using an English-derived structure like LONG TIME instead of the BSL inflection LONG-TIME. It can borrow at the syntactic level too, for example by using English word order instead of BSL sign order (see chapter 3).

Loan translations

Loan translations are found in many name signs. For example, the sign glossed as ICELAND is made up of the signs ICE and LAND, and GREENLAND is made up of GREEN and LAND. This process is very common with referents predominantly known by their English name. The names of television programmes may be translated directly into BSL, so that the Granada soap *Coronation Street* is signed CORONATION STREET, and the snooker quiz game *Big Break* is signed BIG BREAK. It is important to note that BSL does not rely on this process entirely. For example the sign for the BBC soap glossed as EASTENDERS is a visually motivated metonym that uses the shape of the River Thames that appears in the programme's credits (fig. 12.8).

Fig. 12.8 EASTENDERS

Loan translations are also very common when using English idioms in BSL, or when a signer wants to mark an utterance as being a quote from English. Most signers are bilingual to some extent in BSL and English, so we would expect this sort of switching between languages (sometimes called 'code-switching' or 'code-mixing'). A signer, for example, may produce such utterances as CAN'T STAND to mean 'strongly dislike' and DRINK PETROL for a car that is uneconomical on fuel. In both cases, the signing is a loan translation. Some loans of this type become fixed and are regularly used in BSL, while others remain instances of temporary code-switching only.

Some signs may be used in BSL that have been borrowed from English in a different context. The phrase 'key issues' was signed by one fluent BSL/English bilingual as KEY ISSUE, using the sign KEY which refers to locks and keys, rather than the sign KEY which refers to important things. In another example, a signer used the sign BOOSTER (referring to a vaccination booster), to mean a booster session in a part-time university course. In neither case were these errors: the signers chose signs knowing that the conversational partner knew English and BSL and would be able to extract the intended meaning.

Another interesting example of loan translation is the creation of signs from acronyms, using a partial loan translation. Examples include ABSOLUTE from -a-b-s-l-t- (Association of British Sign Language Tutors), and CAP from -c-a-c-d-p- (Council for the Advancement for Communication with Deaf People).

Fingerspelling

We have already seen in chapter 1 that fingerspelling is used in BSL to allow the reproduction of the letters of an English word as part of signing. We have seen that there are many reasons for representing English while signing. We will now consider more of the ways in which BSL uses fingerspelling.

Fingerspelling signs are totally unmotivated visually. There is nothing about their form to link them to the referent except convention. Several handshapes do look like the written letters of the alphabet, but no more than that. There is no connection between the manual letter from the English alphabet and the referent, except convention.

All fingerspelling loans in BSL use the beginning of the English word. We do not know of any that do not use the first letter, except perhaps AUGUST (-g-g-).

The way that the manual alphabet is used is defined by a complicated mixture of at least five factors:

(1) BSL phonology and morphology
(2) English spelling and morphology

(3) the form of the manual letters

(4) the linguistic competence of the signers

(5) the fingerspelling competence of the signers.

Phonology and morphology

BSL phonology permits only two changes in any one basic sign. These changes are usually very easy to see. It has been suggested that many BSL signs are 'disyllabic', in that they can be split up into two definite parts. For example, changes in handshape are often from closed to open (e.g. MAGIC); changes in orientation are from palm up to palm down (e.g. CONFIRM); changes in location are from one area to another (e.g. MORNING). None of these disyllabic features is seen in fingerspelling a whole word because the handshapes change for every letter.

Because of this preference for disyllabic signs in BSL, it is common for fingerspellings to be shortened, and for letters to drop out, especially the vowels. Robin Battison claimed in 1978 that the ideal number of letters in ASL fingerspelling loans was two, in keeping with this idea of a disyllabic sign, but this is not always the case. Acronyms are often three or four letters long, e.g. BBC, RNID, and BDA, and these are fingerspelled using all the letters. We can see here that the 'two part' sign rule is less important than keeping important information. In acronyms, the information contained in each letter is very important, and may even be considered a separate morpheme, so no letter can be dropped without loss of information.

The structure of BSL makes it difficult to borrow fingerspelled verbs. If we think about the three groups of verbs we identified in chapter 8, we can see why fingerspelled verbs are so rare. In almost all spatial verbs the handshape is influenced by the physical appearance of the referent involved. The handshape in a sign from the manual alphabet must be a letter handshape. This creates a clash of requirements. We also know that spatial verbs move through signing space to indicate location and movement of the referent. However, BSL signs do not move through space while the handshape is changing (except from open to closed or vice versa). If a fingerspelled verb were to move through space, the handshapes forming each of the letters would be changing while the sign moved. So fingerspelled spatial verbs cannot occur, because we cannot have both finger movement and movement through space. Lastly, English does not have many verbs that can easily be used by BSL as spatial verbs. Spatial verbs are often glossed using several English words. It would not make sense for BSL to borrow this category of verbs from English, when English does not have a readily identifiable group of these verbs itself.

Fingerspelled loans may be more available for agreement verbs because English does have similar verbs in this category, and the handshapes of these

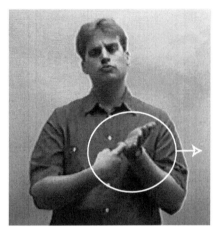 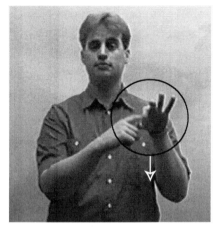

Fig. 12.9a I-RECOMMEND-TO-YOU   Fig. 12.9b QUALIFY

signs are not classifiers. However, there are still very few, probably because of the problems with movement of fingerspelling through space. Information in agreement verbs is shown by movement through signing space (e.g. I-ASK-YOU, as described in chapter 8), and we have just seen that moving fingerspelling is not easy or acceptable.

We know (from chapter 5) that full fingerspelling is not always necessary, and a signer can often use the first letter from the English word, so long as there is an accompanying spoken component. This would solve the problem of combining handshape change and movement through space. However, the very few agreement verbs in BSL that use only the first letter (e.g. RECOM-MEND, or PROPOSE) are limited in the information about subject and object that they can show. Most of them appear only to indicate agreement with first and second person singular (I-RECOMMEND-TO-YOU but not *I-RECOMMEND-TO-ALL-OF-YOU or *SHE-RECOMMENDS-TO-HIM (fig. 12.9a)). In fact, these may not be agreement verbs at all, but just verbs with an arbitrary movement that happens to be away from the signer, in contrast to downward movement, as in QUALIFY where the -q- hand-shape moves down (fig. 12.9b). They may not even be verbs, but rather the nouns RECOMMENDATION or PROPOSAL.

We also know from our consideration of oral components in BSL (in chapter 5) that verbs in BSL are frequently accompanied by adverbial BSL oral components. If this is the case, we cannot have the English spoken com-ponents that are required for a sign that uses the first letter of an English word. Once again, then, we have a clash of requirements.

Plain verbs should be free from most of these restrictions, so it would be more possible to have fingerspelled plain verbs in BSL. However, the only widely used fingerspelled plain verb is DO. The problem may be linked to the required spoken component, or perhaps BSL just does not need to borrow verbs, because there are other preferred ways of creating verbs – most noticeably by aspect and manner inflection, whereas English uses different words. For example, English has different verbs: *look, glance, stare, eye-up, glare* while BSL only alters one basic verb LOOK to give the same meanings, without using entirely different signs.

The restriction on verb loans is not the only influence that BSL has on fingerspellings. We know (from chapter 6) that English and BSL have different ways of showing grammatical information, such as plurals. In English, a plural usually has an -*s* at the end of the word. In fingerspelling, the 's' is often (but not always) left off and BSL grammar is used instead to show the plural. For example, if we were talking about the cells in the body and decided to fingerspell the word, we might use -c-e-l-l-s- but, more often, we would use -c-e-l-l- DIFFERENT DIFFERENT or -c-e-l-l- pro3D^{+++}.

English spelling and morphology

The form of the English word also affects fingerspellings. Short words are more likely to be fingerspelled than long ones. This is probably why many short function words (that is, short 'grammar words') have been borrowed into BSL through fingerspelling, e.g. IF, BUT, OR, and FOR. In many three-letter words, the articulation of the vowel can be significantly reduced in three-letter words, so that the overall effect is a disyllabic sign (e.g. -f-r- or -b-t-, instead of -f-o-r- or -b-u-t-). It is usually very rare for languages to borrow function words from each other but BSL may borrow these words from English precisely because they fit so well into the structure of BSL. In the dialect of some signers, their signs for these function words are these fingerspellings. Other signers only use the fingerspellings for emphasis, using a non-loan sign at other times, for example, BUT and -b-u-t- (emphatic). Yet other individuals use the non-loan signs for emphasis and fingerspell -b-u-t- the rest of the time. Either way, the signers are using the two forms with slightly different meanings. This slight difference in meaning is to be expected when a loan comes into a language where a word with the same meaning already exists.

If an English word is short, it is usually fingerspelled in full (even though the vowel may be reduced). If it is more than four letters long, it is usually abbreviated. This abbreviation is not random. There are definite patterns for abbreviations. The signer may retain the first syllable, for example, -j-a-n-, -f-e-b-, -a-u-g-, -s-e-p-t-, -o-c-t-; -m-o-n-, -t-u-e-, -w-e-d-; -a-b- (ABERDEEN) and -o-x- (OXFORD). These abbreviations are part of 'formal' BSL, in a way that they are not part of 'formal' English.

Where the second letter of a word is an -h-, and therefore combines with the first letter to form a single English speech sound (e.g. ch, th, ph, sh) then the first two manual letters are often retained (e.g. -c-h- for CHAPTER and CHELTENHAM, and -t-h- for THURSDAY or -r-h- for RHETORICAL).

Another way of abbreviating an English word is to retain the first and last letters, e.g. -g-w- (GLASGOW), -b-l- (BRISTOL), -s-(-o-)-n-, -m-(-a-)-y- or -t-(-a-)-x-. This process often happens when the English word is three letters long and has a central vowel. Where the vowel starts a word, all three letters are kept (e.g. -o-w-l-). Vowels are dropped more often than consonants, but the first letter is never dropped. So if the first letter is a vowel, all three letters are usually retained. The retention of first and last letters from longer words is common in place names, but not in many other words.

Another possibility is that the first letter from each syllable or (perceived) morpheme is kept, for example -m-c- (MANCHESTER), -n-c- (NEW-CASTLE), -p-j- (PROJECT).

Form of manual letters

The form of the manual letter is likely to contribute to deciding which letters to select in an abbreviation. For example, if there is a vowel or an -s- at the end of the word, then the last letter is rarely used in the abbreviation. If the letter is symmetrical in manual form (e.g. -h-, -f-, -x- or -z- , where both hands have the same handshape), it is often retained.

In words where the first letter is a vowel and the second letter is a consonant, the first two letters are often retained. This is particularly true where the first two letters are -e-x-, because there is no handshape change (e.g. *executive, Exeter, excuse,* or *example* may all lead to -e-x-).

Another way of borrowing a word from English is by using a single manual letter. Signs borrowed using a single manual letter may be of various types. Most common are signs that only use the first letter unmodified in any way. Single Manual Letter Signs (SMLS) are made using just the first letter, and are disambiguated by context and spoken component, if necessary (as we saw in chapter 5). The Australian linguist Trevor Johnston has observed that they are particularly common in certain semantic groups, e.g. days of the week, measurement of time and space, and family relations. For example, MOTHER, FATHER, DAUGHTER, UNCLE, and NEPHEW/NIECE all have signs made using the first manual letter, as do SECOND, MINUTE, WEEK, MONTH, YEAR, and CENTURY.

At first sight there appears to be a link between the number of times a letter is repeated, and the number of syllables of the English word. For example MOTHER, MEMBER, TUESDAY, BIBLE, DAUGHTER, and TOILET all have two syllables in English and in all the citation forms of these SMLS the letter is repeated, e.g. -m-m, -t-t-, -b-b-, etc. But the link is not that rigid, because there is no such strong relationship in conversational signing. Also, there can be a repetition in a SMLS derived from a monosyllabic word (e.g. -y-y- from *young*), or no repetition in a SMLS from a disyllabic word (e.g. SIX-m- from *six minutes*), and once we get to three syllables or more, the pattern is no longer present (e.g. -g-g- from *government*). It is more likely that the preference for disyllabic signs is the most important factor, creating signs with two movements, even if the handshapes remain the same.

As in previous examples, the form of the manual letter is important in relation to repetition. If the SMLS uses -h- or -j-, there is rarely a repetition, because there is already movement in these letters, e.g. JUBILEE and HARRODS may simply be signed as -j- and -h-, not -j-j- and -h-h-.

Single manual letter signs with the handshape -c- are very common, because the letter is one-handed, which makes it easy to move around the signing space. We will see later that one-handed letters make such good single manual letter signs that several non-standard one-handed manual letters are coming into use in BSL, alongside the existing standard two-handed letters. Manual letters that have only a small surface contact area between the hands when they are articulated (e.g. the vowels and -s-) are rarely used as SMLS, and, again, symmetrical letters (e.g. -f- and -h-) are more favoured over asymmetrical ones (e.g. -d- and -p-).

In some SMLS, however, an extra movement is added to the simple manual letter handshape. This movement may have some sort of meaning, or may be completely arbitrary. Among signs that have a SMLS using meaningful movement are FAMILY, which combines movement representing a group of people with the handshape of the manual letter -f- (fig. 12.10a) and GOLD, which combines the movement of GLITTER with the manual letter -g-.

Signs with an arbitrary extra meaningless movement include FEBRUARY, in which the extended fingers of the dominant hand in the -f- manual letter are rubbed back and forth along the non-dominant hand, and ENGLAND in which the manual letter -e- has a similar rubbing motion (fig. 12.10b). In FRIDAY, the fingers of the dominant hand rub the fingers of the non-dominant hand in a circular movement, but the basic hand arrangement is an -f-.

In these examples, a letter handshape acquires an extra movement. However, the reverse can also occur: a basic sign movement can have the handshape of the first letter added to form a sign, sometimes called 'initialisation'. This is very common in some sign languages that use a one-handed manual alphabet, such as ASL and Irish Sign Language. The use of one-handed manual letters allows languages to add the letter handshape to an existing sign quite easily. For example, in ASL there is a base sign GROUP,

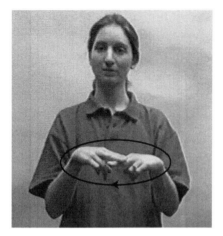

Fig. 12.10a FAMILY

Fig. 12.10b ENGLAND

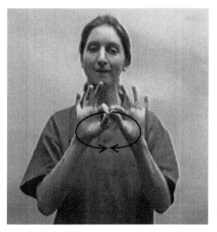

Fig. 12.11a FAMILY (ASL)

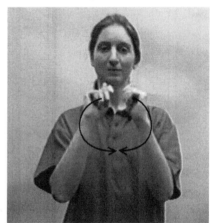

Fig. 12.11b TEAM (ASL)

but if this movement and location is articulated with the .f. manual letter handshape, the sign is glossed as FAMILY. If the handshape for the manual letter .t. is substituted, the sign becomes TEAM etc. (fig. 12.11). This sign-creation system has been in existence for over 200 years. Abbé Sicard used it in the late eighteenth century in Paris in the school for deaf children. There are large numbers of signs in both ASL and Irish Sign Language with these handshapes. Thus PEOPLE, WALK, and HAPPY in ISL have .p., .w., and .h. handshapes respectively. In ASL, PEOPLE, WINE, and INTERVIEW have .p., .w. and .i. handshapes respectively. These letter handshapes have sometimes been inaccurately described as a type of classifier handshape because they represent a 'class' of items that all start with the same English letter.

BSL does not make much use of this process because it has two-handed manual letters which are not so easily added to an existing sign, so many signers of BSL may be surprised by the extent of this use of manual letters in other sign languages.

It is much more common in BSL to sign the first letter of an English word and then add a sign that is a near synonym. The sign becomes 'disyllabic', even if it is monomorphemic. There are many examples in the established lexicon e.g. -h-LONG-AGO, -g-LAND-AREA, -c-LOOK-AFTER, -a-ADD-UP-FIGURES, -e-MONEY, and -p-UNIVERSITY (translated in English as *history, geography, crèche, accountancy, economics*, and *polytechnic*). This process is also productive when signers need to create a sign. Signers who know English well can use this strategy to great effect because they can produce the first letter of the English word, a close or related sign, and also the English mouth pattern.

Fluency of signers in BSL and English

The fluency of signers in BSL and English is very important in determining if a signer will borrow from English by fingerspelling. Signers without a good command of BSL but who know English well are more likely to fingerspell words if they do not have a ready sign for them. This is common among non-fluent signers, but not only among non-fluent signers. While signers with fluent BSL have larger sign vocabularies and are more able to use the productive lexicon, they may still use fingerspelling, if they are also fluent in English.

It may seem odd that non-fluent signers use fingerspelling more than some fluent signers, because non-fluent signers usually cannot fingerspell very well. However, the choice is often one of fingerspelling or nothing, because the non-fluent signer does not know the signs or have the skills to use productive features of BSL sign creation. BSL teachers often try to persuade their students not to fingerspell, but to think of a way to create a sign to express their intention, so that they do not come to rely on fingerspelling.

Skills in fingerspelling determine the form of fingerspelling that is produced. Younger people and people without a strong background in fingerspelling are more likely just to use a first letter (or perhaps an abbreviation), and rely on context and the spoken component. Older signers or English speakers who are very well practised in fingerspelling are more likely to fingerspell a word fully.

NON-STANDARD MANUAL LETTERS IN THE BRITISH
MANUAL ALPHABET

These are used in BSL and are linked to the English alphabet, but are not part of the standard British manual alphabet. One example is the use of different handshapes to represent the letter 'd' in upper and lower case, to mean 'Deaf' (cultural deafness) and 'deaf' (audiological deafness). This is the only use of lower case 'd' as a manual letter (fig. 12.12a).

Non-standard one-handed manual letters also exist and are used productively. They are the '8' hand for -i-, the 'O' hand for -o-, and the 'L' hand for -l-. These handshapes have several advantages over the standard letter handshapes. They can be easily distinguished from other similar manual letters and the 'O' and 'L' handshapes are highly visually motivated. Also, because they are one-handed they can easily be used in signs with movement without the loss of information that would occur if the base hand were omitted in the two-handed letter (fig. 12.12b–d).

The 'O' and 'L' handshapes appear in other manual alphabets (including ASL) and it is possible that they may be loans from other manual alphabets, but the handshapes appear in established BSL signs which are unrelated to foreign signs. Examples of signs synonymous with English words beginning with 'l' and made with a handshape which mirrors the shape of an upper-case 'l' include LIVERPOOL, LANCASTER, BROTHER-IN-LAW, LESBIAN, LASER, LAGER, LEADERSHIP, and LUCK. These might be seen as initialised signs. They are not loans from languages which use this manual alphabet handshape for 'l', but are British signs (unlike LANGUAGE which is based on the ASL .l.).

The 'O' handshape, like the non-standard one-handed 'L', allows signs to move. The hand may simply open and close to repeat the 'O' handshape or it may circle. Established signs with these letter handshapes include OCTOBER, ORPHANAGE, OXFAM, and OFFICE.

The existence of these signs is not, by itself, proof that the handshapes are being used as part of a manual alphabet. However, there is also strong evidence that the 'O' and 'L' handshapes are being used instead of the -o- and -l- of the standard manual alphabet, to make SMLS. Some *ad hoc* signs using the first letter of the English word are made in the same way. They use these handshapes as they would for other standard letters of the manual alphabet.

The 'O' handshape appears particularly productive in place names e.g. OXFORD, OKEHAMPTON, ORPINGTON, and OBAN. The 'L' handshape seems less productive but is still used for place names, as in LEWISHAM and LIVERPOOL.

Fig. 12.12a Non-standard -d-

Fig. 12.12b Non-standard -o-

Fig. 12.12c Non-standard -i-

Fig. 12.12d Non-standard -l-

Stronger evidence still for the role of these handshapes in fingerspelling is that these handshapes may also be used as representations of the letters 'o' and 'l' with other fingerspelled letters, e.g.: 'O'-a-p- for *OAP* using the 'O' handshape for 'o'; and as part of the fingerspelling of *oz* for *ounce*.

For Waterloo Station, one sign compounds WATER with the 'L' handshape (i.e. WATER 'L'), and some younger signers, in fun, may use the non-standard one-handed 'L' and 'O', to spell *loo* as a sign for *toilet*. The non-standard letters occur in the fingerspelled sign COOL, in the sense of 'laid back', creating a sign that is totally one-handed, because the standard manual letter -c- is also one-handed. The 'L' handshape also occurs following the manual letter -y- to produce YOUTH LEADER.

Another non-standard letter is the manual letter representing 'i'. In the standard manual letter, the middle finger of the non-dominant hand is touched by the index finger of the dominant hand. The non-standard form makes 'i' one-handed. It usually occurs as an initialisation, for example for the English words *image, insurance,* and *infection,* always with the accompanying spoken component. It may also be used for place names, e.g. for *Ilfracombe, Islington,* and *Ipswich.*

It may not be a coincidence that 'i' and 'o' are developing new forms. Both -i- and -o- can be easily confused in the standard British two-handed alphabet. In 1845, John Kitto, a Scotsman, described these manual alphabet vowels as being 'in every way a sore evil'. The two non-standard forms are easily distinguished. All three of the non-standard manual letter handshapes are also more easily incorporated into first-letter signs which involve some form of movement, and so lend themselves to the loan process of initialisation.

NAME SIGNS

A study of name signs illuminates many of the processes we have discussed in general terms in this and the preceding chapter. Brand names, place names, and personal names all provide many examples of borrowing and productivity from within BSL.

Brand names

Visually motivated signs are commonly used for creation of new signs for brand names. Because of product innovations, there is a continuous process of creating new signs for new brands. We have seen in chapter 10 that visually motivated signs are often based on the movement of an object, or the appearance of an object. Some signs for brand names are based on a company logo. This is also common, for car and company names (e.g. ROVER, RENAULT, PEUGEOT, MCDONALDS, and ASDA) (fig. 12.13).

Other signs are made by loan translation, such as WATER STONE for the booksellers 'Waterstones' or BOOT for the chemists' chain 'Boots'. Partial loan translation is also possible, such as the (usually jocular) sign -m- AND SPIDER for the company Marks and Spencer (*Spencer* and *spider* look very similar on the lips).

Many other examples use abbreviated fingerspelling (e.g. -s-s- for 'Sainsbury's', -w-w- for 'Woolworth's', or -p-s- for 'Panasonic').

Fig. 12.13a PEUGEOT

Fig. 12.13b MCDONALDS

Place-name signs

It is important to remember that even if a signer knows a sign for the name of a place, the name will often be fingerspelled at least once in full, if there is any doubt about the name, or if the place is being mentioned for the first time and is not local.

Some place-name signs may only be locally known, and for anyone outside the area, a different sign or fingerspelling would be used. Signs for the Bristol areas BEDMINSTER, FISHPONDS, TOTTERDOWN, and KNOWLE, for example, would only be used among Bristol signers. It would be considered bad manners to use these signs with other signers, unless there was an explanation that these were areas in Bristol.

Signs for places are often immediately followed by an index for their location. If the places are local or nearby, signers will point in the direction of the place. If the places are further away, signers will use the vertical plane of signing space as an imaginary map of the country and point to the relevant area.

The name may be based on something associated with the place. PARIS (the Eiffel tower), DERBY (the Derby Ram), SHEFFIELD (a knife, after the cutlery industry), NOTTINGHAM (a bow and arrow, after Robin Hood), and SCOTLAND (bagpipes) are examples. These signs are all visually motivated and they are all metonyms (fig. 12.14).

We have already seen that some place names are borrowed from the language of the place so that MILAN, NEW-YORK, COPENHAGEN, and MUNICH are borrowed from Italian, American, Danish, and German sign languages respectively, even if there are also well-known, commonly used BSL signs (as, for example, there is for New York).

Fig. 12.14a PARIS   Fig. 12.14b DERBY

The signs may be based on a loan translation of the English place name, via an English word. One of the signs for Turkey, as well as the signs for Newcastle (NEW CASTLE) and Swansea (SWAN SEA) are all examples of exact loan translations. The names may also be partial loan translations, based either on the written word, or on an approximation of the spoken component. Examples of signs based on the spoken component include one of the signs for Bristol (PISTOL or PETROL) and one of the signs for Preston (PRIEST). Other partial loan translations include Worthing (WORTH), Washington (WASH), Manchester (MAN CHEST), and Axminster (AXE).

The place name may also be fingerspelled, or at least use fingerspelling for some part. Sometimes half of the word has a manual letter and half has a sign. Shebfield can be signed -s-FIELD, Montrose can be -m-ROSE, and Holberrow can be -h-BARROW. New York and New Zealand combine the sign NEW with a fingerspelled letter in NEW-y- and NEW-z-. The important point is that if part of the name can easily be translated into a sign (like NEW, FIELD, ROSE, and BARROW) then it will be, and if it cannot (like 'Sheb', 'Hol', and 'Zealand') then a manual letter will be used.

Personal name signs

Although there has not been any published research on personal name signs in BSL, there has been a good deal of research into ASL personal name signs, as well as research on some other sign languages including Chinese Sign Language, Swedish Sign Language, and Quebec Sign Language. We can propose some rules for BSL personal name signs, drawing on this research and on everyday experience of BSL.

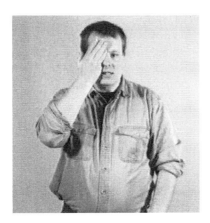

Fig. 12.15 ADMIRAL-NELSON

Personal name signs fall into several categories in sign languages. BSL does not use all of these, but it is interesting to see what processes are available to sign languages in general.

In the past, children in deaf schools did not have personal name signs, but were given numbers (e.g. George Scott, a well-known British Deaf story-teller, was known at school as DB5). This practice has died out now but when older deaf people meet at school reunions, they often know each other by numbers.

A much more common source of personal name signs today is descriptive signs. These may or may not be visually motivated, but they are all metonymic because they use some single descriptive feature associated with a person as a name for the whole person. The descriptive signs have three different sources: a physical characteristic; a character trait of the person; or something identifiable about the person's life.

Physical characteristics include a reference to someone's eyes, the style of someone's hair, or a particular 'distinguishing feature' such as tattoos. Personal name signs based on these characteristics are very common for historical figures, because we often only have a picture of them. Examples include EYE-PATCH for Admiral Nelson (fig. 12.15), and TOOTH-BRUSH-MOUSTACHE for both Charlie Chaplin and Adolf Hitler. Among friends, personal name signs such as LONG-CURLY-HAIR or GOATEE-BEARD or TALL may be used.

Character traits may lead to a personal name sign based on a person's habits. Another sign for Charlie Chaplin represents swinging a cane. One sign for Stan Laurel (of Laurel and Hardy) is made by scratching the head. Among friends or colleagues, an office administrator who is always checking everything may receive the personal name sign CHECK. Another person who is very quiet and withdrawn may be named QUIET.

A name sign may also be based upon personal information. For example if the person comes from another country, but is staying in Britain for a while, they may be given the name of their home country, e.g. BRAZIL, FINLAND, or AUSTRALIA. If they have a special job or hobby, this may be the basis for a name sign.

Sometimes these descriptive signs are not flattering (particularly name signs that are given at school). Adults can reject their name sign if they want to, as we will see in our discussion of uses of names in BSL.

An alternative to basing personal name signs on physical characteristics and personal information is to base them on loan translations from the person's spoken language name. They may be based on an exact one-to-one correspondence of either a first name or surname, e.g. someone called Hope or surnames like Taylor, Driver, or Bird. Alternatively, they may come from a partial, approximate translation of either the written form or spoken component in English, e.g. Gloria may become GLORY, Clive may be named c-LIVE, and Jerry may be named CHERRY.

Personal name signs made using the manual alphabet are common in many sign languages, although this may vary according to the form of the manual alphabet in the different languages. In languages using the one-handed manual alphabet, such as ASL, it is very common to create name signs using the letter handshape of the initial letter of the first name, and then to add a movement or location.

An American researcher, Sam Supalla, has explained that in American Deaf families, all the name signs of the family members are made at the same location and only differ in the letter handshape. The movement may be arbitrary, too. For example the personal name sign of a Frenchman called Bébian (who lived in the late eighteenth and early nineteenth centuries) is a .b. moving downwards.

Many people's personal name signs are just their initials (e.g. -j-d-, or -s-r-), or even the initials of their first name, especially if the letter is either -h- or -j- (e.g. Hilary or Julie could simply be -h- or -j-). These are often used as personal name signs for people who are new to, or peripheral to, the sign language community and who have not yet been given a unique name sign. Short names may just be fingerspelled, e.g. Ann or Bob, since as we have already seen, BSL can readily accept three-letter loans from the manual alphabet into the language.

In BSL, personal names formed by descriptive signs or loan translations are more common than those using the manual alphabet. In some other sign languages, it is much more common to form personal name signs by using an initialised sign with movement.

Finally, it is possible for a person to inherit the name sign of a famous relation or namesake. If a man's father was well known in the community, the son may be given his father's personal name sign. If the person shares a name with someone famous, he may be given that person's name. For example, if someone's name is Churchill, he may be given Winston Churchill's personal name sign (based upon either his cigar, or his 'V for Victory' gesture).

Differences in use of names in signed and spoken languages

Personal names are not used in the same way in BSL and English. There are different social and linguistic rules in British Deaf culture and British hearing culture.

In BSL, personal name signs are not used to address a person, but only to refer to them. In English, in comparison, it becomes very awkward if we cannot address a person by name. Names in English are often used for getting someone's attention, whereas in the Deaf community we get a person's attention in other ways: by waving at the person, or with some other culturally approved action such as tapping their shoulder.

Personal name signs are not essential, because it is possible to use a person's English name; and so not everyone has one. Many deaf people from hearing families who do not mix much with other deaf people do not have personal name signs. Very few hearing people who are not involved in the Deaf community have them (except for some famous people, including politicians and historical figures).

Personal name signs can also change several times during a deaf person's life. If a deaf person dislikes their personal name sign from school, they may elect to change it. If the sign becomes less appropriate because of a change in appearance or interests, a new personal name sign may emerge. In contrast, most people keep their English given name all their lives, even if women may change their surname on marrying. Hearing people may change their names by deed poll, but it is quite unusual.

Personal name signs are not used in all situations. In some social situations, a person's English name is used. Sometimes this is because a conversational partner may know only the English name, and not the personal name sign. In other cases, the English name is more formal, for example if the person's title is needed, like 'Rev. F. W. Gilby' or 'Miss J. Smith'. BSL name signs do not vary according to status or formality. There is no parallel with English titles such as *Mr, Mrs, Dr,* or *Professor.*

Surnames are not as important to the British Deaf community as they are to hearing British people. Some people joke that it is a sign of real intimacy to be on surname terms with someone in the Deaf community. It is possible to know someone's English first name and their personal name sign, and not learn their surname for many years, if at all.

According to Sam Supalla, when a person is first introduced in the American Deaf community, their English name is fingerspelled, and then their personal name sign is given, if they have one. If they have not got one, their initials are used, until a name sign emerges. This differs from Britain. Often there is no introduction by name, but a brief background description is given for context (e.g. 'a friend from work', or 'Emma's mother'). Later, in their absence, they may be referred to as 'you know, the one from Liverpool', or 'with bright red lipstick', and so on. Only later, if the person remained in contact with the Deaf community, would an English name be provided.

SUMMARY

In this chapter we have seen that BSL can borrow from other languages. It can borrow signs from other sign languages or from English. Borrowing from English may be done either through a process of loan translation, or by fingerspelling. By looking at signs for brand names, place names and personal names we have seen examples of all the processes described. We have also seen that personal names are used differently in BSL and English.

EXERCISES FOR CHAPTER 12

1. Manual letters
   (a) List the signs that you know for family relations (e.g. Mother, Father). How many signs use a manual letter?
   (b) List the signs that you know for measurements of distance or time (e.g. yards or metres, and seconds or years). How many signs use a manual letter?
   (c) List the signs that you know for the days of the week and months of the year. How many signs use a manual letter?

2. Place names and personal names
   (a) Find out the place-name signs for your own home town or places where you have lived or recently visited, if you do not already know them. Put each one into the following categories: manual alphabet, metonymy and synecdoche, loan translation, or a mixture. Are these groups enough? Might you need another group?
   (b) If you attend a sign language class, put the personal name signs of students in your class into the following categories: physical characteristics, personality traits, features of a person's life, loan translations, manual alphabet, inheritance, or a mixture. Are these groups enough? Might you need another group?

3. Shortened fingerspelling
   (a) List some examples of shortened fingerspellings in BSL. Think of three that are only two letters long (e.g. TAX t-x), and three that are more than two letters long (e.g. BIRMINGHAM b-h-m).
   (b) List examples where you might use -c-h- to refer to something beginning with 'ch' in English. Do you think it would be possible to use just the -c- for any of your examples?
   (c) List examples where you might use -t-h- to refer to something beginning with 'th' in English. Do you think it would be possible to use just the -t- for any of your examples ?
   (d) List at least six signs where the corresponding English word begins with the letter 'c', and the sign uses the manual letter -c- handshape. Try to identify signs that are not made simply from the letter but have an extra movement added or are made at a new location. For example, COLLEGE is sometimes signed with a -c- handshape at the side of the head.

4. Collect examples of the uses of the non-standard letters 'O', 'L', and 'I' If you have not seen any instances yourself, ask another signer if they have seen some of the examples given in our discussion, and if they know of any others.

5. Watch a video clip of a fluent BSL signer.
   (a) Identify all examples of fingerspelling.
   (b) Try to work out what has been fingerspelled, without slowing down the video. (If you cannot do this easily, try various strategies to help you, e.g. spoken components, context of signs, identifying groups of letters you can catch, etc.)
   (c) What sort of words are fingerspelled (e.g. proper nouns, 'grammatical' words like 'if' or 'so', verbs)?
   (d) Does the signer only fingerspell the word, or is there an accompanying sign too? (If there is an accompanying sign, is there extra information added in the sign?)
   (e) Pick two longer fingerspellings (more than six letters). Does the signer fingerspell every letter fully? (You will probably need to slow the video to see this.)
   (f) Note any signs made using only one manual letter. (Are they accompanied by a spoken component?)

FURTHER READING FOR CHAPTER 12

Carmel, S. 1981, *International hand alphabet charts* (2nd edition), Rockville, MD: Carmel.

Lucas, C., and Valli, C. 1992, (eds.), *Language contact in the American Deaf community*, London: Academic Press.

Sutton-Spence, R., and Woll, B. 1993, 'The status and functional role of fingerspelling in BSL', in M. Marschark and D. Clark (eds.), *Psychological perspectives on deafness*, Hillsdale, NJ: Lawrence Erlbaum Associates, 185–208.

Yau, S., and He, J. 1990, 'How do deaf children get their name signs during their first month in school?', in W. Edmondson and F. Karlsson (eds.), *SLR '87: Papers from the fourth international symposium on sign language research*, Hamburg: Signum Press, 243–54.

Chapter thirteen

Socially unacceptable signs

This chapter will address the different types of socially unacceptable language, why these are used and how. It will not deal with 'rude' or 'coarse' signs, except where it is necessary to give examples of particular linguistic points. Readers interested in taboo signs are referred to Martin Colville's *Signs of a Sexual Nature*, which is still the best source text for this area of BSL linguistics.

Coarse language is an important part of many languages, but it is traditionally not studied by many linguists. To a certain extent, this is because not much coarse language is written down. Also, many people see coarse language as something to use only with their friends, so they will not use it in front of a researcher.

This is particularly true of BSL. Many deaf people are reticent about using rude or coarse language in front of hearing people or any linguist doing research in the language. Some of this feeling may be related to the tradition that the only hearing people in contact with the Deaf community were missioners. Some 'socially unacceptable' signs are included in the *BSL/English Dictionary*. The makers of the dictionary had a responsibility to include these signs, although they also had a responsibility to note that these signs were unacceptable to many people. When the dictionary first came out, some people expressed disquiet because it contained a sign glossed as ˣJEW that many people found offensive. The dictionary-makers defended themselves by saying that they had included a note to indicate that the sign was offensive, but that it was used by some deaf people. From a linguistic point of view this is necessary, because linguists have a duty to describe language as it is used, not as some people might wish it was used. In this chapter, signs which are socially unacceptable in some contexts are preceded by an ˣ, rather than the * which indicates that something is ungrammatical.

Not all cultures use the same amount of coarse language. For example, the Japanese are said not to swear much. The English, on the other hand, are known for using coarse language and as long ago as 1821, it was said that 'The

Fig. 13.1 ^XDISABLED (socially
unacceptable sign)

English ... are rather a foul-mouthed nation.' We might not be surprised if
BSL also had plenty of swearing because British deaf people share so many
aspects of mainstream British culture. However, it is also possible that the cultural differences between hearing and deaf extend as far as swearing, so that
signers and English speakers may use coarse language differently.

Different sections of the community are likely to use different amounts of
socially unacceptable language. For example, it is commonly said that men
swear more than women do, in both the deaf and hearing communities. It is
widely believed in the Deaf community that deaf men swear more, particularly members of football teams.

Older people are also widely believed not to use as much socially unacceptable language as younger people. However, this distinction is not as clear as
we might think. Older people may not blaspheme as much as younger people,
or use 'strong' swear words, yet younger people may see older people's language as full of 'bad' signs, such as 'politically incorrect' signs (which we will
discuss in more depth later). Old-fashioned signs like ^XDISABLED,
^XJEWISH, or ^XCHINESE maybe seen as insulting and unacceptable to
younger people, but older people use them and may not consider them to be
offensive. This demonstrates that the distinction between old and young
signers is not as simple as we might first think (fig. 13.1).

Within any community there are always people who choose not to use
swearing or bad language. People with strong religious beliefs, for example,
often take great care not to use language that they believe to be unacceptable.
This usually involves avoiding sexual swear words, or words that insult God
in any way. (It should be noted, though, that these people can still insult others

if they need to without swear words. For example, many Arabs hold strong religious beliefs, and would not use blasphemy, and yet the linguist David Crystal has said that some Arabs are highly skilled at insulting people, even making insults into an art-form.) In the British Deaf community as well as the British hearing community, people with strong religious beliefs use less 'bad language'.

There are many examples of language that can be termed 'rude', 'coarse', or 'unacceptable', but 'socially unacceptable' language falls into a number of specific categories. We will consider three areas: taboo signs linked to taboo topics, insults, and expletives. For each of these, we can describe what forms a signer may use and why.

TABOO TOPICS AND SIGNS

Taboo topics and taboo words or signs are those which should not be talked about because they are socially unacceptable. In some cultures, their mention is believed to bring bad luck; in British culture today they are more likely to cause hurt, discomfort, embarrassment, or offence.

Taboo topics are topics that might make someone angry, upset, or embarrassed if they were discussed. In many cultures, taboo topics include sex and death or anything linked with the toilet, but each culture has its own taboos. For example, in the Deaf community we might not want to bring up a discussion of BSL and SSE because people might easily end up getting hurt or angry. In some deaf clubs, discussion of sexual matters is not acceptable. For years, topics like women's health and child abuse were not discussed by British people at all, but even when hearing people began to discuss them, they were not mentioned by members of the Deaf community.

Colville's *Signs Of A Sexual Nature* deals with signs from the taboo area of sex. These signs are not necessarily rude, but they are signs that most people would not use in public because they would not discuss the topic in public.

Taboo signs are signs that are not socially acceptable even when the topic is socially acceptable. Many signers find these signs shocking or offensive. They may be used at any time, not only when discussing taboo topics.

Taboo words or signs have a traditional meaning that gives them social impact. Other words can be much more insulting, if their meaning is taken literally, but not have the same swearing force. The linguist Geoffrey Hughes has pointed out that calling someone *thief* is a serious accusation, but it is not a swear-word insult like [X]*bastard*. This idea of force behind a word or sign is important in relation to politically correct language.

Taboo words and signs can lose their original, literal meaning. For example, if we call someone a [X]*wanker*, we mean that we despise them as being childish and annoying. We are not normally referring to other activities. In some cases a word loses its original meaning altogether, so that many people do not see a ^X*bastard* as meaning anything except a hard-hearted or traitorous person. They do not use the word to mean someone whose parents were not married (or at least use this meaning only rarely).

Although deaf people have grown up within the hearing community, the two cultures are not the same and there are 'swear signs' in BSL that are not equivalent to their translations in English. BSL has borrowed ^XBASTARD and ^XBITCH from English with only the taboo meaning of insults and not with the original meanings at all.

In BSL swear signs do not seem to have the same grammatical flexibility as some English swear words. For example ^XF—- can only be used as an expletive in BSL, not as a verb or an adjective. We cannot sign ^{X*}F—-YOU or ^{X*}MY F—-ING CAR BEEN STEAL using this sign. There are other ways of signing the same meaning, but not by using the same sign.

It is possible to talk about things that might be shocking or unacceptable by using signs that society considers more acceptable. When someone refers to something taboo, using words or signs that are not taboo, they use 'euphemisms'. We will discuss this later.

INSULTS

These are taunts to someone whom the speaker or signer despises. Most people have someone whom they despise, and for whom they have insults.

Insults are based on a person's difference from the person making the insult. Insults may be for reasons of almost anything that is different: race, nationality, sex, religion, sexuality, coming from another part of the country, going to a different school, playing for an opposing sports team, supporting an opposing sports team, driving a different car, not driving a car at all, being of a different age, being very rich, being poor, being physically different, having different political beliefs, having views that are too liberal or having views that are too narrow. The list is almost endless.

The aim of an insult is for the person doing the insulting to feel superior, by telling the insulted person very clearly that they are inferior, often by calling them insulting names.

The signer may have the aim of insulting and hurting someone, but sometimes insults happen by mistake. The signer does not mean to insult someone, but the person takes it as an insult. This is obviously unfortunate, and 'politically correct' language has developed in part to avoid this sort of accidental insult.

For an insult to occur, the other person has to feel insulted. If they do not feel insulted then the insult has not really happened. Sometimes the other person does not realise they have been insulted. If an American is called ^X*ginger* by someone from Britain, it would not be offensive, but it might be confusing, because in American English ^X*ginger* only refers to hair colour, while in British English it is an insulting term for a homosexual man.

BSL INSULTS

Many of these develop in schools, and deaf adults see them as something childish that one grows out of. One insult used by some children for pupils at the Mary Hare Grammar School refers to armpit hair (a pun on *hair/hare*). It would seem (from limited research) that BSL has fewer specific signs for insults than English.

It still possible to insult someone, of course, but not by using signs which only have that function. Insults include ^XWANKER, ^XBIG-HEAD, ^XTHICKO, ^XORAL-SIGNER, and ^XRUBBISH (flicking the middle finger away from the thumb in a dismissive movement). It has been said that the Deaf community is more direct than the English-speaking community, and reference to physical features is less insulting than in English. This is not wholly true, and calling someone '^Xfatty' or '^Xbean-pole' can be just as hurtful in BSL as in English. The confusion may arise because many socially acceptable BSL signs appear to have a meaning that, when translated into English, would be insulting. This may be because the non-manual features in BSL are very important in determining whether or not a sign is an insult. English and BSL both distinguish between describing someone as 'heavy-set' and calling them '^Xfatty', or saying that they wear heavy glasses and calling them '^Xfour-eyes' but the difference in BSL is not expressed manually, but rather on the face. This is also true for racial taunts, for example the difference between BLACK or CHINESE and their socially unacceptable forms also lies in the facial expression, not the hands (fig. 13.2). We can insult someone in BSL by using an aggressively contemptuous look coupled with YOU.

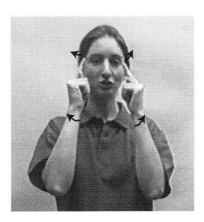

Fig. 13.2 CHINESE

EXPLETIVES

Expletives have the function of allowing people to let their emotions out in times of anger, disappointment, or pain, even when they are alone, just so that they feel better. As well as being used to shock or offend, they are often used in British culture as a sign of a bond with a certain group of people. The function of shocking other people may be quite secondary.

Expletives do not have to be swear words. They can be anything that allows the signer to let their feelings out. They may be signs that are considered very rude, but they could also be very mild signs (one signer reports his mother signing CUSTARD when in situations of great stress). People who do not approve of 'swearing' or 'rude language' still have signs that they use when in pain, anger or frustration.

Some signs are used for expletives in BSL. Several expletives may be found in Colville's book, because signs from this taboo area are frequently used as expletives. Different signs have different levels of impact, so that some may be mild expletives, and some stronger. It is possible to construct a continuum of expletives in BSL, going from mild and acceptable to strong and unacceptable. A series could be SHAME, DRAT (the little finger extended from the fist, moved away from the mouth, with the accompanying mouth pattern 'fzzz'), ?XDAMN, XF—. In each of these, the facial expression can make the sign much stronger. The size of each sign, the tension within it, and the speed of its articulation all serve to alter the strength of the intended impact (fig. 13.3).

One source of possible misunderstanding between signers and non-signers is in the subtle differences between many of these signs. For this reason, interpreters in particular need to be aware of the subtle uses of expletives in both languages. They need to select an English word with the same strength of impact as the BSL sign, and use a similarly appropriate sign in BSL to match an English word.

EUPHEMISMS

Euphemisms are ways of saying something gently in order to decrease the force of something that might be offensive, hurtful, or frightening. Where we find taboo areas, we always find euphemisms, too. BSL euphemisms show some important general characteristics. Compared to taboo signs, euphemisms are much less visually explicit. This may be achieved by replacing a sign with a sign which is not visually motivated, or by changing the location of a sign. The movement of euphemistic signs is usually smaller and less pronounced than taboo signs, and the facial expression is far more 'neutral' or restrained.

Fig. 13.3a SHAME

Fig. 13.3b DRAT

Fig. 13.3c $^{?X}$DAMN

Fig. 13.3d ^{X}F---

Taboo words and signs used when discussing taboo topics are often 'disguised' so that they are more socially acceptable. The less acceptable the word or sign, the more disguises there are. In English, one way of making euphemisms is to use the Latin or French equivalent, instead of the English word, because Latin and French are seen to be high-status languages. The basic meaning is the same, but the force of the taboo is greatly decreased. For example, in English we may use *urinate* instead of ^{X}*piss*, or *conjugal relations* instead of ^{X}*f—-ing*.

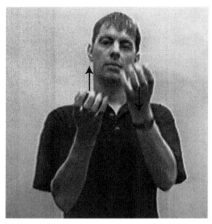

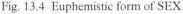

Fig. 13.4 Euphemistic form of SEX   Fig. 13.5 Euphemistic form of
                                           TESTICLES

In BSL, this same reliance on another language is seen when signers use signs based on English to create euphemisms. For example, there are some visually motivated signs that are glossed as [X]SEX that are seen as rather vulgar, and many older people will not use them in public, but fingerspelling -s-e-x- or using a sign based on -s-x- is more acceptable (fig. 13.4). The same is true of 'toilet' which has the neutral sign -t-t-. A recent sign meaning 'disabled' uses -d-, with an added movement. In America the sign meaning 'gay' that is most acceptable to everyone, and least offensive, is one based on fingerspelling.

There are other times, though, when the English term would be inappropriate. For example, using -o-a-p- to a pensioner is considered unacceptable in BSL, and PENSIONER or OVER SIXTY would be more acceptable.

Most euphemisms in BSL have reduced visual motivation. For example, there are euphemistic signs referring to 'menstruation' that may be glossed as TIME (or WHEN), or several other forms, including -p-p- that are not visually motivated. The arbitrary relationship between fingerspellings and their meaning may be another reason why they are used for euphemisms.

Euphemistic signs are also made by changing the location of a visually motivated sign. Some signs can be potentially offensive because of their visual motivation. However, they are made more acceptable by moving the sign into the space in front of the signer e.g. TESTICLES (fig. 13.5). Alternatively an imaginary 'mannequin' can be constructed in the space in front of the signer, with anatomical parts placed on the mannequin.

Euphemisms are often used when a taboo topic, such as abortion, comes up. It is possible to mention this taboo topic by referring to it very vaguely, saying something like 'Do you want to do anything about it?', or 'go to a doctor'. These would be euphemisms. We can also use different signs for ABORTION that are more or less euphemistic. The dominant hand may move from the 'B' hand location (neutral force) or the dominant hand can move from the abdomen (less euphemistic) or the sign can be made deliberately shocking (called a 'dysphemism'), by a representation of stabbing the abdomen. The facial expression accompanying these signs is also important. A neutral facial expression is more euphemistic than one of disapproval or disgust.

If a signer needed to talk about 'women's problems' (a euphemism in itself) it would be possible to sign DOWN-THERE, using a curved 'B' hand, or fingerspell. Again, the accompanying facial expression is important.

POLITICALLY CORRECT SIGNS

Politically correct signs are those that have been changed especially because it is feared that the sign will offend someone. In other words, the person signing is afraid that they may cause an insult without meaning to.

Some signs may be seen as offensive to people from different countries, members of different religions, people of different races (or skin colour), and also to people with disabilities. Politically correct signs are used to avoid this offence.

'Political' signs

There is another area of signs that are also influenced by 'politics', but which is slightly different. This is not concerned with the dangers of offending someone by mistake, but with signs that are considered unacceptable because of Deaf politics and Deaf pride. Deaf politics often involves the rejection of signs that are seen to be 'hearing/social worker' signs. Examples include HEARING (with an 'Å' handshape), PEOPLE (compound of MAN-WOMAN), and signs that are borrowed from English (e.g. ABOUT (from a-b-t)). There are also signs that are seen as being imposed by interpreters. Examples of these include the signs TORY, LABOUR, and LIBERAL-DEMOCRAT. The signs in widespread use have been joined by signs representing the Tory torch, the Labour rose, and the Liberal Democrat bird. The former group are perfectly acceptable linguistically, but some members of the Deaf community reject them because they are seen as 'hearing inventions'.

'PC' signs

Although 'Politics' is an issue in the signs described above, this is not what is meant by 'politically correct signs'. A politically correct sign is a sort of euphemism for something that is feared could be offensive.

PC signs come about for two reasons. Either the person referred to by the sign is offended by it (e.g. a Chinese person objects to being referred to by a sign emphasising the shape of their eyes, or a woman objects to being called a *bird*), or the user of the sign thinks that the person referred to by the sign will object to the sign.

'Inaccurate' signs

Some signs in BSL have been called politically incorrect (PI) because they are 'inaccurate' or are inappropriately visually motivated. This does not really count as PI. For example, it has been said that since Russia is no longer a Communist state, the sign for Russia using a clenched fist is inaccurate; and since not all Asians have a red spot on their forehead, a metonymic sign ASIA using that is inaccurate. This does not necessarily mean that these signs are offensive, however.

Inaccuracy in visual motivation might be a good reason for changing a sign. However, the meaning behind words changes all the time, and the word remains because everyone is used to it. For example, nurses do not wear red crosses on their sleeves any more but we still use a cross on the upper arm in the sign HOSPITAL; jeans are not made in Genoa any more, but English still uses the word *jeans*.

It is becoming common practice to use the country name signs that nationals of that country use. So, for example, more BSL signers are using the Russian sign RUSSIA, the Japanese sign JAPAN, the Belgian sign BELGIUM, and so on. This may be seen as less a PC response than simply a major borrowing process.

Inaccuracy, however, may be one reason for a sign to be seen as unacceptable if it leaves some people feeling excluded. For example, the objection of some Jewish signers to several signs glossed as JEWISH is that they all refer to features associated with men (the beards, the side-curls, or the skull-caps) so that women feel excluded. A sign based on the shape of a menorah (a many-stemmed candlestick) is seen as more inclusive and so more acceptable by some people (fig. 13.6).

The sign glossed as INDIA that refers to the red dot on the forehead is also seen as unacceptable by some because it excludes those for whom this is not part of their culture. Muslims with connections to India may see this as excluding them, for example. A sign outlining the shape of the sub-continent

Fig. 13.6a JEWISH (referring to a beard) Fig. 13.6b JEWISH (referring to a menorah)

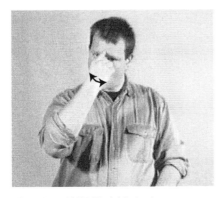

Fig. 13.7a INDIA (old sign)   Fig. 13.7b INDIA (new sign)

is preferred by some, to avoid this exclusion (fig. 13.7). A sign also glossed as ASIAN made on the back of the hand is used by more people now to refer to people from the Indian sub-continent.

Visually motivated signs and PC signs

Signs for races and countries (and other minority groups) that are based on physical features are a sensitive area. Part of the force of insults (as we have seen) is in their intention and their history. In English, to call someone [X]*slitty-eyed* or [X]*a yeller feller* is an insult, mainly because it has been used as an insult in the past.

In BSL there is not the same tradition of this sort of insult, and there is a much greater linguistic tradition of synecdoche, so it could well be argued that no insult is intended. Of course, it is perfectly possible to use visually motivated signs that are insulting, and to fully intend to insult the person by using the sign.

However, it is possible that, despite the lack of intent, disabled, gay, Chinese, Jewish, or Asian people (for example) are offended by some signs. If they are, then it makes sense to explain the basis for the sign, and if they still do not like it, to ask what sign they would prefer. For example, many gay people have made it clear that they do not like the sign GAY that uses the flick of the wrist, and ask people to use another sign. However, not all people in one group have the same opinions about a sign.

An older sign CHINESE refers to the characteristic eye shape of Chinese people. In reaction to some beliefs that this may be seen as insulting, a new sign tracing the shape of the buttons on a Chinese workers' tunic began to spread. Interestingly, however, in a recent discussion with a group of Chinese deaf visitors to Britain, they declared they had no objections to being referred to by the shape of their eyes, and mentioned that their sign for Europeans referred to the round eyes of most Europeans.

Some people have objected to signs in BSL that would be offensive if they were used in English by English speakers. These people have then suggested alternative signs. It is this, in particular, that many deaf people have objected to, because they see it as linguistic imperialism, where English speakers tell signers what their language should be like. Despite the rejection of PC signs imposed by English speakers, some signs in sensitive areas are changing in BSL, as more deaf people become aware of the implications of sign choice, and more minority groups have more control over signs used to refer to them.

SUMMARY

This chapter has covered the sensitive area of socially unacceptable signs. Not all members of a community have the same idea about what is acceptable and what is shocking, or unacceptable. We have discussed the central topics of taboo signs, including insults and expletives, and also considered euphemisms. In each case, we have seen that BSL uses signs to fulfil these functions, just as English does, but in its own way, most particularly by reducing the visual force of the sign in euphemisms. We then considered politically correct language in BSL and changes currently taking place.

EXERCISES FOR CHAPTER 13

1. List some insults that you know in English or BSL (or any other language). What is particularly insulting about these words? What 'difference' is being emphasised by using this insult?

2. List signs that are taboo, or used in taboo situations. If you are not a fluent BSL user, you may find it useful to look at Colville's *Signs of a Sexual Nature*, to find some signs. (Note, though, that there are many taboo signs that are unrelated to sex, and many taboo topics apart from sex.)

    (a) Find five examples of taboo or socially unacceptable signs that are strongly visually motivated.

    (b) Find five examples of euphemistic signs.

    (c) Of the euphemistic signs you find, which are euphemisms borrowed from English, and which are not borrowed?

    (d) Decide if the taboo signs you listed above are taboo only because they refer to a taboo topic, or if they are used as insults or expletives.

    (e) Are there some signs which are only used in some contexts (e.g. medical, educational, to younger people, to older people, telling dirty stories late at night after a lot to drink, etc.)?

3. List five different topics of conversation that might require sign euphemisms (excluding sex or names of body parts).

    (a) Explain why these might use taboo signs.

    (b) For each of those five topics, give five euphemistic signs.

    (c) For each of the signs you have thought of, say why that euphemistic sign is used, explaining how it manages to avoid offence.

4. Find some signs which have basically the same meaning, but have different forms which may be more or less socially acceptable? (Think how facial expression, size of the sign, and location of the sign might vary.)

5. Collect different signs in BSL used to mean Chinese, Indian, Jewish, homosexual, disabled, etc

    (a) Some of these signs might be considered socially unacceptable. By whom? Why?

    (b) How do the more acceptable signs differ from the less acceptable signs?

FURTHER READING FOR CHAPTER 13

Colville, M. 1985, *Signs of a sexual nature*, Northwich: Cheshire Society for the Deaf.
Hughes, G. 1991, *Swearing: a social history of foul language, oaths and profanity in English*, Oxford: Basil Blackwell.

Chapter fourteen

Extended use of language in BSL

For much of the time, language is simply a vehicle for transmitting the thoughts of one person to another. There are times, however, when the language itself, rather than its message, becomes the focus of attention. This is particularly true when the language is used for poetry or jokes. In both these cases, the language user pays particular attention to the form of the language chosen. This final chapter will be concerned with the use of BSL in poetry, humour, and story-telling.

LINGUISTIC FEATURES OF BSL POETRY

Poems are a special part of many languages. One feature of poems is that they often carry a considerable amount of meaning in very few words. However, one of the most important features of a poem is that the language that is used is just as important as (or even more important than) the message in the poem.

There has been little published research on sign language poetry, and the few available linguistic descriptions are of ASL poems. However, the linguistic features seen in BSL poems are sufficiently similar to ASL for us to use the commentary upon ASL poems for consideration of BSL poetry.

The American researchers Edward Klima and Ursula Bellugi carried out an in-depth analysis of ASL and BSL haiku poems (short Japanese poems with a very strict syllable structure) in the 1970s. In this analysis, they found evidence of signing that could be compared to rhyme, assonance ('weak' rhyming) and alliteration (in which words begin with the same letter). Those readers with a particular interest in sign poetry are recommended to look at this analysis in Klima and Bellugi's book *The Signs of Language*. More recently, Alec Ormsby has described several structural features of sign language poetry in an analysis of a poem by a leading ASL poet, Clayton Valli.

Story-telling has always been an important part of British Deaf culture, but poetry has been less significant. However, there is now a growing movement in the British Deaf community for the creation of BSL poetry. Translation of English songs and poems into BSL is another art form, but here we will focus only upon 'pure' BSL poetry. Unarguably, the most important BSL poet of this century was Dot Miles and we will use her work as illustration of our analysis of BSL poetry.

Poetry in sign language exists only in live performance or on video, in the absence of a writing system. The following discussion therefore is based on video recordings of Dot Miles's performances of her own poems.

The first, most immediately noticeable, feature of sign poems is that signs with similar phonological features are used. This occurrence of phonologically similar signs is much higher than would be expected in everyday use of signing. The signs in the poems may use the same, or similar, handshapes, locations, or movement paths.

In Dot Miles's poem 'The Staircase – An Allegory' there is repeated use of the closed fist, seen in the signs DRAW-SWORD, HEAD-ROLL, and, by altering the sign, GIANT (fig. 14.1). GIANT is usually made with a 'B' hand, but here the fist is used to create a link with the other signs. There are also a series of signs made with the '5' handshape as she signs LION, MANE, and CLAW. In another poem 'Evening', the 'V' handshape used in EVENING is echoed in the sign BLIND. In the poem 'Christmas Magic', part of the trilogy 'Christmas', there is repeated occurrence of the '5' handshape, with a fluttering movement of the fingers – evocative of the sparkling feeling of Christmas. This handshape is seen repeatedly in SHIVER-DOWN-ARM, MAGIC-FLOWING, EMBERS-DYING, and FEEL-ALONG-CHRIST-MAS-STOCKING (fig. 14.2).

The examples above also show repeated movement paths, which is a device also seen in many of Dot Miles's poems. In 'Christmas Magic', there is a repeated downward sloping movement of many signs, such as SHIVER-DOWN-ARM, SANTA'S-SLEIGH-FLIES-DOWN, RUN-DOWN-STAIRS, and FEEL-ALONG-CHRISTMAS-STOCKING. In 'Afternoon', there is a repeated set of movements, in three different locations, with three different handshapes, as first the narrator, then her dog, and finally a sparrow, all eat and sit back replete. In 'Morning' the same external movements of similar handshapes in similar locations are used to show how rain and wind both slowly die down.

There may also be a repeated pattern of non-manual features, such as repeated head movements, direction of eye gaze, facial expression or mouth pattern. In 'The Staircase' the signer repeatedly looks left and right for several signs, and then looks up and down during several more signs. This repetition of these phonological features may be considered as a parallel to such features as rhyme, alliteration, and assonance in spoken or written poetry.

Fig. 14.1a GIANT

Fig. 14.1b DRAW-SWORD

Fig. 14.1c HEAD-ROLL

Fig. 14.2a MAGIC-FLOWING

Fig. 14.2b EMBERS-DYING

Fig. 14.2c FEEL-ALONG-CHRISTMAS-STOCKING

As well as the repetition and pattern of phonemic features, there is also a greater balance in the use of the two hands. In normal signing, as we have seen before, one hand dominates. In poetry, the non-dominant hand is used considerably more, to produce greater symmetry. In 'The Staircase', the left hand and right hand are balanced as signs are repeated on each hand: a person walking forwards on the left, then one on the right; two on the left, then two on the right; three on the left, then three on the right, and so on. In 'Afternoon', we see this again when the activities of the dog are shown by one hand, and this is balanced by the identical activities of the bird on the other hand.

Although the movement of articulators in sign languages in everyday signing is rarely staccato, in poetry there is often a deliberately smooth and graceful fluidity of movement of the hands. The movement of one sign may be especially chosen so that the next sign starts where the first finishes, with no break in the flow of signing. We see this in a beautiful construction in 'Evening' where the sign DARKNESS blends almost imperceptibly with the sign BAT. The same smooth flow is seen as the movement of the hands during the sign LION blends with the sign MANE in 'The Staircase'. In 'Evening' a series of signs moves across signing space, with each sign beginning at the end point of the previous sign. For example, in the phrase SUN LIKE FLOWER FLOWER-FOLDS (fig. 14.3), the sign FLOWER moves from right to left across the nose, and this is a device used to move the signing from the right side of the signing space to the left.

As well as being smoother, movements are often slower and (to use a term from Ormsby) more 'fastidious'. Many signs in conversational signing bear little resemblance to the 'citation form' found in a dictionary. Contrasts are often reduced as the sign handshapes, movements, and locations blend into preceding and following signs. Although the blending of signs is deliberate within a poem, casual blending does not occur, and each sign is clearly made. This clear signing is a noticeable feature in all Dot Miles's poems.

In conversational signing, there are many signs that would be described as visually motivated in some way. However, many of them have become less clearly visually motivated over time, as movement is reduced or changes occur in handshape or location. In poetic signing, however, the visual motivation is strongly emphasised for many signs. This may be partly because the signer is deliberately trying to create strong visual images. However, Ormsby suggests that it is done to draw attention to the form of the sign itself, so that the signs become less simple vehicles of communication and more performance art. There are two very clear examples of this in 'Evening'. In the first example the poet signs LIKE FLOWER FLOWER-FOLDS, and in the second LIKE -b-a-t- BAT-FLIES. On both occasions, she emphasises a visually motivated image, and then signs it slowly, clearly, and for a noticeably long time.

SUN

LIKE

FLOWER

FOLDS

Fig. 14.3 'The sun, like a flower, folds.'

Fig. 14.4 TWIN-TREES

Signs may also be created for a poem, to draw attention to the richness of the language and the ability to manipulate form in BSL. In 'Morning' the sign TWIN-TREES is a novel creation (fig. 14.4). The audience's attention is particularly drawn to this new sign by the look of complete delight on the signer's face. The facial expression might be interpreted as pleasure at seeing the reflection of one tree in the pool, but there is also a definite feeling of the poet's great satisfaction at creating such an elegant sign.

We have seen on several earlier occasions (e.g. in chapters 1 and 9) that BSL signs are constrained to a limited signing space. However, in poetry, signs may move out of the usual signing space. In the poem 'Out of the Shell', written for the centenary celebrations of the British Deaf Association, the final line OUT-OF-THE-SHELL moves out of the signing space (fig. 14.5).

In another device to make the audience focus on the form of the signs, rather than on their content, the signer's eye gaze can be on the hands, rather than the audience, as we would expect in conversational signing. As the signer focuses on the hands, the audience is invited to do the same. In 'Morning', there is a noteworthy example of this when the poet signs TWIN-TREES and during this sign looks at her hands, looks up at the audience, and then back to her hands.

Fig. 14.5 OUT-OF-THE-SHELL

At a different level of analysis, BSL poems have definite overall structures. Poems in English have rules, not only about rhyme, alliteration, assonance, and rhythm, but also about stanzas or verses. Stanzas are also marked in BSL poetry. Ormsby has remarked upon the use of stanzas in Valli's ASL poem 'The Snowflake'. In this, there are three stanzas of 20 seconds, 40 seconds, and 20 seconds. The first concerns reflection on the present, the second moves to the past, and the third to the future for resolution. This same three-part structure can be seen in Dot Miles's 'Christmas magic' with an initial introduction, followed by a shift to Christmas in the past, and finally a return to the present. The same triple structure is seen in 'Morning', 'Afternoon', and 'Evening'. These three stanzas are accentuated by the poet's performance of the first while standing, the second seated, and the third standing again.

Mood changes are also seen between stanzas. We see three very different moods in 'Morning', 'Afternoon', and 'Evening' as the mood passes from fresh excitement at a new day, to peaceful contentment and companionship in the afternoon, to isolation and fear as darkness falls, paralleling youth, middle age, and old age. In 'Christmas magic' the mood changes in each stanza, from peaceful remembering, to the child's excitement at Christmas, and finally to the adult's wiser perspective.

BSL HUMOUR

Another heightened use of sign language is in humour. In this section we will consider the use of language in humour in the Deaf community.

The Deaf Comedians, a troupe of comedians working in the British Deaf community, base much of their humour on the shared experience of many deaf people, particularly miscommunication with hearing people and the oppression that many deaf people have suffered in the 'hearing world'. Although this is a very important part of Deaf humour, the humour is not necessarily based on language.

By linguistic humour, we mean using the language itself to create amusement. Linguistic humour in English includes riddles, puns, and word games.

There are very few 'Deaf jokes' in BSL that are told as stories with a punchline based on language rather than solely upon the content. One well-known joke is an exception. A deaf giant falls in love with a human girl. She is terrified, but he gently picks her up, holds her on the palm of his left hand, lifts her up to his face and using his right hand signs to her that he loves her and wants to marry her. This leads to an unfortunate accident because the sign MARRY in BSL is two-handed, and the palm of the non-dominant hand faces downwards. As the giant says he wants to marry the girl, he turns his hand palm down and she falls off his hand and plunges to the ground.

Such jokes are not common, but there are many other forms of humour in sign languages that rely on language. There are references to puns in ASL in Klima and Bellugi's book, mentioned earlier. For example, the signs meaning 'age 13' and 'ejaculation' in ASL are very similar, and combining them can serve as a source of considerable amusement. Other examples of puns include changing the movement of a sign (e.g. in UNDERSTAND, where more and more fingers can open as the person understands more and more) and the orientation (e.g. in the sign NEW-YORK where, in reference to the seamy, underworld side of New York, the sign can be turned upside down) (fig. 14.6).

In BSL there are similar signs that are equivalent to puns in English. Many puns rely on a slight difference in form, creating a different (but somehow related) meaning. In one example, the sign FOOTBALL changes to the sign DISABLED, to show how badly the team was playing. In another, one hand signs DRINKING (alcohol) and blends with the other hand in the sign CONVERSING until the sign CONVERSATION becomes totally disorientated.

Another BSL pun, with a serious side to the humour is the rather bitter change of handshape from the sign INTEGRATION to the sign MAINSTREAMING, referring to placement of individual deaf children in hearing schools. The lower hand changes from a '5' hand to a 'G' hand, to show how

Fig. 14.6a NEW-YORK   Fig. 14.6b The New York underworld

deaf people can feel when they are individually mainstreamed. In this case, the person feels less integrated, and more oppressed (fig. 14.7).

We have already seen in chapter 10 that productive signs may be seen as humorous, especially in the creative use of metaphor. A good signer will be able to pick up on a certain aspect of a situation and turn something mundane into an amusing situation, using a well-chosen metaphor. A parallel in English would be the use of similes in the *Blackadder* comedies on BBC television where the idea of 'stupid' and 'we have not moved very far' are transformed into humorous ideas with similes *as thick as a whale omelette* and *we have advanced as far as an asthmatic ant with heavy shopping.*

Fig. 14.7a INTEGRATION   Fig. 14.7b MAINSTREAMING

Fig. 14.8 LIMBER-UP

A signer might sign that they were preparing to give a presentation and lim-
bering up for the performance, but a more humorous metaphor would be to
sign oiling the joints in the hands and arms with a small oil can (fig. 14.8).
Another signer might sign that they were getting ready for a party, but rather
than putting on party shoes and party clothes, they take their party hands
from the peg and put them on, ready for a wild evening of signing. Much of
the humour of this metaphor relies on spontaneity and visual presentation for
its effect, but it is an important part of linguistic humour in BSL.

Another use of metaphor in BSL humour is the use of 'anthropomorphism'
by signers. In this type of humour, things that are not human are treated as
though they are. The signer 'becomes' the object and signs as though that
thing were human, and gives its feelings or actions. For example, the office
joker might describe the feelings of the chairs in the office coffee area after
they have been sat on all day, by 'becoming' the chair, and showing the feelings of the chair. The skill and humour lie in the ability to describe the feelings of the chairs as though they were human.

Recently, some deaf and hearing people were sitting in a summer garden
under an apple tree, when an apple fell and hit a member of the group on the
head. It sparked off two simultaneous jokes. The hearing person whose head
was hit looked up with mock inspiration and signed -g-r-a-v-i-t-y-! The
hearing people laughed, but the deaf people merely smiled politely. Even
though they understood the joke, they did not find it very funny. However, a
deaf person 'became' a big apple in the tree, and, with an expression of

disdain, nudged her elbow to knock the other little apple out of her way off the tree. The deaf people laughed, and the hearing people smiled politely. This is an illustration of the different senses of humour that one may see in Deaf and hearing communities.

Another source of linguistic humour in BSL is bilingual language play. This can occur because most fluent signers are bilingual in BSL and English, and there is amusement to be had from literal loan translations between English and BSL. A similar parallel in English is Miles Kington's 'Let's parler Franglais' which relies on the reader's knowledge of both French and English. In BSL, we may see signs such as FELLOW SHIP instead of FELLOWSHIP, or ONE-PERSON-MEET-FOUR-PERSON instead of METAPHOR (*met a four*) or I CAN'T STOP instead of MENOPAUSE (*me no pause*) or MY CROW WAVING and VERY-SMALL-WAVE instead of MICROWAVE. This humour clearly only succeeds if the conversational partner can reconstruct the original meaning.

Language games are also a source of amusement in sign languages. Some of them may be seen as partly bilingual games, but others are solely within BSL. In one bilingual game, the signer must make a story containing signs whose English translation starts with each successive letter in the alphabet. For example, AWAKE BECAUSE CAR DRIVE EUROPE FOREIGN, or AUNT BUY CAT DEAF EQUAL FRIENDS, and so on. The signs follow an order dictated by English, but the story is in BSL, and must make sense in BSL.

In another 'alphabet' game, which uses BSL only, the signer must make a story using successive handshapes from the BSL manual alphabet, but without using an initialised signs. One example might be FIRST STUDY-ING CONTINUE-LONG-TIME WHISKY! QUICK! NONE-TO-BE-SEEN... MAKE-IT SMOOTH (*Well, I was studying all night and needed whisky desperately, but there wasn't any, so I decided to make some, and it turned out to be smooth stuff* ...). Each of the signs uses the handshapes seen in -a-b-c-d-e-f-g-h-, etc (fig. 14.9). This game is not easy, because many of the hand-arrangements of manual letters are quite specific. However, the successful completion of the story is a source of considerable admiration, coupled with amusement at the ludicrous story that is created as a result of the limitations imposed on the signer.

A similar 'story' game can be played using the American manual alphabet handshapes (a little easier because this alphabet only uses one hand) or numeral handshapes (that is, a sign using the same handshape as ONE then TWO, THREE, etc.) without ever using them solely as a numeral. For example: I-SEE AMERICAN-INDIAN MOTHER (ASKS) REALLY AMERICAN? I'M-WRONG (*I see an American Indian and my mother asks, 'Is he really American?', but I'm wrong* ...) (fig. 14.10). Each of these signs is

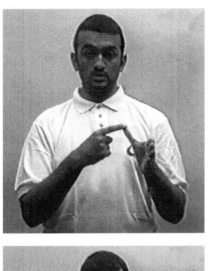
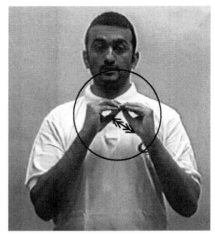

Fig. 14.9 Two-handed alphabet game:
FIRST (-a-) STUDYING (-b-)
CONTINUE-LONG-TIME (-c-)
WHISKY! (-d-) QUICK! (-e-)

Fig. 14.10 Numeral game: I-SEE (1) AMERICAN-INDIAN (2) MOTHER
(ASKS) (3)

made using the consecutive handshapes for the numerals ONE, TWO,
THREE, FOUR, FIVE, SIX, etc., but, like the alphabet games, completion is
difficult and the story produced by the constraints often hilarious.

The cultural differences between deaf and hearing people mean that sometimes jokes in BSL are not easily appreciated by hearing people, even if they
understand the meaning of the signs. However, there is no doubt that BSL is
used by signers as an important part of humour.

STORY-TELLING

Descriptions of story-telling in BSL show us how sentences are combined into larger units, which in turn have their own features and rules. In a community, like the British Deaf community, in which there is no written literature, story-telling is an important part of cultural and linguistic life.

BSL signed stories or 'narratives' share features with stories in English, but there are some important differences. This section will only provide a very brief introduction to some of the characteristics of BSL stories.

In a story, the narrator tells about a series of events (real or not), in the order in which they were supposed to have happened. They usually tell about people acting and interacting. Stories may be on any topic, and of varying lengths. Some anecdotes or stories may be new to the audience, but others may also be old stories where the content is already known, and the pleasure comes from seeing a familiar story told in a new and skilful way. For our discussion of stories here, we will focus upon the telling of the well-known children's story 'Little Red Riding Hood'. We will draw particularly upon the telling of this story by Jerry Hannifin to a class of children at the Royal School for the Deaf, Derby, and broadcast as part of a BBC *See Hear! Christmas Special* television programme. The story is a familiar one, but part of the pleasure of this story is that it is told purely for entertainment and Little Red Riding Hood and all the characters in the story are Deaf.

Theories of story-telling expect a well-formed story to have three parts: an introduction, one or more episodes, and a conclusion. This is certainly true in the example of 'Little Red Riding Hood'. It is even more strongly marked by the story-teller signing the raising of curtains at the start of the story, and signing a lowering of curtains at the end.

In the introduction of a story, eye contact is made with the conversational partner (in this case, a class of children). When the episodes start, the eye contact moves away from the conversational partner. If the story-teller interrupts the telling of an episode to make an aside, or comment, or add more background information, they look at the conversational partner again.

There may be a number of characters in a story, and the narrator must make it clear to the audience which character is being referred to at any time. This is true in story-telling in English too, of course. English-speaking story-tellers may use devices such as *the Wolf said*, or *Little Red Riding Hood asked the Woodman*. The narrator may also use different speaking styles when quoting the speech of different characters. Little Red Riding Hood might have a soft, piping voice, Grandma might have a quavering voice, while the wolf would have a menacing, snarling voice.

In the story we consider here, there are six characters in the story (Little Red Riding Hood, the Mother, the Grandma, the rabbit in the forest, the wolf, and the Woodman), and the narrator also has his own role. The narrator needs to be able to refer to the different characters and also to be identified by his audience as the narrator too, when necessary.

Gary Morgan, who has made a detailed study of BSL narratives, has summarised ten different ways that a narrator can identify characters in a story. It should be emphasised that many of these different ways are used in conjunction with each other.

(1) **Full noun phrases.** The use of a full noun phrase to identify a character works in the same way as in English language stories. The name of a referent can be spelled out, e.g. -r-a-b-b-i-t-; or a name sign can be used for a referent, e.g. RED-RIDING-HOOD. The narrator can also use phrases like THE-GIRL (or less specific phrases like A-GIRL which Morgan notes are distinguished largely by facial expression) or simply a single lexical item like GRANDMOTHER or MOTHER. These named characters will be established in space by indexing in the signing-space, either after the identifying sign, or at the same time as the sign.

(2) **Index points.** Once the exact identity of the character has been established and assigned a location in the story's signing space, an index point for reference can be used. When this index is used, it identifies the character assigned to that location, as well as locating it simultaneously.

It is often said that once the characters have been named, and located, they do not need to be named again, and the story-teller can just point back to their location. In fact, this is not always the case, and even skilled story-tellers telling stories to audiences fluent in BSL will use the character's name again, with the pronoun. For example, in a story in Swedish Sign Language described by Inger Ahlgren, one episode includes a waiter, the manager, and two diners. Even after all the characters have been named and given an identifiable location in syntactic space, the story-teller still signs WAITER Index when referring to the waiter later on.

(3) **Verb inflections.** We have already seen in chapter 8 that some verbs are inflected in space in BSL. Verbs such as GIVE, LOOK, or ASK can give information about which characters are referred to by the use of inflection in syntactic space. If a character placed on the left looks to a character placed on the right, the verb LOOK will agree with these locations.

(4) **Proforms** (also called **classifier pronouns**). These may be used to establish the character's identity while simultaneously telling the audience where the character was and how they moved. At the end of the story discussed here, Little Red Riding Hood and the Woodman go off home together, and this is shown by the use of two 'G' hand 'person' proforms, moving through the signing space.

Morgan refers to these four markers as 'manual'. However, he points out that these manual markers are not the only markers, and they are almost always used with other non-manual markers. The next group of markers that he describes are often collectively referred to as 'role shift'. By this we mean that the narrator signs actions and interactions with the narrator himself acting as the character. Specific postures, facial expressions, and styles of signing are allocated to each character, and the signing space is used as seen from each character's point of view.

We have seen in our earlier discussion of humour that signers frequently take on the characteristics of people and things they are talking about, in order to entertain. This entertaining aspect of role shift is also frequently seen in narratives, however, the shift into the roles of others is also an important grammatical tool in story-telling.

(5) **Body shifts.** The body can be used to show the identity of the chosen character. Body shifts can be a left-to-right shift or a forward-to-back shift. Body shifts are particularly important for contrasting characters, and Morgan describes a continuum ranging from large side-to-side movements to subtle, finer forward-to-back shifts. In the story discussed here, the shifts between the wolf and Little Red Riding Hood during the classic 'what big eyes you have' exchange are very subtle, back and forward movements, while the shifts between other characters (such as Mother and Little Red Riding Hood, or the rabbit and Little Red Riding Hood) are much larger and more obvious. The differing heights of the characters in this story enable the story-teller to use body shift very successfully and clearly. When the narrator takes on the character of Mother talking to Little Red Riding Hood, he leans his body forwards and to one side and leans down; when he shifts to Little Red Riding Hood replying to her mother, he turns his body to the other side, and leans back to look up. However, although Little Red Riding Hood is much shorter than her mother, she is much taller than the rabbit that she meets in the forest. During her exchange with the rabbit, the signer's body shift is forward and to one side, leaning down, to identify Little Red Riding Hood, and to the other side and up to identify the rabbit. At Grandma's cottage, the wolf and Little Red Riding Hood are of the same height, and the body shifts are far less obvious. In this case, other features also serve to identify the two characters. Later, when Little Red Riding Hood meets the (much taller) Woodman, her identifying body shift is again upwards, while the Woodman's identifying shift is leaning down.

We have seen that agreement verbs can inflect to show subject and object in space and so serve to specify characters. However, other verb signs can also be directed at specific parts of the signing space, to show who is saying what to whom. There are many instances of this in the story described here. When Little Red Riding Hood leaves home, the signer, in the role of the Mother, signs WAVE-GOODBYE directly ahead and then almost turns his back on his audience to sign WAVE-GOODBYE while in the role of Little Red Riding Hood. This is appropriate, because the visual scenario of Little Red Riding

Hood walking away from the Mother has been set up by an earlier use of pro-forms. When Little Red Riding Hood meets the rabbit, she asks the animal its name and this question is signed with the signs directed downwards to the specified height of the rabbit. When the rabbit replies, the signs are directed upwards towards the specified height and location of Little Red Riding Hood.

(6) **Shoulder shifts.** As well as turning the whole torso, a shift of the shoulders can also be used to represent different characters.

(7) **Head orientation.** The head can also be used to represent characters in the story. It is less explicit than body movements but performs the same task of contrasting characters for their location and height. In all of the examples given here of body shifts, there is an accompanying head movement in the same direction. Indeed, it would look unnatural if the body shifted but the head did not.

(8) **Eye gaze orientations.** Eye gaze alone can be used to identify referents. However, this is the most reduced, and least obvious, of these shift markers. In the story here, eye gaze alone is never used (perhaps because the audience is a large group of children, where such a subtle marker could easily be missed) but it is used on most occasions in conjunction with all the other character markers. In more sophisticated, adult-orientated narratives, eye-gaze can be the sole identifier of a character. The signer looks to the area of signing space allocated for a character, and that is sufficient for identity. Once the signer has taken the role of a character, the signer's eye gaze can also represent the eye gaze of the character, so that, for example, if in the story a character looks down, then the signer looks down.

(9) **Facial component.** Facial expression also accompanies the other manual and non-manual markers. The story-teller can use specific facial expressions to identify different characters, and also uses them to show the character's emotions in the story, which can be used to identify the character in context. For example, Little Red Riding Hood's actions and conversation are frequently accompanied by a wide-eyed, innocent, happy facial expression, whereas the wolf's actions have a menacing face, and the rabbit's conversation is signed with a wrinkled nose and 'buck teeth'. Little Red Riding Hood's carefree expression changes to terror when she realises she has encountered the wolf, but where there are two contrasting facial expressions of 'innocent' and 'menacing', and later 'terrified' and 'menacing', there is no doubt from the story's context that both the innocent and the terrified expressions refer to Little Red Riding Hood.

(10) **Character style** (also called **character play**). Morgan notes that the age, physical, and psychological state of a character can be shown by the style of signing. For example, the character of an old signer might be shown by the story-teller always using fingerspelling articulated in a small area of space at waist height, while the character of a younger signer might be shown by larger,

expansive signing. A French character's role might be signed in a stereotypically 'Gallic' way, with use of a great deal of shoulder shrugging, or a hearing character might be shown using stereotypically 'hearing' signing (perhaps with over-articulated spoken components). In the story discussed here, we see two very clear examples of character style being used to identify characters. When the rabbit fingerspells its name, the signer curves his hands into 'paws' and signs with these paws, making an identifiable rabbit signing style. Towards the end of the story when Little Red Riding Hood rushes to the Woodman, she fingerspells -w-o-l-f- in a careful, deliberate childlike way.

In all this discussion of characters, it is also important to remember that the narrator must be identifiable and contrasted with all the characters. The audience needs to know when the plot is being moved along by the narrator and when the signs should be interpreted as an utterance by a character. In narrator role, the narrator typically looks ahead at the audience, with a 'neutral' body posture, and only looks away or shifts body posture to become characters in the story.

Although the narrator is the person telling the story, they do not necessarily occupy the most important signing space. The spatial viewpoint of the main character in the story is the most important one, and all other signing space is set up in relation to the main character. This is why the main character has to be set up near the beginning of the story. According to Ahlgren, the main character need not be given an identifying location in the signing space, because the narrator's body is used for the main character. The other characters involved are given their place in the signing space relative to the main character. We see exactly this during the telling of the Little Red Riding Hood story. Although there is not a single 'main character' in the story as a whole, we do see that whenever a character becomes the main focus of an episode, the use of space and the direction of verbs is seen from the perspective of that character.

According to Ahlgren, the number of places used to show characters in an episode in the signing space is always one less than the number of characters in that episode, that is: marking reference is for number of characters, minus one. This means that if there are two characters in an episode, only one will be placed, if there are three, two will be placed, if there are four characters, three will be placed, and so on. Four people at any one time is usually the maximum.

SUMMARY

In this chapter we have looked at the heightened use of language. We have seen how BSL can be manipulated as an art form, and as a source of humour. BSL poetry is created by using signs with phonological similarities, to create forms that may be seen as parallel to rhymes or alliterations in spoken languages. It also contains many other features that draw attention to the beauty and form of the language. Deaf humour is widely regarded as being very different from hearing humour, especially because so much humour requires a shared cultural experience before an conversational partner can really appreciate a joke. However, we have seen here that BSL can be used for humour, especially by humorous use of creative metaphor. Puns are made within the language, and there are also puns made bilingually with BSL and English. Language games, demanding skill and imagination from the language user are also sources of great amusement.

An important function of stories in any community is to share and remember experiences, and this is true also of the British Deaf community. The stories do not need to be new. The idea is to include everyone in a shared experience. For example, when a group of people from school get together, the stories are often about their time there. In many ways, the social function of the story, and how it is told, is more important than its content.

From our brief discussion of characters in narratives, we have seen that BSL uses space, body movement, and non-manual features in order to tell a story concerning a sequence of episodes and various characters. We have focused here especially upon a story designed to entertain, and have seen how the story-teller draws upon a range of linguistic markers to make the story both clear and entertaining.

EXERCISES FOR CHAPTER 14

1. Watch the video 'Deaf Humour'.
    (a) When does the humour rely upon 'slapstick'?
    (b) When does the humour rely upon shared life experiences?
    (c) When is the humour based upon the extended use of BSL?

2. Watch a video clip of a fluent signer telling a story. Observe how the signer identifies the characters in the story.
    (a) When are they named explicitly?
    (b) When are they given a place in signing space that is pointed to?
    (c) When is body shift (or shoulder, head, or eye-gaze shift) used to identify them?
    (d) When does facial expression identify them?
    (e) When does style of signing identify them?
    (f) How do you know when the signer is in the role of narrator, and not in the role of a character?

3. Watch a BSL poem. Analyse it, and pick out instances of the use of the following:

(a) signs with the same (or similar) handshapes, locations, or movement paths
(b) balance of both hands (i.e. the non-dominant hand is used unusually 'actively')
(c) smooth, fluid movement
(d) specially created signs or signs that leave the conventional signing space.

FURTHER READING FOR CHAPTER 14

Klima, E. S., and Bellugi, U. 1979, *The signs of language*, Harvard University Press.

Ormsby, A. 1995, 'Poetic cohesion in American Sign Language: Valli's "Snowflake" and Coleridge's "Frost at Midnight"', *Sign Language Studies* 88, 227–44.

Valli, C. 1990, 'The nature of the line in ASL poetry', in W. Edmondson and F. Karlsson (eds.), *SLR '87: Papers from the fourth international symposium on sign language research*, Hamburg: Signum Press, 171–82.

Bibliography

Aitchison, J. 1981, *Language change: progress or decay?*, London: Fontana.

1983, *The articulate mammal*, London: Hutchinson.

1992, *Introducing language and mind*, London: Penguin.

Aramburo, A. 1989, 'Sociolinguistic aspects of the Black Deaf community', in C. Lucas (ed.), *The sociolinguistics of the deaf community*, San Diego, CA: Academic Press, 103–21.

Bergman, B. 1983, 'Verbs and adjectives: some morphological processes in Swedish Language', in J. G. Kyle and B. Woll (eds.), *Language in sign*, London: Croom Helm, 3–9.

Bergman, B., and Wallin, L. 1985, 'Sentence structure in Swedish Sign Language', in W. Stokoe and V. Volterra (eds.), *SLR 83*, Silver Spring, MD: Linstok Press, 217–25.

Bouchard, D., and Dubuisson, C. 1995, 'Grammar, order and position of Wh- signs in Quebec Sign Language', *Sign Language Studies* 87, 99–139.

Brennan, M. 1983, 'Marking time in BSL', in J. G. Kyle and B. Woll (eds.), *Language in sign*, London: Croom Helm, 10–31.

1990, *Word-formation in British Sign Language*, Stockholm: University of Stockholm.

1990, 'Productive morphology in British Sign Language', in S. Prillwitz and T. Vollhaber (eds.), *Current trends in European sign language research*, Hamburg: Signum Press, 205–30.

1992, 'The Visual World of BSL: an introduction', in *The dictionary of British Sign Language/English*, London: Faber & Faber, 1–134.

1994, Pragmatics and productivity', in I. Ahlgren, B. Bergman, and M. Brennan (eds.), *Perspectives on sign language usage*, Durham: ISLA, 371–90.

Brennan, M., Colville, M., and Lawson, L. 1984, *Words in hand: a structural analysis of the signs of British Sign Language*, Edinburgh: Moray House College of Education.

Brentari, D. 1994, 'Prosodic constraints in ASL', paper presented at the Fourth European Congress on Sign Language Research, Munich, September 1994.

Brien, D. (ed.) 1992, *The dictionary of British Sign Language/English*, London: Faber & Faber.

Carmel, S. 1981, *International hand alphabet charts* (2nd edition), Rockville, MD: Carmel.

Chomsky, N. 1976, *Reflections on language*, London: Fontana.

Coerts, J. 1990, 'Analysis of interrogatives and negations in SLN', in S. Prillwitz and
     T. Vollhaber (eds.), *Current trends in European sign language research*, Hamburg:
     Signum Press, 265–78.
Colville, M. 1985, *Signs of a sexual nature*, Northwich: Cheshire Society for the Deaf.
Cornett, O. 1967, 'Cued speech' *American Annals of the Deaf* 112, 3–13.
Crystal, D. 1988, *Rediscover grammar*, Harlow: Longman.
     1992, *The Cambridge encyclopaedia of language*, Cambridge University Press.
de l'Epée, C. M. 1784, *La veritable manière d'instruire les sourds et muets, confirmée par
     une longue experience*, Paris: Nyon.
Desloges, P., cited in Lane, H. 1984, *The Deaf experience*, Harvard University Press.
Deuchar, M. 1977, 'Sign language diglossia in a British deaf community', *Sign
     Language Studies* 17, 347–56.
     1977, 'Is British Sign Language an SVO language?', in J. G. Kyle and B. Woll (eds.),
     Language in sign, London: Croom Helm, 69–76.
     1984, *British Sign Language*, London: Routledge & Kegan Paul.
Ebbinghaus, H., and Hessman, J. 1990, 'German words in German Sign Language',
     in S. Prillwitz and T. Vollhaber (eds.), *Current trends in European sign language
     research*, Hamburg: Signum Press, 97–114.
     1996, 'Signs and words: accounting for spoken language elements in German Sign
     Language', in W. Edmondson and R. Wilbur (eds.), *International review of sign lin-
     guistics, Vol. I*, Hillsdale, NJ: Lawrence Erlbaum Associates, 23–56.
Edwards, V., and Ladd, P. 1983, 'British Sign Language and West Indian Creole', in J.
     G. Kyle and B. Woll (eds.), *Language in sign*, London: Croom Helm, 147–58.
Emmorey, K., Corina, D., and Bellugi, U. 1995, 'Differential processing of topo-
     graphic and referential functions of space', in K. Emmorey and J. Reilly (eds.),
     Language, gesture and space, Hillsdale, NJ: Lawrence Erlbaum Associates, 43–62.
Engberg-Pedersen, E. 1990, 'Pragmatics of nonmanual behaviour in Danish Sign
     Language', in W. Edmondson and F. Karlsson (eds.), *SLR '87: Papers from the
     fourth international symposium on sign language research*, Hamburg: Signum Press,
     121–8.
     1991, 'Some simultaneous constructions in Danish Sign Language', in M. Brennan
     and G. Turner (eds.), *Word-order issues in sign language*, Durham: ISLA, 73–87.
     1993, *Space in Danish Sign Language*, Hamburg: Signum Press.
Fischer, S., and Janis, W. 1990, 'Verb sandwiches in American Sign Language', in S.
     Prillwitz and T. Vollhaber (eds.), *Current trends in European sign language research*,
     Hamburg: Signum Press, 279–94.
Friedman, L. 1975, 'The manifestation of subject, object and topic in American sign
     language', in C. Li (ed.), *Subject and topic*, New York: Academic Press, 125–8.
Fromkin, V., and Rodman, R. 1993, *An introduction to language*, London: Holt,
     Rinehart and Winston.
Hay, J., and Lee, R. 1994, *A pictorial history of the British manual alphabet*, Edinburgh:
     The British Deaf History Society.
Hockett, C. F. 1968, *The state of the art*, The Hague: Mouton.
Hughes, G. 1991, *Swearing: a social history of foul language, oaths and profanity in
     English*, Oxford: Basil Blackwell.
Jackson, D. 1992, (ed.), 'The history of the residential school for Jewish Deaf people',
     London: Reunion of the Jewish Deaf School Committee.
Jackson, P. 1990, *Britain's Deaf heritage*, Haddington: Pentland Press.

Jepson, J. 1991, 'Urban and rural sign language in India', *Language in society* 20, 37–57.

Johnston, T. 1989, 'Auslan: the sign language of the Australian deaf community', Ph.D. thesis, University of Sydney.

1989, 'Spatial syntax and spatial semantics in the inflection of signs for the marking of person and location in Auslan', *International Journal of Sign Linguistics* 2, 129–62.

Joos, M. 1968, 'The isolation of styles', in J. Fishman (ed.), *Readings in the sociology of language*, The Hague: Mouton, 185–91.

Kitto, J. 1845, *The lost senses*, Edinburgh: Oliphant, Anderson and Ferrier.

Klima, E. S., and Bellugi, U. 1979, *The signs of language*, Harvard University Press.

Kyle, J. G., and Pullen, G. 1984, 'Young Deaf people in employment', final project report to the Medical Research Council.

Kyle, J. G., and Woll, B. 1985, *Sign language: the study of deaf people and their language*, Cambridge University Press.

Lakoff, G., and Johnson, M. 1980, *Metaphors we live by*, University of Chicago Press.

Le Master, B., and Dwyer, J. 1991, 'Knowing and using female and male signs in Dublin', *Sign Language Studies* 73, 361–96.

Liddell, S. 1980, *American Sign Language Syntax*, The Hague: Mouton.

1985, 'Compound formation rules in American Sign Language', in W. Stokoe and V. Volterra (eds.), *SLR 83*, Silver Spring, MD: Linstok Press, 144–51.

1990, 'Four functions of a locus: re-examining the structure of space in ASL', in C. Lucas (ed.), *Sign language research: theoretical issues*, Washington, DC: Gallaudet University Press, 176–98.

Liddell, S., and Johnson, R. 1989, 'American Sign Language: the phonological base', *Sign Language Studies*, 64, 195–277.

Lucas, C., and Valli, C. (eds.) 1992, *Language contact in the American Deaf Community*, London: Academic Press.

Mandel, M. 1977, 'Iconic devices in ASL', in L. Friedman (ed.), *On the other hand*, New York: Academic Press, 57–108.

McIntire, M., and Reilly, J. 1988, 'Non-manual behaviours in L1 and L2 learners of American Sign Language', *Sign Language Studies* 61, 351–76.

Miller, C. 1994, 'Simultaneous constructions and complex signs in Quebec Sign Language', in I. Ahlgren, B. Bergman and M. Brennan (eds.), *Perspectives on sign language usage*, Durham: ISLA, 131–48.

Morgan, G. 1996, 'Spatial anaphoric mechanisms in British Sign Language', in S. Botely, J. Grass, T. McEnery, and A. Wilson (eds.), *Approaches to discourse anaphora 8*, University of Lancaster Press, 500–6.

in press, 'Discourse cohesion in sign and speech, *International Journal of Bilingualism*.

Nowell, E. 1989, 'Conversational features and gender in ASL', in C. Lucas (ed.), *The Sociolinguistics of the deaf community*, San Diego, CA: Academic Press, 273–88.

Ormsby, A. 1995, 'Poetic cohesion in American Sign Language: Valli's "Snowflake" and Coleridge's "Frost at Midnight" ', *Sign Language Studies* 88, 227–44.

Padden, C. 1988, *Interaction of morphology and syntax in American Sign Language*, New York: Garland.

1989, 'The relation between space and grammar in ASL verb morphology', in C. Lucas (ed.), *Sign language research: theoretical issues*, Washington, DC: Gallaudet University Press, 118–32.

Paget, Lady G., and Gorman, P. 1976, *The Paget-Gorman sign system*, London: Association for Experiments in Deaf Education.

Pimiä, P. 1990, 'Semantic features of some mouth patterns in Finnish Sign Language', in S. Prillwitz and T. Vollhaber (eds.), *Current trends in European sign language research*, Hamburg: Signum Press, 115–18.

Pizzuto, E., and Volterra, V. 1996, 'Sign Language Lexicon: cross-linguistic and cross-cultural comparisons', report prepared for the Commission of the European Communities, Human Capital and Mobility Programme Project: Intersign: Multi professional study of sign language and the deaf community in Europe (Network).

Poizner, H., Klima, E. S., and Bellugi, U. 1987, *What the hands reveal about the Brain*, Cambridge, MA: MIT Press.

Schermer, T. 1990, *In search of a language: influences from spoken Dutch on Sign Language of the Netherlands*, Delft: Eburon.

Schermer, T., and Koolhof, J. 1990, 'The Reality of time-lines: aspects of tense in Sign Language of the Netherlands', in S. Prillwitz and T. Vollhaber (eds.), *Current trends in European sign language research*, Hamburg: Signum Press, 295–306.

Schroeder, O. 1985, 'A problem in phonological description', in W. Stokoe and V. Volterra (eds.), *SLR '83*, Silver Spring, MD: Linstok Press, 194–201.

Stokoe, W., Casterline, D., and Croneberg, C. 1965, *A dictionary of American Sign Language on linguistic principles*, Washington, DC: Gallaudet College Press.

Stokoe, W., and Jacobowitz, L. 1988, 'Signs of tense in ASL verbs', *Sign language studies* 60, 331–9.

Supalla, S. 1992, *The book of name signs*, San Diego, CA: Dawn Sign Press.

Supalla, T., and Newport, E. 1978, 'How many seats in a chair? – the derivation of nouns and verbs in American sign language', in P. Siple (ed.), *Understanding language through sign language research*, New York: Academic Press, 91–132.

Sutton-Spence, R. 1994, 'The role of the manual alphabet and fingerspelling in British Sign Language', Ph.D. thesis, University of Bristol.

Sutton-Spence, R., and Woll, B. 1990, 'Variation and recent change in British Sign Language', *Language variation and change* 2, 313–30.

   1993, 'The status and functional role of fingerspelling in BSL', in M. Marschark and D. Clark (eds.), *Psychological perspectives on deafness*, Hillsdale, NJ: Lawrence Erlbaum Associates, 185–208.

Valli, C. 1990, 'The nature of the line in ASL poetry', in W. Edmondson and F. Karlsson (eds.), *SLR '87: Papers from the fourth international symposium on sign language research*, Hamburg: Signum Press, 171–82.

Valli, C., and Lucas, C. 1992, *Linguistics of American Sign Language*, Washington, DC: Gallaudet University Press.

Vogt-Svendsen, M. 1990, 'Eye-gaze in Norwegian Sign Language interrogatives', in W. Edmondson and F. Karlsson (eds.), *SLR '87: Papers from the fourth international symposium on sign language research*, Hamburg: Signum Press, 153–62.

Wallin, L. 1983, 'Compounds in Swedish Sign Language', in J. G. Kyle and B. Woll (eds.), *Language in sign*, London: Croom Helm, 56–68.

   1990, 'Polymorphemic predicates in Swedish Sign Language', in C. Lucas (ed.), *Sign language research: theoretical issues*, Washington, DC: Gallaudet University Press, 133–48.

Watson, J. 1809, *Instruction of the deaf and dumb*, London: Darton and Harvey.

Wilbur, R. 1990, 'Metaphors in American Sign Language and English', in W. Edmondson and F. Karlsson (eds.), *SLR '87: Papers from the fourth international symposium on sign language research*, Hamburg: Signum Press, 163–70.

    1996, 'Evidence for the function and structure of Wh-clefts in American Sign Language', in W. H. Edmondson and R. B. Wilbur (eds.), *International review of sign linguistics, Vol. I*, Hillsdale, NJ: Lawrence Erlbaum Associates, 209–56.

Woll, B. 1981, 'Question structure in British Sign Language', in B. Woll, J. G. Kyle and M. Deuchar (eds.), *Perspectives on British Sign Language and deafness*, London: Croom Helm, 136–9.

    1983, 'Change in British Sign Language', final project report to the Leverhulme Foundation.

    1987, 'Historical and comparative aspects of BSL', in J. G. Kyle (ed.), *Sign and school*, Clevedon: Multilingual Matters, 12–34.

    1991, 'Variation and change in British Sign Language', final project report to the Economic and Social Research Council.

    1990, 'International perspectives on sign language communication', *International Journal of Sign Linguistics* 1, 107–12.

Woll, B., and Allsop, L. 1990, 'Recent variation in BSL in the light of new approaches to the study of language', in J. G. Kyle (ed.), *Deafness and sign language into the 1990's*, Bristol: Deaf Studies Trust, 72–8.

Yau, S., and He, J. 1990, 'How do deaf children get their name signs during their first month in school?' in W. Edmondson and F. Karlsson (eds.), *SLR '87: Papers from the fourth international symposium on sign language research*, Hamburg: Signum Press, 243–54.

Zimmer, J. 1989, 'Toward a description of register variation in American Sign Language', in C. Lucas (ed.), *The sociolinguistics of the deaf community*, San Diego, CA: Academic Press, 253–72.

Subject index

Index of signs in the text